World War I
UPDATED EDITION

PETER I. BOSCO

REVISED BY
ANTOINETTE BOSCO

JOHN S. BOWMAN
GENERAL EDITOR

Facts On File, Inc.

Note on Photos
Many of the illustrations and photographs used in this book are old,
historical images. The quality of the prints is not always up to modern
standards, as in some cases the originals are from glass negatives or are damaged.
The content of the illustrations, however, made their inclusion important
despite problems in reproduction.

Facts On File, Inc.
132 West 31st Street
New York NY 10001

Library of Congress Cataloging-in-Publication Data

Bosco, Peter I.
World War I / by Peter Bosco ; revised by Antoinette Bosco.
p. cm. — (America at war)
Includes bibliographical references and index.
ISBN 0-8160-4940-8
1. World War, 1914–1918—United States—Juvenile literature. [1. World War,
1914–1918—United States.] I. Title: World War One. II. Title: World War 1.
III. Bosco, Antoinette, 1928– IV. Title. V. Series.
D570 .B64 2003
940.3'73—dc21   2002005106

Facts On File books are available at special discounts when purchased in bulk
quantities for businesses, associations, institutions, or sales promotions. Please call our
Special Sales Department in New York at (212) 967-8800 or (800) 322-8755.

You can find Facts On File on the World Wide Web at http://www.factsonfile.com

Text design by Erika K. Arroyo
Logo design by Smart Graphics
Maps by Jeremy Eagle

Printed in the United States of America

MP FOF 10 9 8 7 6 5 4 3 2 1

This book is printed on acid-free paper.

Contents

To all the people who inspired and nurtured my love of history when I was in my teens, especially my three high school social studies teachers, Robert Carr, Al Ainbinder, and David Rood, and the late historian Barbara W. Tuchman.

—P. B.

Preface
TO THE UPDATED EDITION

The destructive conflict that Americans know as World War I and Europeans know as "the Great War" erupted in August 1914 when a long-standing quarrel between Austria-Hungary and neighboring Serbia took a deadly turn. On June 28, 1914, a Bosnian-Serbian student named Gavrilo Princip, furious at Austria-Hungary's interference in Serbia's affairs, shot the heir to the Austrian throne and his wife. With this act, he set off an explosion that would rip Europe apart in the next four years and be felt around the world. It took only one month before escalating anger and cries for retaliation for the dual murders caused a war to break out between Serbia and Austria-Hungary. In the next few weeks, this war, considered at first to be only a localized conflict between these two countries, spread to the major countries of Europe.

This book shows why this happened, and why it led to a world war that eventually engaged the United States, bringing Americans to fight bloody battles in foreign countries. Storm clouds had already been gathering over Europe for several years as nations, long concerned with the preservation of their power and prestige, had taken major steps to keep rivals at bay. In fact, by 1914, two powerful military alliances had been formed: on one side, Germany and Austria-Hungary, calling themselves the Central Powers; on the other, France, Britain, and Russia, which would later be called the Allies. With Germany bound to support Austria-Hungary, and Russia concerned with the autonomy of Serbia, all it took was an assassin's bullet to light the spark of a major war by having the big nations come to the defense of their little allies.

In the beginning, most of the men in charge of the military in these countries believed that this would be a relatively short war. The reader learns, though, in this book, just how wrong they were. The Great War went on for four years of slaughter and destruction, defying many of the past rules of war. The world was literally remodeled by this great war that pitted Germany, Austria-Hungary, and Turkey against France, Great Britain, the United States, China, and Russia, with many other smaller nations joining in and taking sides. Raising questions about the reasons these countries entered into this war is one of this book's goals.

This updated edition has added box features that illuminate certain aspects of the war. One of these covers technology. This was the first time in history that a war would be fought on an increasingly brutal scale because of the new technology that had become a fascination of all the major countries. Scientific experimentation had led to developing tangible products which held the promise of both practical and entertaining uses. Some of the most notable successes were automobiles, airplanes, wireless communication, and motion pictures. These incredible inventions were expected to create new and better relationships among peoples worldwide. But World War I turned even positive technology into weapons of war, as automobiles were converted into tanks and fast-moving military vehicles, airplanes became the means of hurling death from the skies, and wireless communication and movies fed hate-filled propaganda.

Having machines in the air that could hurl bullets and bombs from the skies brought about a rapid and radical change in thinking about war, which until then had been seen as a contest in which casualties were confined to the military. It became clear that war would no longer be confined to soldiers on one side fighting against enemy peers on the other side. The new military word on all sides was "strategic bombardment," in which explosive weapons from the air would now be aimed not just at military targets but also at civilian targets believed to be sites of the enemy's war industries. War would be inclusive, a threat to everybody—civilian and military—because bombs dropped from a fast-moving airplane could not hit targets with perfect precision. Cities and towns would now be hit, in addition to military targets. Bombardments from the skies would pile up the dead, the wounded, and cause starvation in the cities and towns and on the farms.

Technology also led to impressive innovations in military weapons that made the old-style rifles virtually obsolete and would forever change war from a shooting battle at a relatively close distance to one of deadly competition from afar. Heavy artillery—weapons too heavy for

PREFACE TO THE UPDATED EDITION

individuals to move—became a major factor, as both sides, developing ever better levels of technical efficiency, produced self-propelled guns and howitzers that could fire killing projectiles long distances. The goal of weapons development was mass destruction, and no sooner was one introduced than there was a plan for a better, more deadly one. In this book the reader will see how new, rapid-firing machine guns were developed that could kill with great efficiency. Fire-throwing weapons could produce horrific deaths for men in confined spaces. Even the submarine, which in 1914 was still considered a technological experiment, within a few years became a matchless destroyer of commercial ships.

The development of all these instruments of destruction was rapid and produced changes, not only in the way war was fought, but also in the way in which it was thought about. The technology of World War I showed that humans had made an exponential leap in learning and inventiveness and that, therefore, never again would there be a certainty about how a war would be fought. Scientists went on produce the atomic bomb in World War II and since then, the world has lived under the threat of nuclear bombs. In World War I scientists also developed varieties of poison gas as a way to disable and kill soldiers. These were the forerunners of currently feared chemical and biological weapons.

World War I began as a war on two fronts, west and east. The western front was a battle line in France, in effect separating the Germans and the Allies. The line was actually a double track of trenches, constructed by both sides to maintain their defensive positions, with the area between called no-man's-land. This book attempts to paint a clear picture of the madness of trench warfare, showing the hellish conditions soldiers of both sides were forced to endure both in the trenches and at the times when they were ordered to go "over the top," basically becoming targets of the deadly weapons on the other side. The battles of this war often measured victory simply by the side that had killed the most. For more than three years neither side advanced very far from their defensive positions, and World War I's trench warfare remains a sad synonym for slaughter.

The eastern front was a large area between Russia and Austria-Hungary, extending as far north as Germany and Poland and as far south as the mouth of the Danube River in the Black Sea. While Czar Nicholas of Russia felt justified in warring against Austria-Hungary and Germany, he was either unconcerned or oblivious to the fact that his country was a powder keg about to explode. As the military and civilian deaths mounted from battles, starvation, and freezing, and as people began marching in protest or gathering in food riots, revolution swept the country. Vladimir Lenin stepped into this chaos in Russia with his dream of replacing capitalism, which he saw as the cause of wars, with socialism. He promoted his vision with the slogan that socialism would give the people peace, land, and bread. Revolution in Russia replaced the war against the Central Powers when the Bolsheviks—meaning "the majority"—under Lenin took power. By December 1917 Russia's involvement in the war was over, freeing Germany from having to fight on the eastern front. Lenin had emerged as the victor in establishing the socialist government that he had fought for, now renamed the All-Russian Communist Party. World War I had pushed his country too far, bringing to a climax all the anger, misery, corruption, and abuse that the mass of Russians had so long endured. The Russian people opted for a new social and political order, one that few predicted would make such an impact on the rest of the 20th century.

If there were one word to associate with World War I, which involved about 93 percent of the world's population and left some 38 million soldiers and civilians killed or wounded it would be *casualties*. As this book underscores, the war decimated a generation of Europe's youth and left more than 120,000 U.S. servicemen dead. Largely unreported was the fact that the Allies' losses were nearly three times more than those of the Germans, who were consistently superior in training, weapons, tactics, and leadership. The French and British commanders too often ordered actions out of military incompetence or sheer pride. In the Battle of Verdun, for example, the British army's dead and wounded on a single day numbered more than 60,000 because of the stubbornness of the British generals.

It is generally agreed that it was the coming of the "Yanks" that saved the Allies from defeat. The United States did not want to enter the war, and President Woodrow Wilson seemed determined to keep the nation out of the conflict, getting reelected in 1916 on that promise. But things changed. Germany not only tried to get Mexico to invade the United States but also proclaimed that its submarines would attack U.S. merchant ships. U.S. self-interest was threatened when Germany would no longer respect the rights of American shipping, and the pressure on Wilson to confront Germany gave him no choice but to declare that the United States would join the Allies in war. Examining the dilemma faced by Wilson should prompt students to reflect on how other U.S.

presidents have responded to assaults on U.S. self-interest, whether they were indirect—such as the threats to oil supplies that led to the Gulf War—or direct, such as the September 11, 2001, attacks that led to the war in Afghanistan.

Because so many of the American people did not want to get involved with a European war, Wilson had a problem. He had to get the people behind him by convincing them that the United States was confronting an evil enemy. He set up the Committee on Public Information to whip up patriotism. It demonized the enemy, building up hate, all focused on the "evil" people, some of them at home. Patriotism had Americans turning viciously on neighbors with German names in World War I.

This suspicion of neighbors whose origins or ancestry were an enemy country set a tone that would be seen in other 20th-century wars, most notably in World War II, when Japanese-American residents were moved from their homes and confined in camps. Even Americans of German and Italian heritage sometimes felt antagonism from fellow workers, neighbors, and school classmates during World War II. In the war on terrorism that was launched in 2001, many people of Middle Eastern heritage were arrested and detained, often without cause. Others experienced prejudice or hate crimes. The fueling of fear, anger, and prejudice by a propaganda machine was yet another legacy of World War I.

The Great War radically changed the role of women. Women took over many of the jobs that had been men's work before the war. The war had come at a time when many American women were boldly marching for the right to vote, pointing to the dozen or so countries that had already taken this step. Women were proclaiming in action and words that they were not going to fade back into the home when the war ended. Several decades would pass before women gained a more equal position. It took the women's liberation movement to help them achieve greater rights in education and employment. But World War I had reshaped and permanently changed the role of women, who, before the century was over, would be donning military uniforms and joining men in the military.

While the Allies forced the Germans to accept an armistice, due in great part to the intervention of the United States, they proceeded to rack up a great failure in the Treaty of Versailles. As this book shows, Wilson's Fourteen Points for a just and lasting peace were effectively ignored as the British and French governments opted for revenge and punishment. They carved up the Middle East, solidified their colonial empires, and humiliated Germany by making it take full moral and financial responsibility for the war.

In such negotiations, the choice is often either fairness or sowing new seeds of destruction. The World War I treaty proved this, as the book shows by relating how a former German army corporal who fought the doughboys in the Argonne was determined to settle scores and regain all and more that Germany had lost at Versailles. His name was Adolf Hitler. Seeing "revenge, greed, and stupidity" in the Versailles treaty, Pope Benedict XV said prophetically, "Nations do not die; in humiliation and revenge, they pass from generation to generation the sorrowful heritage of hatred and retaliation." Hitler fit this prophecy. World War I's most devastating legacy was to become the direct cause of World War II.

Many Americans today know little of World War I because, as some have noted, it fell between the United States's two major crises, the Civil War and World War II. Yet, the war inspired a number of creative works that are still familiar to many Americans. A new, expanded further reading list in this edition includes some of these. Fiction and poetry are often appealing ways for students to gain greater perspective on history. Writers such as Ernest Hemingway, John Dos Passos, and Edith Wharton produced World War I novels that remain relevant. Notable writers—both men and women—from countries on both sides of the hostilities emerged as journalists and war correspondents. Great poetry was written by various men who saw action, such as Wilfred Owen, killed in the war, and Siegfried Sassoon, who suffered later in life from shell shock. One of the most oft-quoted lines in American poetry—"I have a rendezvous with death"—comes from "Rendezvous," written by Alan Seeger, who did indeed die in combat in 1916. Wrenching poetry was also written by women from all the major countries involved in the war, one most notably by Britain's Dame Edith Sitwell, called "The Dancer," with its haunting first line, "The floors are slippery with blood. . . ."

In 1927, T. E. Lawrence, the legendary "Lawrence of Arabia," published *Revolt in the Desert,* his first person account of his World War I service in the Middle East. Earlier nonfiction books and articles had been written by women seeking peace, like Clara Zetklin of Germany and America's Jane Addams, a peace activist who helped found the American Civil Liberties Union in 1920. One of the most powerful novels to come out of World War I was *All Quiet on the Western Front,* by a German, Erich Maria Remarque. Its international success led to a Hollywood movie, one of several that portrayed the waste and futility of the war as

PREFACE TO THE UPDATED EDITION

experienced by the mass of soldiers on both sides. The British scholar J. R. R. Tolkien affected by his experience at the Battle of the Somme, where some 19,000 soldiers were killed in one day, years later created his masterful *Lord of the Rings,* a mythical account of how the struggle between good and evil can shift the balance of power in the world.

Movies about World War I have long since been displaced by movies of more recent wars, although occasionally there is some recognition of the war in the popular media. World War I was the first war to be recorded by moving pictures; the History Channel on television periodically carries programs that show graphic newsreel films of the war. In 2001, the Arts and Entertainment Channel (A&E) featured a special movie, *The Lost Battalion,* the story of American soldiers trapped in the Argonne forest.

In the 1980s, recording artist John McCutcheon produced a CD with a touching song titled "Christmas in the Trenches," about a beautiful moment in World War I. It was Christmas 1914, when the soldiers of both sides began singing Christmas songs and walked into no-man's-land without weapons, but with brandy, chocolates, and musical instruments to share, both sides joyful for this brief time of peace before they got back to killing each other. This same event was recounted in a book by Stanley Weintraub, *Silent Night: The Story of the World War I Christmas Truce* (2001), one of the hundreds of books written about World War I.

There is much still to be learned from World War I, as this book suggests, because the issues that emerged early in the 20th century have not gone away. The Great War showed how deep nationalist feelings can be and how these can escalate when people sharing a certain kinship feel threatened by another labeled "the enemy." The conflicts that triggered World War I were relatively minor at first, but the war itself turned these into issues of great magnitude. The lessons of World War I still must be studied so that its tragic history will never be repeated.

Foreword
TO THE FIRST EDITION

World War I is the name given to the fire that consumed Europe from 1914 to 1918. Before it was over, the flames would spread to six continents.

Mighty nations locked themselves into a titanic struggle. As the months and years passed, it was called simply the Great War—the only description that seemed appropriate. Not until the outbreak of a second struggle in 1939 was the "Great War" recognized as the first of two world wars.

World War I destroyed people, resources, and empires. It rocked the political balance of Europe, interrupted its economic growth, and decimated a generation of its youth. It started the disintegration of the colonial system that seemed so permanent in 1914. It also released communism as a world force.

The war brought about spectacular shifts of power. Most notable was the rise of the United States to military and economic leadership. As the war reduced the great powers of Europe to a state of impotency, it thrust the United States, unprepared, into a position of world responsibility.

This is the story of that terrifying conflict, and the important role that America played in it.

1

THE SINKING OF THE *LUSITANIA*

Fog enveloped the British ship *Lusitania* the entire morning of Friday, May 7, 1915. Capt. William Thomas Turner felt greatly relieved when the blinding mist lifted shortly before noon. He was guiding his ship through troubled waters that morning. His grand vessel, a luxury ship of the Cunard line, was carrying 1,257 passengers— 159 of them Americans and 168 infants and children.

The ship was on course to its destination, Liverpool, England. Now, as it approached the coast of Ireland, the liner entered waters that were known to be infested with torpedo-laden German submarines, called U-boats (from the German for submarine, *Unterseeboot*). Captain Turner felt uneasy.

Great Britain was at war with Germany, which had issued orders to interrupt all British trade. The plan was to prevent any supplies, from food to arms, from getting to the enemy. Every ship was suspect, even passenger liners, which would make a good cover-up and might secretly be carrying much-needed supplies.

The fog had made some of the passengers and many of the 702 crewmen on the ship nervous. Many of them had listened to the photographers and reporters at Pier 54 in New York on Saturday, as the ship was being prepared to begin its journey. These journalists had claimed this would be the "last voyage of the *Lusitania*."

By early afternoon, the mood had changed to near giddy confidence. The fog cleared away, the day got bright, and the ship was close enough to land for the captain and passengers to see the Irish coastline, with its trees, rooftops, and church steeples. Some people went to the dining room to eat lunch, expressing to each other their relief at having crossed the Atlantic safely. Others went to their rooms to pack their bags, anticipating their arrival in Liverpool early the next morning.

On deck, 63-year-old Captain Turner felt uneasy. The Irish Coast Patrol, charged with protecting ships in this area, was not in sight. The *Lusitania* remained alone on the flat, blue-green water. Why were there no other ships? he wondered.

To add to the captain's worries, his wireless operator had received several messages the evening before from the British Admiralty, telegraphs that warned of "Submarines active off south coast of Ireland." This was precisely where his ship now cruised. Captain Turner would have been even more nervous had he known that in the past week 23 merchant vessels had been torpedoed in the waters where he was now traveling.

He tried to dismiss his fears, gazing at his vessel, which had made 201 successful trips since being launched in 1907. The 790-foot *Lusitania* was big enough to carry a flotilla of U-boats on its deck, he reasoned; the bridge was as high as a six-story building. It was fast, with a top speed of 25 knots. That gave the *Lusitania* a considerable margin over the fastest U-boats.

The captain smiled wryly as he remembered being questioned by a reporter about the U-boat threat six days earlier, just before sailing. Breaking into laughter, he had responded, "Do you think all these people would be booking passage on board the *Lusitania* if they thought she could be caught by a German submarine? Why, it's the best joke I've heard in many days, this talk of torpedoing!"

Captain Turner quickly brought his thoughts back to the present, shaking his head in disbelief that not a single escort ship was in sight. One thing became clear to him. On his present course, at full speed, he would arrive at Liverpool far ahead of full tide. That could mean dangerous circling in these unsafe waters for several hours. He had no choice. He had to change course and backtrack. At 1:45 P.M. the helmsman, on the captain's reluctant orders, swung the *Lusitania* away from the coast.

Some passengers had come on deck by this time, having finished lunch. With heavy hearts, they watched the friendly green land disappear.

Within 10 minutes, it was the *Lusitania* that was being watched. Kapitänleutnant Walther Schwieger, the 32-year-old skipper of the *U-20*, a 650-ton U-boat stationed in the coastal waters of the British Isles, had sighted something in his binoculars. It was a rapidly materializing

THE SINKING OF THE *LUSITANIA*

The British passenger liner *Lusitania,* launched in 1907, docks for the first time in New York City. *(Library of Congress)*

speck coming in from the west that the skipper noted in his log to be "a large passenger steamer."

The 35 men and three other officers on the U-boat came immediately alive as they heard the skipper's command, "Diving stations."

This was Commander Schwieger's first patrol aboard a U-boat in the nine-month-old war. His mission was clear. Any ship believed to be carrying cargo that would aid the enemy must be sunk. Since even food supplies came under that category, all ships were in jeopardy. The *Lusitania*, in fact, was carrying 4,200 cases of small-caliber cartridges and other munitions.

On the *U-20*, Commander Schwieger prepared himself for the command that would send one of his boat's torpedoes—packed with 290 pounds of a powerful new explosive—zooming toward the enemy ship. He stood, his eye tight against the periscope. At 2:09 P.M. came the shout "Torpedo ready!" A moment later, Commander Schwieger ordered "Fire!" He heard the hiss of air in the forward torpedo room. The whole sub shuddered from the release of its deadly projectile.

Courage aboard the Lusitania

WHEN THE BRITISH LUXURY LINER *LUSITANIA* WAS HIT, the ensuing chaos was incredible to describe. With inexperienced, panic-stricken passengers trying to cut the lifeboats loose on a ship that was tipping on its side, a second tragedy ensued. Many of the lifeboats, loaded with frightened people, swung out and then crashed back against the ship. The people were thrown into the water, and most of them were killed.

Yet, coming out of this horrendous scene were stories of remarkable human courage. The story of the wealthy, dashing 37-year-old Alfred Vanderbilt is well known: He directed his valet to "Find all the kiddies you can, boy!", directed women and children to the lifeboats, gave his lifebelt to a lady, and then joined hands with four other men and looked ahead, saying, "Why fear death?"

But there were many instances of less celebrated courage. Elizabeth Duckworth, a 52-year-old widowed cotton weaver from Connecticut, saved a child before getting on a lifeboat herself and being rescued by a fishing trawler. As Duckworth stepped into the trawler, another lifeboat with three people drifted by. They screamed that the boat had capsized, spilling all the others into the water. They needed help to row back and try to save them. The officer on the boat replied that he could not spare anyone.

Duckworth yelled, "You can spare me!" She held up her skirts and jumped across the few feet of water separating her from the lifeboat. Once aboard, she immediately reached for an oar. Published reports later said that with the help of this courageous woman, 40 people were pulled from the water and saved.

THE SINKING OF THE *LUSITANIA*

Captain Turner was looking back at the barely visible Irish coastline, as he stood on the port side of the lower bridge. Then he heard the message shouted through a megaphone on the starboard side. One of his seamen had seen a telltale white streak in the water, coming straight toward the ship. "Torpedo coming on the starboard," he screamed into the megaphone.

As the captain looked up, the torpedo was so close he could see the foam it raised just before it hit. A deafening explosion was followed shortly after by a second explosion. The ship immediately began to list badly to one side, while plunging ahead erratically. The coast was again in sight. Captain Turner, in the first few minutes after impact, believed he could get the ship to shore, if it could only stay afloat another hour.

That never happened. The captain and his remaining crew could not right the ship. It took only 18 minutes to sink the incredible ship, which like the *Titanic,* had been called unsinkable.

It was 18 minutes of tragedy. Dozens of seamen skilled in lifeboat launching and handling were killed below by the first impact of the torpedo. Those remaining, and some of the passengers, tried to release lifeboats.

A debacle followed, as the lifeboats, cut loose on a moving ship that was tipping on its side, swung out and back. The boats crashed against the ship, spilling the people who had climbed into them and then falling on the passengers as they floundered in the water. Of the 48 lifeboats, only six made it to sea intact with survivors.

Some of the passengers and crew found ways to save themselves in the cold waters by hanging on to pieces of wood or some other material that floated. Captain Turner stayed with his ship to the bitter end. Once in the sea, he saved himself by hanging on to a chair. Eventually, rescue boats reached the few, badly shaken survivors.

When the final count came in, the tally was grim—1,201 dead. Of the 129 children, 94 were gone; of the 35 infants on board, 31 had died; of the 159 Americans, 124 had perished.

To understand how such an event could have happened in a civilized world calls for a close look at the war then in progress. Only then can the scope of this tragedy be realized, and what effect it would have on the United States.

2

STORM CLOUDS OVER EUROPE

The First World War was about nine months old when the *Lusitania* became one of its countless victims. The origins of the war, however, went back to the 1800s.

The nations of Europe changed immensely in the second half of the 19th century. Improvements in health care and nutrition prompted a population boom. The Industrial Revolution was making the European nations more powerful than ever before. The need for new markets and raw materials to keep their factories busy spurred competition among the growing empires for new territory and for influence among smaller nations.

This competition inevitably led to friction. As the British, French, and German empires carved up Asia and Africa, heated disputes arose over colonial boundaries. In eastern Europe the disputes between the Austro-Hungarian and Russian empires were even more heated as they vied for control and influence over the little countries of southeastern Europe.

It was Germany that grew most spectacularly. Germany soon became the dominant political power of continental Europe, as well as the strongest industrial and military power on Earth.

Germany's military machine had won a shocking string of victories culminating with the defeat of France in 1871. Frenchmen could never forget the sight of German soldiers in their menacing spiked helmets marching in triumph through the streets of Paris. As part of the price France had to pay for losing the war, Germany added to its empire a

Kaiser Wilhelm II *(Library of Congress)*

whole French province and most of another. This conquered territory, called Alsace-Lorraine, remained a constant thorn to French pride.

From the 1890s onward, Germany's emperor, Kaiser Wilhelm II, symbolized his country's militaristic character. Wilhelm was a tense and immature man who was known for his frequent temper tantrums. His black mustache jutted upward from under his sharp nose. He always stood straight and rigid. He almost always wore a military uniform.

The kaiser's bristling mustache, stiff posture, and gaudy, medal-bedecked uniform was made familiar throughout the world by foreign cartoonists, who used him as a convenient symbol of Germany. Throughout his reign, he was preoccupied with enlarging Germany's combat forces. He delighted in flaunting his army and navy.

The intensity of Germany's military buildup worried the other countries of Europe. The French feared another German invasion. The Russians were disturbed by the kaiser's growing friendship with Russia's rival, Austria-Hungary. The British were extremely unsettled by the expansion of the German navy, which might one day be used to challenge Britain's traditional rule of the seas.

As suspicions festered, each nation increased its armed forces to keep pace with its neighbors. As a result of this arms race, armies grew tremendously in size and strength. The generals believed victory would go to the army that was strongest when war broke out.

Politicians tried to arrange a balance of power by forming alliances between countries. They hoped that if no group became stronger than the others, peace could be maintained. Yet, rather than prevent war, the alliance system seemed to increase the risk of a conflict. If a nation felt itself threatened, it might decide to attack first. Allies, bound by agreement, might then be drawn in. A widespread conflict might result, even if none of the countries concerned really wanted it to happen.

The summer of 1914 was a particularly lovely one in Europe. In the fertile fields cows fattened and crops ripened under the warm sun. In the cities commerce flourished and business boomed. Europeans basked in prosperity and peace.

But a terrible storm was looming on the horizon. By this time, two powerful, opposed military alliances had formed: Germany and Austria-Hungary (the so-called Central Powers) on one side, and France, Britain, and Russia (later known as the Allies) on the other. Europe had become a huge armed camp, divided against itself. It was an extremely dangerous situation, based on mutual distrust, suspicion, rivalry, and fear. It was a keg of gunpowder waiting to explode. Only a spark was needed for a massive, all-destructive war to erupt.

An assassin's bullet was to be the spark. For some time trouble had been brewing between Austria-Hungary and Serbia, a small country on its southern border. The Serbs, like the Russians, belonged to the Slavic race. In the Austro-Hungarian provinces that bordered Serbia lived several Slavic peoples, including Serbs, called South Slavs, or Yugoslavs.

STORM CLOUDS OVER EUROPE

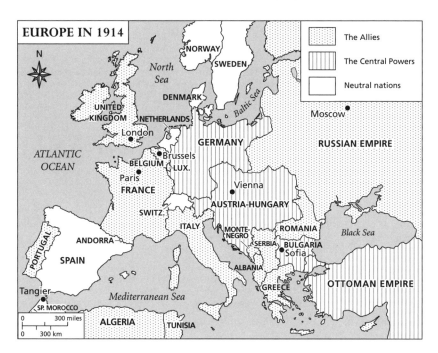

With the spread of nationalism these people came to think of themselves as one. Neighboring Serbia pledged to free all Yugoslavs from the control of the Austro-Hungarian empire.

On June 28, 1914, the heir to Austria-Hungary's throne, Archduke Franz Ferdinand was assassinated by Gavrilo Princip, a Bosnian-Serbian student. The murder was linked to Serbia. After a bitter month of confrontation and tension, Austria-Hungary declared war on Serbia on July 28. Kaiser Wilhelm gave the Austrians his pledge of support.

Russia rose to Serbia's defense and began to assemble troops on Austria-Hungary's eastern frontier. Germany demanded that Russia withdraw its army. Not receiving a reply to this demand, Germany declared war on Russia on August 1. France and Britain honored their agreement to stand by their ally, Russia. Within three days they, too, were at war with the Central Powers.

World War I had begun.

3
THE OPENING CLASH

"You'll be home before the leaves have fallen from the trees," Kaiser Wilhelm told his troops departing for the front. Both sides, in fact, expected it to be a short war. German, French, and Russian military planners assured their governments that their enormous forces would need only a few months to vanquish the enemy.

Even before the official declarations of war, the involved countries began to assemble armies on their frontiers. For the huge armies of 1914, this process, called mobilization, was a complex operation.

The monumental task of pulling together millions of people and thousands of tons of equipment and supplies would not have been possible without the recent expansion of the European railway system. Large units could be concentrated or shifted around very quickly by railroad. Once away from the railroad stations the armies could move no faster than those of Caesar or Napoleon.

For this reason, control of key rail centers was a central feature of military planning throughout the war. The railroads also helped give World War I a dimension previously unthinkable. For example, in 16 days (August 2 through 18) France transported 3,781,000 persons under military orders, in 7,000 trains.

The German army was the best fighting force in the world. Its soldiers had a high level of both fitness and vigorous training. It also had more heavy artillery than all the Allied countries combined.

The Austrian army was, in general, of poor quality for a major country. Troops lacked adequate training. Also, it was an army drawn from more than a dozen different ethnic groups. Most of its officers could not speak the same language as their troops.

France's army was second only to Germany's. The French army had a long and proud history. Its soldiers were full of dash and courage. However, because of France's much smaller population, its potential military manpower was only 60 percent of Germany's.

Russia mobilized the largest army that had ever existed. This Russian army, however, was not well prepared for war. It had crippling shortages of equipment, ammunition, and other necessary supplies. There would be times when many soldiers had to march into battle without rifles.

Britain's army was much smaller than those of the other powers. The British had always relied on their navy, the largest in the world, for protection. Britain was the only nation in Europe that did not have compulsory military service. In August 1914, it had only about 100,000 men available to fight in France. Though small in numbers, these men, called the British Expeditionary Force (BEF), were probably the best-trained professional soldiers in the world.

As the Earth's mightiest armies were preparing to annihilate each other, Americans all across the United States followed the events in Europe with keen interest. American newspapers faithfully reported every detail of the crisis. The declarations of war in August 1914 were the biggest news story of the young century.

Some of the fascination with Europe's troubles stemmed from the close connection between the American people and Europe. One of every nine people living in America had been born in Europe. Six million came from central and eastern Europe, 4.2 million from northwestern Europe, and 1.5 million from southern Europe. In addition, more than 18 million native-born Americans had foreign-born parents.

The U.S. government for a time feared that the warring countries would try to stir up trouble in the United States by appealing to the loyalties of their former subjects. But most foreign-born Americans had come to the United States to escape what they felt were petty squabbles of corrupt and greedy Old World states.

As Europe plunged into war in the first weeks of August 1914, the United States declared that it would not interfere. The majority of American citizens supported the government's policy of neutrality. While the situation in Europe was making headlines, most Americans were content to just read about it.

The fighting began on August 4. On that day the Germans invaded the neutral country of Belgium. Germany had no quarrel with Belgium. Yet German military strategists had long planned the invasion, because they wanted to use Belgian territory as a sort of "shortcut" to Paris by outflanking the main French forces farther south.

Germany did not want to go to war with Belgium, but Germany's generals needed Belgium's flat, open landscape and fine rail network to maneuver its tremendous army against France. The kaiser made several pleas to Albert, king of the Belgians, to let German forces pass peacefully through his nation to the French border.

Albert refused. The proud king would not allow German soldiers to trample through his little country without a fight. Although Belgium's

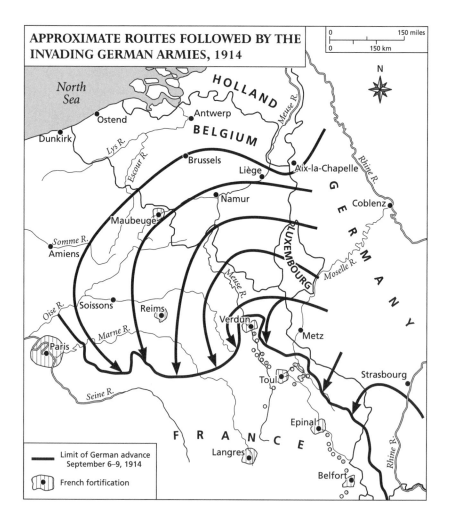

APPROXIMATE ROUTES FOLLOWED BY THE INVADING GERMAN ARMIES, 1914

THE OPENING CLASH

King Albert of
Belgium, who
organized stiff
resistance to the
German invasion,
1914 *(photo courtesy
of the New York
Public Library)*

small army was no match for its gigantic opponent, the Belgians fought on harder and longer than anyone expected. King Albert's soldiers made a brave and gallant effort to hold back the invaders. Germany's superior arms and greater numbers finally overwhelmed them.

On August 20 the German army entered Brussels, Belgium's capital. Albert and his army eventually retreated to the westernmost tip of his country. They refused to surrender and held out there for the rest of the war. The Germans would try, but never succeeded, in dislodging Albert and his men from that last tiny patch of Belgian soil.

Americans were shocked by the invasion. Germany's violation of a harmless, neutral country seemed uncivilized. Far worse was the barbaric behavior of German soldiers. Soon after they marched into Belgium, accounts of German atrocities began to appear in American newspapers.

The German army ravaged and plundered the countryside as it advanced. Soldiers tried to terrorize townspeople by randomly taking hostages. They executed about 5,000 hostages, including many Catholic priests. In addition to murdering civilians, the Germans destroyed many buildings and historic landmarks.

One of Belgium's most cherished national treasures was the medieval library in Louvain, founded in 1426. It contained many priceless ancient manuscripts. German troops burned it to the ground, and much of the city as well. On August 28, three days after the sacking began, Hugh Gibson, a diplomat from the U.S. embassy in Brussels, came to see Louvain for himself. The city was still burning. Black smoke and soot were everywhere. Even where the flames were gone, the pavement was still hot. The bloated bodies of dead civilians and dead horses lay strewn about.

German soldiers were going street by street, house by house, breaking down the doors and kicking out the people living there. In each house these soldiers first stuffed their pockets with whatever valuables they found there, then set fire to the house. One German officer in charge of this systematic looting and destruction said to Gibson: "We will teach [the Belgians] to respect Germany . . . People will come here to see what we have done!"

Such reports horrified the American people. Newspapers across the United States condemned the savagery of the Germans. The brave Belgians, who had stood up against the big German bully, were hailed as heroes. Cartoons showed Kaiser Wilhelm as a sinister, overbearing brute

German soldiers attempt to defend their exposed position against French attack, somewhere on the Western front in 1914. New rapid-fire weapons made this kind of defense obsolete and led to trench warfare. *(National Archives)*

German machine gunners face Russian troops on the eastern front, 1915. *(National Archives)*

trying to stretch his greedy hands, stained with Belgium's blood, across the European continent.

President Woodrow Wilson urged Americans not to take sides. "Be impartial in your thoughts as well as action," he said. Yet he was, himself, deeply disturbed by Germany's actions.

Britain and France belatedly sent troops to help defend Belgium. They could not hold their ground against the German "bulldozer." On August 22, the French were defeated at Charleroi, Belgium, and forced to retreat. The Germans attacked the British the next day at Mons, Belgium. The British Expeditionary Force fought well and honorably, but was also forced to retreat.

By August 25, 1 million German soldiers had crammed into Belgium, poised to pounce on Paris. They swept into northern France, toward the French capital, crushing all resistance.

Meanwhile, in the east, the Russian army was marching into German territory. The early success of this invasion raised the hopes of the Allies fighting in France. Then the Russians suffered a disastrous defeat at the Battle of Tannenberg (August 25–31). A large part of the Russian force

French troopers under General Gouraud with their machine guns amid the ruins of a cathedral near the Marne, driving back the Germans
(National Archives)

disintegrated, losing about 125,000 men, the majority taken prisoner. Russia never completely recovered from this catastrophe.

Ironically, the only Allied army not defeated in that first month was Serbia's. Austria-Hungary's invasion of its little neighbor was a fiasco. By the end of August the Austrian army had lost a humiliating 40,000 men and was hurled off Serbian soil.

The first days of September were dark, desperate hours for the Allied armies fighting in France. One German unit came within 15 miles of Paris. The exhausted German troops, however, had been pushed to their limit by their commanders and stopped along the Marne River northeast of Paris.

The Allies counterattacked. The Battle of the Marne (September 6–10) stopped the Germans in their tracks and forced them to pull back and reorganize their position. The threat to Paris dissolved, along with the kaiser's hope for a quick, victorious war. But the Allied armies were too weak and tired to chase the Germans as they withdrew from the Battle of the Marne. This gave the Germans time to dig in.

The early weeks of autumn saw many vicious clashes as both sides tried to hold on to as much ground as possible. The Germans' attempt to push the Allies off the last little piece of Belgium resulted in the first battle of Ypres (October 17–November 21). Casualties were astounding on both sides. The British Expeditionary Force was practically wiped out, but the Allied line held.

By December 1914, trench warfare—the horrible deadlock that characterized the First World War—had arrived. Both sides carved a line of fortified trenches across western Europe. It was a scar that stretched more than 400 miles from the Swiss border to the North Sea coast. Along these lines millions of men and thousands of artillery pieces were put into position.

This poster shows Lord Kitchener appealing to the British public for enlistment. *(Library of Congress)*

The proud armies that marched to war in August were all but gone. Their best soldiers were killed, mutilated, and maimed. Each nation had to draft more recruits into its army to replace the losses. Many volunteered, but most were drafted. Younger, inexperienced, less well-trained men had to be sent to fill the ranks.

On Christmas Day 1914, both sides declared a 24-hour armistice, or cease-fire. For the freezing troops huddled in their damp dugouts eating canned food, it was not much of a holiday. At least there was no shelling from enemy guns. On December 26 the shooting and shelling resumed. It was if the exasperated armies had paused for a moment to take one last, deep breath before continuing a struggle that would stretch on for years.

4
THE GREAT NEUTRAL
—◆—ᴔᴔᴔ—————————————————

The year 1915 arrived to find Europeans still shooting at each other, and Americans still distant from the war and wanting to keep it that way. America had always tried to steer clear of Old World conflicts. The United States had embraced a policy of isolationism since the earliest days of the Republic.

The president, peace-loving Woodrow Wilson, concentrated his efforts on domestic programs and issues. Following George Washington's advice, he vowed not to involve the nation in "foreign entanglements."

Yet America had changed a lot since Washington's day. At the time of the Revolution there were 3 million people in the United States. In 1915 the population reached 100 million, larger than any European country, save Russia. Washington's America of the 18th century was a rural society based on small farms. Wilson's America of the 20th century had become a great industrial power. America's global trade had rapidly expanded. The U.S. economy was increasingly intertwined with Europe's. The days of America's isolationism were numbered.

The most immediate effect of the war on the United States was the disruption of international trade. The Allies and the Central Powers obviously stopped trading with each other. The Allies also wanted neutral countries to stop trading with Germany.

Neutrals had a legal right to conduct business with whomever they liked. The United States, the wealthiest and most important neutral, insisted that the Allies respect that right. Yet the Allies were determined to get their way.

The British navy attempted to starve out the enemy by blocking off all German ports. That blockade was probably the most effective and

Peace-loving
President Woodrow
Wilson tried to keep
the United States
out of the war
in Europe for as
long as possible.
(Library of Congress)

devastating use of naval power of the war. In this way the Allies cut the Central Powers' outside sources of supply. The gigantic amounts of food and raw materials essential to sustaining a prolonged war would have to be found at home or come from neutral states that could be reached by land.

The United States resented Britain's high-handed tactics. Preventing neutral countries from trading with the Central Powers was a violation of international law. American ships were being stopped, boarded, and searched. Even cargoes of grain or beans were considered contraband and confiscated. President Wilson became furious with Britain.

The situation paralleled a crisis 102 years earlier when the British navy blockaded the ports of Napoleon's French Empire, and boarded American merchant ships. That, of course, resulted in the War of 1812.

In 1915, however, Britain's diplomats were shrewd and clever men. Time and again they skillfully avoided confrontation over the blockade issue. They did not want to offend the Americans, but their main objective was to gain American support for the Allied cause.

Soon, increasing commerce with the Allies compensated the United States many times over for the loss of trade with the Central Powers. Economic ties grew stronger every month between the Allies and the "Great Neutral."

Germany, too, saw the necessity to starve out Britain. Unable to block its ports with surface ships, the German navy launched an aggressive campaign of submarine warfare.

Unlike massive battleships, submarines were very small and frail. There was no room for cargo, so a submarine could stop a shipment only by sinking the ship. At first, when a U-boat sighted an enemy vessel, it would surface and fire a round from its one small cannon as a warning. The passengers and crew were then supposed to evacuate the ship while the U-boat finished it off.

Some ships were faster than the underpowered U-boat and could escape while it was surfacing. Merchant vessels also began to carry

British Dismay at Wilson's Neutrality

IN LESS THAN 23 HOURS AFTER THE *LUSITANIA* WENT down, President Woodrow Wilson had a telegram in his hand from his ambassador to Great Britain, Walter H. Page, who did not mince words about how the English felt. "The freely expressed official feeling," he emphasized, "is that the United States must declare war or forfeit European respect." His communication was beyond unwelcome. Wilson burned his telegram.

Page wanted to go back to the United States and present his—and England's—case in person. Wilson said no, from then on literally ignoring this man who had been his friend for 40 years, since when, as young men, Page, then editor of the *Atlantic Monthly,* and Wilson, an academic and writer, discussed philosophic and social issues.

A year later, Page got to see Wilson. The Germans had struck a medal to commemorate the sinking of the *Lusitania.* In the letters he left, it is noted that Page particularly wanted to see the president alone to show him this memento that denigrated the United States. Wilson was not impressed. Ironically, in April 1917, when Wilson did ask Congress to declare war on Germany, he used the arguments Page had been sending him for two and a half years.

German U-boat sinks an Allied merchant ship in blockade of British Isles.
(Library of Congress)

large-caliber deck guns that could blow an exposed submarine out of the water. Therefore, surfacing was not only dangerous, but also deprived the U-boat skipper of his two best weapons: surprise and his torpedoes (which could be fired only while submerged).

In February 1915, Germany began unrestricted submarine warfare. Berlin announced that it considered the waters around the British Isles a "war zone." British ships would be sunk on sight, and the safety of neutral ships could not be guaranteed. The Germans made it clear that merchant vessels would be attacked without warning or regard for the fate of their crews.

On March 28, 1915, the first American life was lost in the sinking of a British ship. A month later, German airplanes attacked an American steamship, and on May 1, the U.S. tanker *Gulflight* was sunk by a torpedo. That same day, the *Lusitania* set sail. From New York to San Francisco the press condemned this "slaughter," "murder," and "piracy" of the Germans. Continued sinkings kept the public anger high. After the loss of the *Lusitania*, the *New York Times* reported that "a grave crisis is at hand."

The Women Who Worked for Peace

WHEN THE WAR IN EUROPE STARTED, MANY IN THE United States were outspokenly opposed to their country's getting swept into the hostilities and began working actively to promote peace. One of the most vocal advocates of pacifism was Jane Addams, a noted social reformer who, based at Hull-House in Chicago, had brought hope and help to poor immigrants. Early on, she led a procession of women through the streets of New York City in protest against the war and then went on to present this message in lectures at a dozen colleges. Addams cofounded and became chairperson of the U.S. Women's Peace Party, which, because it advocated pacifism, soon faced negative public opinion.

Undaunted, Addams, in March 1915, reached out to women in Europe to gather as the Women's International Congress for Permanent Peace. Their first assembly was planned for April 28 to May 1 at The Hague in the Netherlands. The U.S. delegation's ship was halted in the English Channel. Newspaper reporters came aboard, as did officials, sharply opposed to the women's congress, "lest it weaken the morale of the soldiers," Addams later reported. The women were ridiculed as "Peacettes," and for three days the ship was held at anchor. When the congress finally convened, women representing 12 different countries were there, including a German delegation.

After the United States entered the war, the women were increasingly maligned, being called traitors and cowards, although, as Addams said, they were only "urging a reasonable and vital alternative to war." After the war, when peace became popular, Addams was seen as something of a hero. In 1931, she received the Nobel Peace Prize for her longstanding commitment to and efforts for peace.

Jane Addams, pacifist and social reformer *(Library of Congress)*

The sinking of the *Lusitania* had a profound effect on many Americans. German atrocities against civilians in Belgium and other occupied areas were fresh in the public mind. Together these horrors irreversibly damaged Germany's reputation and image. The American press began to portray the Germans as savage, barbaric "Huns."

Late in May the German government apologized about the two U.S. ships and said that they had been attacked by mistake. Berlin even offered to pay for the loss of the *Gulflight*. Yet Germany made no excuse for the *Lusitania*. As a British ship, it had been fair game.

The president wanted to preserve America's neutrality, yet he knew that he had to take a tough stand. He called these ocean ambushes a "violation of the sacred principles of justice and humanity." Wilson sent several stiff protests to Germany. The kaiser fumed but he too, wanted to preserve America's neutrality. In September 1915, Berlin grudgingly called off the unrestricted U-boat campaign.

American neutrality was safe again. Yet just how neutral was America? The majority of Americans, including President Wilson, sympathized with the Allied cause. War relief groups raised money to send to French and Belgian refugees who had been displaced by the German advance. American banks made huge loans to Allied governments.

The kaiser had good reason to be upset. Germany's blockade of Britain had been provoked by Britain's blockade of Germany. President Wilson scorned Germany, but tolerated the British.

The United States was Britain's number-one trading partner. Thus, the U-boats were also hurting American commerce. Many shippers would not risk sending their cargoes into submarine-menaced waters. This tied up business. During periods of peak U-boat activity, American ports became congested with tons of snarled freight. On U.S. docks, meat spoiled and produce rotted.

Not all Americans were pro-Allies. Many Irish-Americans, for example, had come to the United States because they could no longer tolerate Britain's longtime mistreatment of Ireland. They would be happy to see the British take a licking. Many German-American communities even raised money to send back to the Fatherland.

Even Americans sympathetic to the Allies believed that the United States should not in any way intervene militarily. Extending credit and trade with the Allies was one thing. Going to war on their behalf was quite another.

THE GREAT NEUTRAL

Pacifist demonstrations and movements sprang up across the nation. Most Americans clearly still cherished isolation. A popular song expressed the public attitude:

> I didn't raise my boy to be a soldier.
> I brought him up to be my pride and joy.
> To live to place a rifle on his shoulder.
> To shoot some other mother's darling boy . . .
> There'd be no war today
> If mothers all would say,
> I didn't raise my boy to be a soldier.

Secretary of State William Jennings Bryan privately favored Great Britain. Yet he and many others pressed for total noninvolvement. He sponsored a ban on loans to countries that were at war, and urged the president to forbid American citizens from traveling on ships of warring nations. When Wilson rejected both of these sensible suggestions, Secretary Bryan resigned from the cabinet.

In December 1915 a delegation of American pacifists called the Peace Ship, headed by Henry Ford, sailed for Europe intent on ending the slaughter there. They believed that the greatest neutral nation owed it to humanity to try, at least. The belligerents' governments rejected the famous automobile manufacturer and his "peace pilgrims." Ford left Europe's inhospitable shores with a head cold five days after he arrived.

5

DEADLOCK

1915

While Americans were busy avoiding war, the Europeans were trying to win one. On the western front, the year 1915 saw the opposing lines of trenches become stronger and deeper.

The French spent the year trying to liberate some of their country, only to learn the futility and costliness of massed infantry attacks against a well-fortified trench line. France spent the lives of hundreds of thousands in useless efforts that gained only a few miles.

Meanwhile, the British had been building up their forces by drawing soldiers from every part of their far-flung overseas empire. By spring, Britain's forces in northern France numbered some 500,000 and were ready to take the offensive.

The German army struck first. It launched a major attack against the British line at Ypres, the city in northwest Belgium where the British army had been all but eliminated five months earlier. The 21 days of sheer slaughter that followed became known as the Second Battle of Ypres.

On the first day of the battle, April 22, 1915, the men in the British trenches could not have imagined the horror about to befall them, for on that day occurred a gruesome event in the history of warfare.

Sentries were peering through their rifle sights, watching for German infantry that they were told might be coming. Instead, they saw a greenish-yellow vapor rolling toward them from the enemy trench. Some who witnessed it said they were transfixed by its eerie beauty. Taking advantage of the westerly winds, the Germans had released a bank of deadly chlorine gas four miles wide.

Salvation Army representatives with steel helmets and gas masks
distribute pies for the soldiers of the Twenty-sixth Division, in France.
(Library of Congress)

The heavier-than-air gas cloud dipped into the Allied trenches. The
soldiers in the trenches did not know what hit them. Drawing chlorine
gas into their lungs caused acute bronchitis, congesting their faces until
they were livid purple and producing the most intense pain.

The left flank of the line broke and fled. This was a terrible mistake.
By fleeing in the direction of the drifting gas, they prolonged their exposure. Running and gasping caused heavy breathing, which made them
inhale even larger quantities of the deadly fumes.

The men of the right flank held their ground despite great suffering.
(Many saved themselves by breathing through handkerchiefs soaked in
their own urine, which helped to neutralize the gas.) Because of the
courage of the men on the right flank, the Germans could not fully
exploit the gap created on the left. Frustrated in the attempt to penetrate the Allied line, they called off the attack on May 13.

The use of poison gas and the excruciating pain it produced horrified
Americans. Then, on May 7, came the news of the *Lusitania*. It seemed

to the United States that the Germans were determined to give one proof after another that they were callous to the feelings of humanity and the esteem of civilized peoples.

The Second Battle of Ypres did more than introduce a fearsome new weapon, it gave birth to a new mode of military thinking. The Germans did not need the city of Ypres, but they knew the British would try to hold it all costs. The goal of the German generals had not really been to gain territory, but rather to waste the strength of the British army, wearing it down, man by man. This ghastly strategy is called attrition.

There were many Americans who got to see the horror of the western front for themselves, young men and women who went there to serve as volunteers. Many worked for the American Red Cross. Another volunteer organization was the American Ambulance Corps. The ambulances were purchased and outfitted through fund-raising in the United States by private groups that supported the Allied cause.

Some Americans wanted to fight, even though their country was officially neutral. A way to get around that was to join the French foreign legion. (Made up of nationals from many countries, it asked only that a man obey his commanding officer.) As early as August 1914, a number of American men donned the red cap and blue overcoat of France's most famous colonial unit.

American volunteers were stunned by what they witnessed. Upon returning to the United States, they would give firsthand accounts of the war. Yet, words could scarcely describe the pitiful conditions of trench warfare. Life was cheap in the trenches. Dead bodies were used to build support walls. Yellowing skulls and limbs could be seen packed into the dank, black soil. Everywhere lingered the smell of decomposing corpses, or the lime used to disinfect them.

Every day men lived in the presence of death. There might be a pair of boots lying in a trench—with the remains of feet still in them. No one would take any notice. Fat, well-fed rats scurried everywhere. It was said that they favored the eyeballs of the dead.

The filthy, overcrowded trenches were ideal breeding grounds for disease and parasites. Men were covered with lice and bugs. Many also suffered from "trench foot," caused by the dampness, in which they lost all sense of feeling in their feet.

Death could come suddenly, from a sniper's bullet, a grenade fragment, or an artillery shrapnel. A direct hit by an artillery shell exploded a man into nothing, so that no traces of his body could be found. A shell might collapse a dugout roof, burying alive the men sleeping inside.

Also deadly were attacks from hand grenades, flamethrowers, and poison gas. Both sides started to use chlorine gas on a large scale. Another chemical, phosgene gas, could seep through many of the crude masks

The Descent into the Abyss
TRENCH WARFARE

THE TRENCHES ON THE WESTERN FRONT WERE PRIMITIVE, horrendous underground "housing" for the soldiers on both sides. Ironically, it was "progress" that gave them no choice but to fight a war stationed under the Earth's surface if they hoped to survive. New and devastating weapons had been developed, with firepower that blasted everything in range above ground. Thus, armies were reduced to building elaborate trench systems, where soldiers tried to fight and survive in these subhuman conditions.

Underground conditions varied according to the land. In a few places like Picardy in northern France, where the soil was hard chalk, trenches could be neatly designed. But mostly, troops had to deal with dank earth and the problem of drawing away water. They constructed dugouts in deep underground chambers, lined with boards and strengthened with sandbags. Death was always imminent from artillery fire, but just as threatening was illness from rat bites, bad food, vermin, and the dampness.

"Trench warfare saw more cruelty, terror and more barbarism than any war from the beginning of time," wrote war correspondent Matthew Holden. And yet, life went on for thousands of soldiers, many of whom lived in trenches for months at a time. They sometimes found a noble fellowship that helped them tolerate their hellish conditions. Some soldiers composed their own humorous newspapers. Some put up a light-hearted "hotel for sale" sign on an abandoned dugout.

Author Gregor Dallas wrote of his experience 80 years later, when he was led by historian Frank Gilson into some of these trenches in Picardy, "terrifying places unknown to the public and untouched in 80 years . . . As we emerged . . . Gilson said to me, in his lovely, quiet way, 'Listen, these fields are singing,'" poetically expressing his belief that the spirits of the soldiers who died in this horror were in a way still present.

Front-line trenches in the forest of Chausseau, France *(National Archives)*

then being worn. The Germans also developed vomiting gases. These made men sick so that they had to take off their masks, after which they could be attacked by other chemicals.

Trench life was relatively safe between big battles. For the men on both sides, the odds of surviving during a major attack were much. slimmer. In an attack, the defending trench would first be pounded by an artillery barrage that would often last days without pause. This would "soften up" some of the defensive earthworks and obstacles. For the defending soldiers huddled in the darkness of their deep, damp dugouts for the duration, it was a nightmare from which they could not awake.

The constant shelling also deprived men of sleep and regular meals. This helped to reduce their effectiveness in combat. Some snapped under the pressure and went mad. Many were killed. Yet the majority survived. When it was over, the fatigued, deafened men would pop back up behind their machine-gun placements.

Nurse Edith Cavell

A VICTIM OF HATE SPAWNED BY WAR

AT THE OUTBREAK OF WORLD WAR I, EDITH CAVELL, a nurse, was safe in her home country of England on a visit. Her family tried but could not persuade her to stay away from the Belgian hospital where she ran a training school for nurses. She went back to Brussels, then under German occupation, and turned her institution into a hospital for wounded soldiers. She treated them all: Belgian, French, British, or German. But she did more. With the aid of friends, she helped many recovered Allied soldiers to escape to Holland from where they could rejoin their armies.

Then a betrayer turned her in to the Germans, who arrested her. In spite of efforts by the British and U.S. governments to free her, Cavell was convicted of treason and executed by firing squad on October 12, 1915. Even in a war marked by many horrendous actions, this stood out as especially despicable.

Although she was a victim of war's hatred, Edith Cavell's last words to a British chaplain were, "Standing as I do in view of God and eternity . . . I must have no hatred or bitterness toward anyone." A monument to her memory stands at Trafalgar Place in London, and Hollywood made a movie about her heart and courage.

Edith Cavell, killed by the Germans in Bruxelles on October 12, 1915 *(Library of Congress)*

"No-man's-land," between two deadlocked armies, France, 1915
(National Archives)

The moment the bombardment stopped, the infantry in the attacker's trench would go "over the top." The cratered, obstacle-covered strip between the friendly and enemy trenches was called no-man's-land. Men would form into long lines and move forward in waves at a walking pace.

It was always rough going. No-man's-land was pocked by thousands of shell holes, which were very often filled with water. Constant cannon fire churned the landscape into a quagmire of muck and mud that sometimes literally swallowed men alive. As best they could, the attackers would stumble forward. Fog, smoke, or the steamed-up goggles of their sweat-filled gas masks made visibility almost zero.

No-man's-land was stitched with barbed-wire entanglements. The advancing infantry would try to penetrate the barbed wire through gaps that the artillery shells were supposed to have blown. Usually, few of these gaps could be found. The men would bunch up to go through. The enemy's machine-gun fire would concentrate on them, and the gaps would soon become clogged with bodies.

Some men would try to climb over the unbroken wire. Stuck on the sharp barbs, they would jerk around like flies in a gigantic spider's web, until enemy bullets riddled them.

Some would make it to the defenders' trench to face hand-to-hand combat. Others would take cover and crawl back to their own trench after dark. Many wounded would be left for dead, moaning for days among the craters.

This was the horror of trench warfare. Once they had seen enough, American volunteers not enlisted in one of the armies could always go

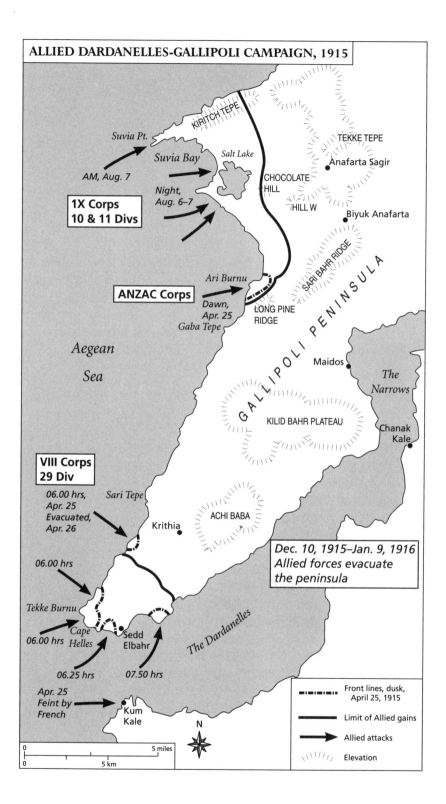

ALLIED DARDANELLES-GALLIPOLI CAMPAIGN, 1915

Suvia Pt.

KIRITCH TEPE

TEKKE TEPE

Suvia Bay

Salt Lake

Anafarta Sagir

AM, Aug. 7

CHOCOLATE HILL

Night, Aug. 6–7

HILL W

1X Corps 10 & 11 Divs

Biyuk Anafarta

SARI BAHR RIDGE

Ari Burnu

GALLIPOLI PENINSULA

ANZAC Corps

Dawn, Apr. 25

LONG PINE RIDGE

Gaba Tepe

Aegean

Sea

Maidos

The Narrows

GALLIPOLI

KILID BAHR PLATEAU

Chanak Kale

VIII Corps 29 Div

06.00 hrs, Apr. 25
Evacuated, Apr. 26

Sari Tepe

ACHI BABA

Krithia

06.00 hrs

Dec. 10, 1915–Jan. 9, 1916
Allied forces evacuate
the peninsula

Tekke Burnu

Cape Helles

06.00 hrs

Sedd Elbahr

The Dardanelles

06.25 hrs

07.50 hrs

Apr. 25
Feint by French

Kum Kale

N

| | 0 _____ 5 miles |
| 0 _____ 5 km |

▪▪▪▪▪▪ Front lines, dusk, April 25, 1915

▬▬▬ Limit of Allied gains

➤ Allied attacks

〟〟〟 Elevation

home. After all, it was not really their war. For Europeans, however, the war was inescapable, and it was just beginning to heat up.

After giving up the attack on Ypres in May, the German army went over to the defensive on the western front for the rest of 1915 so that large numbers of soldiers could be sent east. Austria-Hungary was proving to be a disappointing ally. It had again failed to beat the little Serbian army. Now the eastern part of its empire was being overrun by the Russians. Supported by the better-quality German troops, the Austrians were able to drive out the Russian army and crush Serbia completely.

In May 1915 Italy entered the war on the side of the Allies. Italian forces set out at once to attack Austria-Hungary. Their largely mountainous common border, however, hindered open warfare and greatly favored the defense. To the misery of the Italian army, its unimaginative commander in chief was dedicated to the strategy of attrition. In June began the First Battle of the Isonzo (named after the Isonzo River). By the end of the Fourth Battle of the Isonzo in December the Italian army had lost more than 280,000 men, the Austrian defenders about 160,000.

The war also saw a tragic sideshow that year in Turkey. The Allied armies and navies planned an amphibious invasion intended to knock the Ottoman Empire (which had joined the Central Powers in November 1914) out of the war. Beginning on April 25, 1915, an Allied force consisting of French, English, New Zealand, and Australian soldiers landed on the Gallipoli Peninsula, situated about 100 miles southwest of Constantinople (Istanbul).

The Allied operation was an epic of confusion, mismanagement, and bad timing. Also, the kaiser generously supplied German armaments and military advisers to the defending Turks, as well as one of his best generals to command them. After eight months of hard fighting and 214,000 casualties, the Allied forces had not even advanced off the beachhead. In November the Allies decided to pull out. In a belated show of competence, they completed the evacuation by January 9, 1916, without losing a man.

6

ATTRITION

1916

The beginning of 1916 saw the German army at the height of its success against the Russians on the eastern front. The German High Command decided, therefore, to renew its effort in the West. The chosen target would be the fortress-city of Verdun, France.

There were certainly more strategic places at which to launch a major attack. France could afford to lose Verdun without jeopardizing its overall defensive position. The French, however, were emotionally attached to Verdun. It was one of their oldest and most sacred cities. Attila the Hun had burned the city in the fifth century. Now the "Huns" were back. This time France was determined to keep Verdun if it took the entire fighting force.

This is precisely why the Germans chose it. They knew the French would try to hold it at all costs. The target was Verdun, but the goal was to inflict a mortal defeat on the French army by bleeding it white. The object was not to take ground, but to get as many men killed as possible. Once again, the tactic was calculated, cold-blooded attrition.

The battle began on February 21, 1916, with the most intense artillery barrage yet seen. Over the six-mile front more than 2 million shells rained down on the French defenders at the incredible rate of 28 per second. (Most contained high explosives; the rest, poison gas, which by this time was usually delivered by artillery fire.)

Soldiers on both sides marched into the furnace. Never before or since did so many die in so small an area—the inferno of hell itself to those that survived.

Of the returning soldiers, a French general wrote: "Their expressions . . . seemed frozen by a vision of terror: their postures betrayed a total dejection; they sagged beneath the weight of horrifying memories."

A German survivor wrote: "Verdun transformed men's souls. Whoever floundered through this morass full of the shrieking and dying . . . had passed the last frontier of life, and hence bore deep within him the leaden memory of a place that lies between life and death." A French army chaplain recalled grimly: "Having despaired of living amid such horror, we begged God to let us be dead."

Nearly every unit of the French army took its turn at Verdun. The French systematically rotated fresh troops from "quiet" sectors and put them into the battle. Units that had already seen a lot of action would then be sent to the quiet sectors. Soon, along almost every section of the western front were Frenchmen who had "done time" at Verdun. They were recognizable by their blank, empty expressions and the hollow eyes that had seen too much.

A German soldier at Verdun predicted that the battle would continue "until the last German and the last Frenchman hobbled out of their trenches on crutches to exterminate each other with . . . teeth and fingernails." It might have been so had events not forced the Germans to pull many troops out of the battle to fight elsewhere.

The British, determined to relieve pressure on the French army, launched a huge offensive along the Somme River, about 60 miles north of Paris. Months of careful and intensive preparation went into the operation. On June 24 an artillery barrage began that pounded the German positions for six days with a total of 1,508,652 shells.

At 7:28 A.M. on July 1, 1916, the Allied infantry went over the top. It was a catastrophe, the worst day in the history of the British army. On the average, some 83 British soldiers were killed or wounded every minute. It was the most terrible one-day loss for any army during World War I. (The British army's dead and wounded for that single day numbered more than 60,000—nearly one-third killed in action—which was more than all the American soldiers killed during the entire Vietnam War.)

The British generals should have called off the offensive that night and cut their losses, but they were too stubborn to quit. In the first week, they advanced only a mile, and after a month, only two and a half miles.

Meanwhile, the Russians were doing their part to relieve the hardpressed French at Verdun. In June they invaded eastern Austria-Hungary once again. It was Russia's final, desperate, all-out effort, and it achieved stunning success. Some 400,000 Austrians surrendered. Germany again had to send troops from the western front to save its ally.

In September, the British army surprised the Germans on the Somme front with a new secret weapon that was supposed to break the deadlock of trench warfare—the tank. Although the tanks performed well in a

New Weapons of Ground Warfare

WORLD WAR I IS THE STORY OF WEAPONS, DEADLIER and of greater variety and magnitude than could have been anticipated. The long fuse was lit when the Germans routed the invasion of France through Liège, Belgium, a city guarded by 12 forts equipped with 78 mm artillery pieces. On August 15, 1914, the Germans began to bombard the forts with 420 mm guns, heavier than any used before. The Belgians raised the white flag on August 16.

The handwriting was on the wall—weapons would determine who won and who lost in this war. Both sides began the rush to get the best brains developing the ever more powerful weapons that would handle larger shells, loaded with more powerful explosives, that would go a longer distance. The most devastating weapon of the war, constantly improved by both sides, was the machine gun, designed with a belt feeder containing multiple rounds of ammunition.

But the most inhumane of the war weapons was poison gas, produced by the German chemical genius Fritz Haber. In 1915, he provided the German army with chlorine gas; then with a more effective choking gas, phosgene; and by 1918, the most devastating of all, the dreaded mustard gas. After the Germans' first use, the Allies also resorted to poison gas. The Germans also introduced another deadly weapon, the flamethrower.

The British came up with a new defensive weapon—the tank. Officers of the Royal Engineers had been working for some time on the idea of a moveable fortress with the mobility of the American farm tractor. Introduced as "Little Willie" in December 1915, the tank was greatly improved in the months to come and became a superior weapon for the Allies. The Germans neglected tank development until late in the war. Finally, they developed a monstrous tank, poorly modeled after a British tank that they had captured, putting it in the battlefield in March 1918. Finally seeing its potential as a battle weapon, Germany developed and perfected powerful tanks used two decades later in World War II.

number of small-scale engagements, there were too few of them to make a difference.

By the end of October, the Russians had been driven from Austria-Hungary. The campaign had cost the Russian army a million men. In mid-November, the British finally gave up on the Battle of the Somme. They had gained less than eight miles along a 12-mile front, at a price of nearly 600,000 casualties.

In mid-December, the Battle of Verdun ended. The forts in front of the city, at last recaptured by the French, were useless mounds of rubble, with thousands of attackers and defenders entombed inside. The opposing lines were now roughly the same as they had been 10 months earlier. For this, about 950,000 French and German soldiers had been killed, wounded, or captured.

Meanwhile, on the southern front, the Italian army had renewed its war of attrition against the Austrians. From April to November 1916 raged the Fifth through Ninth Battles of the Isonzo. Little ground was taken but, as usual, casualties on both sides were enormous.

The Italian offensives, however, along with Russia's early success on the eastern front, convinced Romania that Austria-Hungary would soon be defeated. In August 1916, Romania joined the Allies. It was a fatal decision.

Once the Russians were in full retreat (by October), Germany and its allies Turkey and Bulgaria dealt with the Romanians. By December 1916, their country was completely overrun. Germany might not have been able to continue the war much longer had it not been for Romania's vast supply of wheat and its rich oil fields, which the Germans now possessed.

The Allies did get some good news. Although World War I was fought mainly in Europe, there were many smaller battlegrounds around the world. In 1914, for example, all of Germany's possessions in east Asia were captured by British and Japanese forces. In Africa, some German colonial forces stubbornly resisted until the end of the war. By 1916, however, the French and British had conquered most of Germany's African colonies.

Also in 1916 came good news from Allied troops fighting battles in Asia Minor against the Turkish Ottoman Empire. British forces had gained ground in Mesopotamia and Arabia, while the Russian army pushed deep into Turkey itself.

Another battleground in 1916 was in the North Sea. On May 31 the German and British fleets ran into each other off Denmark's Jutland Peninsula. The Battle of Jutland was the only major naval engagement of the war. Both sides claimed victory. In this clash, German gunners proved they were better shots, sinking twice as many warships as they lost (61,180 tons of German ships sunk, versus 117,025 tons of British). Yet the German fleet would never leave port again.

As usual, the war in Europe was the big story for American newspapers throughout 1916. Not all of the fighting, however, took place on battlefields.

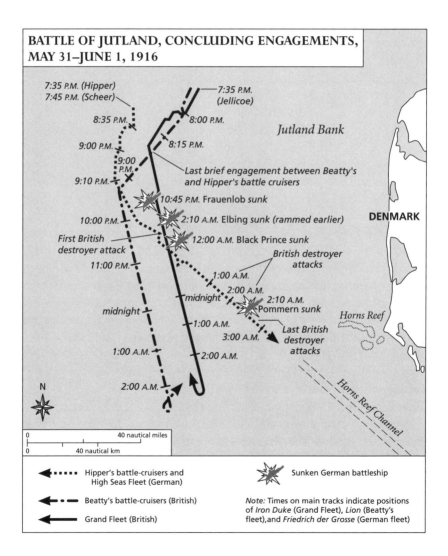

BATTLE OF JUTLAND, CONCLUDING ENGAGEMENTS, MAY 31–JUNE 1, 1916

ATTRITION

Submarine chaser (foreground), starboard side, at Brest, France *(National Archives)*

On April 23, a group called the Citizens Army took control of Dublin and declared Ireland's independence from the United Kingdom. They proclaimed it the Free Irish Republic and appointed a president. England quickly sent troops to stamp out what it called the Easter Rebellion. The American press blasted the English for this bloody act, calling them "tyrants" and "oppressors." American sentiment for Britain hit its wartime low.

That year the U.S. Army made a few headlines of its own. On March 9, 1916, followers of the Mexican bandit and revolutionary Pancho Villa raided Columbus, New Mexico. Fifteen Americans were murdered and 13 wounded. President Wilson sent a 12,000-man military expedition 300 miles into Mexico to find Villa. The commander of the expedition, Brig. Gen. John J. Pershing, entered the public eye and became a hero.

Although Americans were temporarily distracted from the war, Germany managed to make its presence felt again. On March 24, 1916, a German submarine torpedoed the British liner *Sussex,* killing several American citizens. The incident brought the friction between Berlin and Washington to a head.

President Wilson, backed by Congress, issued an ultimatum to the kaiser. The U.S. government threatened to break off diplomatic relations

Engine room of an oil-burning German submarine *(National Archives)*

with Germany if it did not comply. On May 4 the Germans gave in. They promised to abide by international law and not sink merchant and passenger vessels without attempting to warn them first.

The "Sussex pledge," as it was referred to, was not a very good formula for peace. Wilson's ultimatum made the issue of war or peace dependent on decisions made in Berlin. German military officials might decide that the submarine campaign was more important than the risk of American involvement in the war.

For a while it seemed to work. In November 1916, the president ran for reelection under the slogan "He Kept Us Out of War," and won by a narrow margin. Wilson would use the Sussex pledge as a token of the Germans' good faith, a trust they would soon break.

7
AN AMERICAN
CRUSADE

Throughout the war President Wilson pressed for peace negotiations between the warring powers, without success. He also offered to mediate discussions. And in January 1917, with the war in its third year, the president made a final attempt to bring about peace talks.

Again he failed. It became apparent to Wilson that the governments on both sides would not settle for anything less than the total and unconditional surrender of the enemy. He gave up all hope that there could be a "peace without victory." But if one side must lose the war, Wilson was convinced that it should be the Central Powers.

If the Allies lost, it could be damaging to the United States economy. While the Europeans were preoccupied with killing each other, American commerce had benefited greatly. Its overseas trading surplus had increased from $690 million in 1913 to $3 billion in 1916. (The first three years of the war saw no less than 8,000 new American millionaires.)

The basis of this prosperity was the dependence of the Allied countries on American imports. Many of those imports were purchased with money the Allies were borrowing from American banks. By January 1917 the Allied debt stood at $2 billion. American business, therefore, had a stake in an Allied victory. Should the Allies be defeated, large American investments would be at risk.

There was also a deep concern among many Americans, including the president, over Germany's conduct during the war. Many saw the Allied cause as a crusade against German militarism. Yet many Americans still thought the United States should not have a political or military role in the outcome of the war.

President Wilson felt differently. He believed the United States must have a hand in shaping postwar peace. Like most Americans, he believed in the superiority of the American way and the corruption of the Old World. The war had revealed the disastrous consequences of the old diplomacy of secret treaties and intrigue. Wilson thought that the world was marching upward on an evolutionary path toward democracy, liberalism, and open diplomacy.

A devout Presbyterian, Wilson believed that the years of horror and devastation caused by the war should be put to a higher end. It was as if the war was a transitional phase between the old order and a new and better world.

As war weakened the European powers, America emerged stronger. Wilson began to see the United States not as an ordinary mediator, but as an active peacemaker. He envisioned America as an architect with the power to construct a new world on the ruins of the old one.

True, Wilson had failed to use America's neutral position to bring the warring nations to the conference table. Now he realized that the United States could play a major role in a postwar peace conference only if it had helped to win the war. He began to consider military involvement on the side of the Allies.

Yet Wilson knew that it would take more than his lofty ideals about postwar peace and reconstruction to unite the country's many diverse ethnic groups behind the idea of American intervention. There could be no "hyphenated loyalty." German Americans, Irish Americans, Italian Americans, Scandinavian Americans—all Americans—would have to be galvanized into one nation, behind one cause.

Wilson knew that going to war would be a test of America's solidarity. (After all, he had won the election just two months earlier with a promise to keep the peace.) By the end of January, the president began thinking of how he could convince the American people that the United States should help defeat Germany. Then the Germans did the convincing for him.

On February 1, 1917, Berlin announced that it would resume unrestricted submarine warfare. The United States immediately broke off diplomatic relations with Germany. As one Allied ship after another sank, it was only a matter of time until an American ship was hit. It seemed to many people in the United States that war lay only one torpedo away.

AN AMERICAN CRUSADE

Then an extraordinary development took place. British Intelligence intercepted a message from German Foreign Secretary Zimmermann to the German ambassador in Mexico City. The note urged Mexico to declare war on the United States if the United States sided with the Allies. It offered Mexico generous financial support and the return of its "lost territory" of Texas, New Mexico, and Arizona.

It was a bizarre message. Mexico had no organized military power. Overrun by revolutionaries, it was a country on the verge of anarchy. Wilson was outraged. He thought the message might have been a hoax, but Berlin clumsily admitted its authenticity.

On March 1, the Zimmermann telegram made headlines across the country. Its chief result may have been the elimination of the small minority in Congress that had opposed America's growing involvement with the Allies, but the public went wild. War fever heightened. Suddenly, the war in Europe seemed to be a clear-cut contest between good and evil.

On March 16, German submarines sank three American ships. Among them was the oil tanker *Illinois,* homeward bound to Texas. A large pair of American flags and the initials "U.S.A." were painted on its side. It had not been sunk by mistake. It had been stopped by a U-boat, boarded, and plundered. Then the Germans destroyed it by setting off bombs in the oil compartments.

Former president Theodore Roosevelt thundered: "There is no question about going to war. Germany is already at war with us." Marchers took to the street carrying banners that read: "Kill the Kaiser!"—"On to Berlin!"—"Let's Get the Hun!"

On the night of April 2, 1917, a seething multitude formed outside the Capitol, while inside the president asked the Congress to declare war on the Central Powers. The packed gallery listened silently. Most of the congressmembers wore small stars and stripes on their lapels. The Supreme Court justices were also present. Chief Justice Edward Douglas White, a Civil War veteran, cried as he listened to the president's address.

"There is one choice we cannot make, we are incapable of making, we will not choose the path of submission," Wilson said. "It is a fearful thing to lead this great peaceful people into war, into the most terrible and disastrous of all wars, civilization itself seeming to be in the balance. But the right is more precious than peace, and we shall fight for the things which we have always carried nearest to our hearts."

One line from Wilson's war address people remembered most of all: "The world must be made safe for democracy." For many, this single sentence gave reason enough for America to enter the war.

The principles for which European governments were fighting were alien to the average American. But the triumph of democracy over dictatorship was an ideal that a nation of free citizens thought worth fighting for. So different was this truly American reason for war that Wilson made the symbolic gesture of calling the United States an "associate" rather than an ally.

On leaving the rostrum, he got the greatest ovation of his life. He was pleased, but his heart was heavy with sadness. Later, at the White House, he said to his secretary, "Think of what they were applauding. My message today was a message of death for our young men. How strange it seems to applaud that."

Congress reached its decision at 3 A.M. on April 6. Some lawmakers still held that America should stay neutral. When the voting came, the only congresswoman of that time, the pacifist Jeannette Rankin of Montana, whispered a gentle "no." (Twenty-four years later, on December 8, 1941, Rankin, back in Congress and still a pacifist at heart, cast the only "no" vote when the U.S. declared war on Japan.)

After a Senate vote of 82 to 6, the House voted 373 to 50 to support the president. The nation was at war.

President Wilson addresses a joint session of Congress and asks for a declaration of war against Germany, April 2, 1917. *(Library of Congress)*

8

CRISIS

1917

The Allies were jubilant. America's long-awaited entrance into the war had finally come. Yet most Americans were not quite sure what was expected of their country. The United States would, of course, continue to supply the Allies and loan them money. America's large navy could be of immediate help. A token expeditionary force would probably be sent to fight in France.

The Allies, however, were counting on the United States to send hundreds of thousands of troops to fight on the western front. America was not at all ready for such a war. The country was physically unprepared to support its verbal declaration.

The U.S. Army in April 1917 was a quiet, sleepy institution where old soldiers killed time until they began drawing their pensions. It numbered less than 200,000 men. Among the world's standing armies, it ranked only 17th. It was not much larger than King Albert's brave little Belgian army, and much less prepared to fight in a modern war. Its firearms were outdated. Its few cannon were antiques. Of its 55 airplanes, 51 were found to be hopelessly obsolete.

At first the United States did not recognize the scope of the job involved in mobilizing, training, supplying, and transporting troops, arms, and equipment across the Atlantic. When President Wilson asked how many troops could be sent to France immediately, he was told 24,000 men—at most—with only a one-day supply of ammunition. America may have been ready to fight, but it was not "fighting ready."

This fact had not escaped the German High Command. Germany had long noticed American sympathy for the Allied cause. German military experts had made careful calculations of the length of time it would take the United States to achieve a stable war footing should it become involved. The minimum estimates were six to eight months. More likely it would take 12 months before America could put its full resources behind the war effort.

This period of security had given the Germans the confidence to resume unrestricted submarine warfare, which they knew would likely draw the United States into the war against them. It was a calculated risk. They knew that, if the tactic failed, American involvement would ultimately mean defeat for the Central Powers.

The Allies started the war with about 21 million tons of shipping, well over the minimum necessary to feed Britain and keep the armies supplied. Their shipbuilding program had not kept up with the loss rate from submarines. The Germans calculated that if their U-boats could sink 500,000 tons of shipping a month, Britain would be brought to its knees well before the United States got into full swing.

This mad policy nearly succeeded. The U-boats sank 540,000 tons of merchant shipping in February 1917, 578,000 tons in March, and a strangling 874,000 tons in April. One in every four ships leaving British ports was sunk. Britain suffered crippling shortages. By May, there was enough food supply to last only six more weeks.

Germany, however, underestimated the effect of America's naval contribution. At Britain's most desperate moment, the U.S. Navy came to the rescue. Working together, the American and British fleets were able to cut monthly shipping losses in half by early fall of 1917.

On water, the Allies were beginning to turn the tables against Germany. On land, however, the Allies were in trouble. For them, 1917 would be the most critical and dangerous year of the war.

Discontent and unrest were reaching a climax in Russia. By January 1917, the Russian army had lost at least 5 million men, killed, wounded, captured, and deserted. On the home front, the cost of living had increased seven times what it had been in 1914. Food supply to the cities had broken down. Workers everywhere went on strike. Troops and civilians began to riot.

On March 15, 1917, the Russian emperor, Czar Nicholas II, gave up his throne. A government of liberal aristocrats and politicians was formed. The new leaders wanted to keep up the fight against the

Central Powers. The Russian army, however, was showing signs of severe strain. Just when the United States was joining the struggle against Germany, it looked as if Russia, a crucial ally, might soon be out of it.

The Allies now feared that Germany would be able to move hundreds of thousands of troops that had been busy at the eastern front to the western front. The French generals decided to gain ground while they still had the advantage. They made plans to launch a huge offensive.

The plan was to "pinch off" a bulge in the German line. Once surrounded, the defenders would be forced to surrender. It might have worked had the Germans not caught wind of the plan. The German army pulled back its line. The readjusted position was no longer an awkward bulge, it was now a death trap.

Despite pressure from the French government to reconsider the offensive, the French High Command chose to go ahead with the attack. On April 16, masses of French infantry went over the top—but not much further. In 10 utterly futile days, the French army lost another 187,000 men. The soldiers had taken more than they could stand, not from the Germans but from their own generals.

On April 29, a full-scale mutiny spread through the French army. The troops had seen their fellow soldiers massacred by following the inhuman and senseless orders of

Revolution breaks out in Russia, after heavy war losses and a breakdown of the food supply. Rioting troops and civilians take cover from gunfire, leaving dead and wounded in the streets. *(National Archives)*

Gen. Robert-Georges Nivelle, the commander in chief of the French armies. They rebelled against that by refusing to continue suicidal attacks against the Germans who fired machine guns from safe, entrenched positions, suffering few casualties as they slaughtered thousands of French soldiers. The horror and uselessness of the Nivelle Offensive brought other grievances to the surface, including the lack of medical care, hunger from the shortage of food, and no leave time.

As word of the mutiny spread, 54 other French divisions joined the protest, paralyzing the French western front. Not less than 100,000 soldiers were later court-martialed. Some soldiers deserted over to the enemy. The stories they told about the extent of the mutiny seemed so incredible that the Germans did not believe them. As a result, Germany missed its best chance of the war for a decisive breakthrough on the western front.

In May, Nivelle, the French commander who had bungled the offensive, was replaced by Gen. Henri Pétain, a hero of the battle of Verdun. Pétain restored order and regained the confidence of the soldiers. He worked to improve their food and increase their leave time. Most of all, he promised them that there would be no new French offensive for the rest of the year. Pétain's strategy was summed up in one sentence: "We must wait for the Americans."

It was now up to the British to carry the western front. Eager to draw the Germans' attention away from the shaken French army, Britain's generals decided to launch a major attack. They chose for their offensive the wretched bogs and wetlands just east of Ypres in Belgium. Three years of war had churned the countryside around Ypres into one big, mangled mud pit. It was the sorriest possible ground for an operation.

Three miles south of the town, the Germans were poised menacingly on a crest called Messines Ridge. The British knew that before they could push east of Ypres they would have to take the ridge. The Germans had been there for two years and were well entrenched.

For months, English and Welsh miners, drafted into the army for their digging skills, worked like moles to run tunnels under the German positions. Because the sudden appearance of mounds of dirt would give them away, every ounce of soil and chunk of rock had to be bagged and transported far to the rear.

In all, they dug five miles of tunnels, without being detected by the Germans. The tunnels were then packed with 1 million pounds of high explosives.

CRISIS

The blast that followed was so powerful that people as far away as London heard the rumble and felt the quake. Not only did it make history, but it changed geography. It made craters 100 yards across and 100 feet deep. More than 20,000 German soldiers were killed or maimed by the explosion.

After taking over what was left of Messines Ridge, the British prepared for the main assault. As usual, it was preceded by an intense bombardment lasting many days. While the British artillery "softened up" the battlefield, the weather did its share. Rain came down in torrents for days.

By the time the Third Battle of Ypres finally got under way on July 31, 1917, no-man's-land had dissolved into ooze. British soldiers had to advance through mud that was often up to their knees. Some men drowned in shell craters that had filled up with water. British tanks, stuck in the muck, were easy targets for German gunners.

Two years earlier, during the Second Battle of Ypres, the same field saw the first use of chlorine gas. The Germans now introduced the most terrible chemical—mustard gas.

Because it could penetrate clothing, gas masks gave only limited protection. It caused blindness, severe burns, and large, festering blisters. Affected soldiers were told not to touch the irritated areas, as it only made the burns spread, but victims often could not control themselves. They would scratch frantically and tear at the wounds until they had clawed themselves to death. Even today there is no adequate treatment for mustard gas wounds.

The battle raged on for more than three months until, finally, the British gave up the attack in November. It had not been the breakthrough the generals had hoped for. The British army had lost another 244,897 men to gain 9,000 yards of blood-soaked marshland.

While the British and Germans were slugging it out in Belgium, Italy made its last lunge at the Austrian line on the Isonzo sector. The 11th Battle of the Isonzo (August 19–September 12) drained the Italian army's manpower, but brought the Austrian army to the very point of collapse.

Once more, Germany had to come to the rescue. The Austrians were beefed up with German troops released from the eastern front. The Austro-German force struck a sledgehammer blow at Caporetto. The Italians were overwhelmed.

The Battle of Caporetto (October 24–November 12, 1917) was an unnerving disaster for the Allies. Italy lost 305,000 soldiers, 275,000 of whom had surrendered. What was left of the Italian army retreated 100

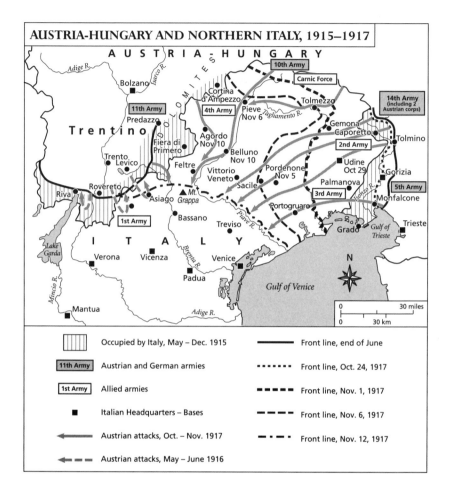

AUSTRIA-HUNGARY AND NORTHERN ITALY, 1915–1917

Occupied by Italy, May – Dec. 1915		Front line, end of June
Austrian and German armies		Front line, Oct. 24, 1917
Allied armies		Front line, Nov. 1, 1917
Italian Headquarters – Bases		Front line, Nov. 6, 1917
Austrian attacks, Oct. – Nov. 1917		Front line, Nov. 12, 1917
Austrian attacks, May – June 1916		

miles. Thousands of French and British troops, badly needed on the western front, were sent to Italy to check the enemy advance.

The Allies were clearly in a desperate position. Then, on November 7, 1917, the government of Russia was overthrown by Bolsheviks (communists). The next day, the new Bolshevik government announced its plan to make a separate peace and, in December, it signed an armistice with the Central Powers.

Now, help from the United States was needed more than ever. Both sides waited, one with hope, the other with fear, for the arrival of the Americans.

9

MOBILIZING A NATION

You're in the army now,
You're not behind a plow . . .

—popular song of 1917

Having entered the war, the United States had the task of mustering its full resources behind the war effort as soon as possible. There was more to be done than raising an army. More ships would have to be built. Factories would have to be converted to manufacture armaments. Industry and agriculture needed to be reorganized to meet the demands of a wartime economy. "It is not an army we must shape and train for war," said the President, "it is a nation."

In the emotional fervor that followed the declaration of war on April 6, many young men rushed to volunteer for the armed forces. Yet, it was only a fraction of the number needed. Americans had heard three years of stories about the horrors of trench warfare, so it is hardly surprising that more men did not run to join up.

President Wilson proposed national conscription, otherwise known as a *draft*. Many members of Congress objected to the bill. The Speaker of the House asserted that there was "little difference between the conscript [draftee] and the convict." "You will have the streets of our American cities running red with blood on registration day," warned one senator.

Yet on May 18, 1917, Congress ratified the Selective Service Act, requiring all able-bodied males between the ages of 21 and 31 to register for active duty. Later in the war, the age limits were extended to include men from ages 18 to 45.

Surprisingly, there were no antidraft riots anywhere, not even, as had been expected, in the cities with large German-American populations. Some credit must be given to the secretary of war, Newton Baker, who enlisted the support of chambers of commerce and other local agencies "to make the day of registration a festive and patriotic occasion." The occasion did, in fact, go off more like a holiday than a grim mustering for war.

This portrait of Uncle Sam by James Montgomery Flagg was so popular it was used again by recruiting stations in World War II. *(National Archives)*

On the appointed day, June 5, 1917, some 9,660,000 men registered. On July 20 came the first drawing of the "great national lottery." Blind-folded, Secretary Baker reached into a big glass bowl containing 10,500 numbers in capsules and pulled out number 258. In each registration district throughout the country, the man holding number 258 was the first to be called into service.

Racism

A BLEMISH ON THE U.S. ARMY
AND THE HOME FRONT

MORE THAN 370,000 BLACK AMERICANS SERVED IN THE military between 1917 and 1918, but the conditions they found in the U.S. Army camps and later overseas were clearly "separate and unequal," despite the 1896 Supreme Court decision in *Plessy v. Ferguson* that mandated "separate but equal" facilities. Wanting to maintain strong control over possible dangerous altercations between black and white soldiers, the army kept a "safe ratio," meaning a camp would have about one black soldier for every 10 white ones. Every camp had separate facilities for blacks and whites, and when there were shortages of anything from food to blankets, it was the black soldiers who did without.

Black soldiers were also expected to take on noncombatant duties, because military leaders, reflecting the country's racial attitudes, falsely believed black soldiers were lazy, unintelligent, and not courageous enough to fight. Most black soldiers were assigned to the Services of Supply (SOS), loading trains, getting the mail through, constructing railroads and barracks, and similar tasks. One regiment, however, the 369th Infantry, was the first black unit to go to France, where its men fought with the French army and became famous for their bravery.

On the home front, black Americans were called upon to work for the war effort, but they were given wages way below that of white workers. The Red Cross, greatly needing nurses, still refused to accept black nurses. Worse, blacks were still being lynched in the South—44 in 1917, 64 in 1918. The brutality and injustice of lynching—when one in seven soldiers serving the country was black—moved President Wilson to address the nation, asking to end "this disgraceful evil." Not until after World War II, however, would the U.S. armed forces be desegregated.

The War Department designated 16 army camps to be built in the North and 16 in the South. Each was near a railroad, on 8,000 to 12,000 acres of land with a good water supply. The southern camps were called "tent cities," mostly because they lacked wooden barracks. By contrast, the northern camps had some 1,200 buildings each.

It was the largest government undertaking since the building of the Panama Canal. It took 12 trains a day, each 50 cars long, to transport the construction materials. Thousands of civilian workers were needed. Some 200,000 carpenters and other workmen (more than the combined strengths of the Union and Confederate armies at the battle of Gettysburg), labored continuously. They laid enough roofing to cover Manhattan and Atlantic City, with some to spare.

When the new recruits arrived to see the muddy, unpaved campsites that would be their new homes they often found the barracks not yet ready. Many would have to sleep on the cold, wet ground, wrapped in blankets. And army chow, they found, was nothing like the food back home.

The winter of 1917–18 was particularly hard in the northern camps. For many of the southerners, it was their first time seeing snow. Measles, meningitis, influenza, and pneumonia spread rapidly through the crowded camps. Many recruits died of disease.

Much equipment, artillery pieces in particular, was not yet available. New soldiers trained on wooden replicas of the weapons they would be using. Even uniforms were sometimes in short supply. At one camp, some soldiers were issued old, blue Civil War uniforms.

The men were given complete physicals, most for the first time in their lives. Many had never been to a dentist. It was probably not a pleasant first experience. Overworked army dentists simply pulled out any tooth that looked like it might give trouble.

Some recruits had never been to a doctor. Instruments for taking blood pressure or listening to the heart filled these men with fright. Vaccinations were the worst. One recruit recalled his first shots:

> As we went by, single file, the doctor would stick us with a long needle on the right arm. We had a little patch of iodine there, but the fellow in front of me was so frightened he forgot to move on after being stuck, and when the doctor turned around, he stuck the first brown spot that he saw with the result that the man got a double dose and nearly fainted. He fell on the floor, everyone laughing at him ... but I was next and did not feel like laughing much.

"The Biggest Drum in the World" beats for a 1917 Liberty Loan Drive in New York, to help finance the war through the sale of U.S. Treasury Bonds. *(National Archives)*

Underprivileged men from rural areas probably had the hardest time adjusting to camp life. Many of them had never had a hot shower or a full suit of clothes or pair of shoes. Many could not read or sign their name. A few did not know their birthdays or only had first names. Birthdates and last names were assigned to these men by the army.

Geoffrey Perret points out in *A Country Made by War* that only 4 percent of the 2.8 million draftees had a high school diploma; in fact, most had no more than a grade school education.

The camp instructors did their job of turning raw recruits into soldiers. The men learned to drill, shoot, dig trenches, lay barbed wire, and construct latrines. They also learned that *kitchen police* (KP) did not mean guarding the kitchen—it meant performing menial kitchen tasks, such as peeling potatoes or washing dishes.

Meanwhile, the government's primary concern was how to raise the tens of billions of dollars the war was going to cost. About one-third of the funds would come from new taxes on income, alcohol, tobacco, and

Another patriotic poster by James Montgomery Flagg appealed to Americans' deepest sentiments. *(Library of Congress)*

various other goods and services. The rest of the money would be borrowed from the people, through the sale of war bonds.

Clubs and civic groups of all types, as well as federal and local government agencies, organized "Victory Loan" and "Liberty Loan" drives to encourage citizens to buy war bonds. Popular stars of the movie industry, like Charlie Chaplin and Mary Pickford, made public appearances to urge Americans to invest in America's future through War Bonds.

World War I gave birth to a centralized bureaucracy of unprecedented size. New federal agencies assumed unheard-of power. The War Industries Board, for example, seized raw materials, took control of production, and created new industries to meet war demands. The War Trade Board controlled imports and exports. The Federal Fuel Administration supervised efficient use of resources like coal and oil by industry and the public. Even the railroads were taken over and run by the government.

MOBILIZING A NATION

The Federal Food Administration was created to assure adequate food supplies for military needs and to send agricultural aid to the Allies. It monitored farm production and regulated prices. It asked Americans to plant "victory gardens" and observe "wheatless" and "meatless" days.

All this was the United States' first experiment with a government-directed economy. Some of the experts who staffed these wartime emergency boards would later use the valuable experience they gained to fight the economic depression of the 1930s.

Public opinion, an intangible but important resource, also had to be mobilized. This was the mission of the most controversial of the new government agencies, the Committee on Public Information. It hired hundreds of writers and artists who turned their talents to wartime propaganda. Pro-war leaflets and posters were widely circulated. The committee also sent skilled orators around the country to make speeches intended to rally the nationalistic emotions of the American people.

The spirit of "100 percent Americanism" promoted by the committee had an ugly side effect. German Americans, the country's largest

Women of Boston collect peach stones to be used in the production of gas masks. *(National Archives)*

Blurred Lines

NEWS OR PROPAGANDA?

NATIONS HAVE ALWAYS KNOWN THE IMPORTANCE OF creating patriotic fervor when they have declared war. One of the best ways was to make sure that the news people got was carefully censored—in particular, that it is embellished to bring out the atrocities of the enemy and the heroism of their own soldiers.

In World War I, the British and French propaganda machine was highly effective at painting the Germans as beasts in human form. However, the British military believed that the true story of the outrageous slaughter of Allied soldiers by the Germans had to be suppressed or they would be judged "incompetent" and lose the support of the people.

The control of news was so strong early in the war that public criticism developed, especially in the United States. Former president Theodore Roosevelt complained that the only real war news was from the German side. He had a point, because to try to win the United States over to their cause, the Germans had welcomed American correspondents and even assisted them. Eventually, to avoid more criticism, Britain and France agreed to accredit some American correspondents, but they were made to know that they were to write stories of heroism and glory to keep up the enthusiasm for the war.

When the United States entered the war, it also became guilty of the manipulation of news that Roosevelt had complained about. And propaganda was not restricted to news reporting. In the United States, President Wilson created the Committee on Public Information eight days after entering the war. It became a propaganda agency to hammer home American war aims, both in the United States and overseas. The irresponsible propaganda caused Hiram Johnson, a three-time U.S. senator from California, to say in 1917, "The first casualty when war comes is truth."

single group of foreign-born citizens, numbering 2.3 million at the time, became the target of patriotic frenzy. People of German origin felt the suspicion, scorn, and hatred of their neighbors.

German Americans tried to prove their loyalty with gestures like buying war bonds and having the German language banned from school curriculums. They even changed the name of sauerkraut to "liberty

A government-issue
poster encourages
Americans at home
to buy war bonds.
(National Archives)

cabbage." In spite of these efforts many German-American citizens were harassed. Thousands of German Americans who were not yet naturalized U.S. citizens were arrested and placed in internment camps.

Mobilizing the nation for war was a painful growing experience. But America would emerge from it stronger and more united than ever before.

10
THE BATTLE OF THE ATLANTIC

The Allies were pleased with the energy America was putting into its mobilization in the spring of 1917. However, an army in North America was of no use to them if the kaiser made good his promise to block the Atlantic sea lanes. Germany was counting on its U-boats to sink American troopships before they could land in Europe. Unless the battle of the seas was won, the war on land would be lost.

An effective antisubmarine tactic was the convoy. In a convoy, the most important vessels, the loaded troop transports, were surrounded by smaller, fast-moving combat ships called destroyers. Destroyers were designed and equipped to attack submerged submarines.

Also, by sailing on the outside of the convoy, a destroyer could, if necessary, block a torpedo with its own hull. The idea was that it was better to lose a destroyer than a huge transport with its tons of supplies and many hundreds of soldiers.

Because the naval war was to be directed against submarines, the navy suspended the building of battleships. Instead, it planned construction of 250 more destroyers. It also planned to build 400 smaller boats called submarine chasers.

American scientists developed simple underwater listening devices, the forerunner of today's sonar. Munitions experts developed effective depth charges. These were canisters of TNT that could be hurled into the water from the deck of a destroyer and set to explode at various depths.

Many of the new ships were still under construction when the war ended. Even so, the navy by then had 834 combat vessels on convoy duty.

The overall strength of the U.S. Navy in 1918 reached some 2,000 ships and 533,000 men.

The first U.S. Navy vessels to see wartime service were 34 destroyers sent to Queenstown, Ireland, in May 1917 and stationed there. From this base they went out on convoy duty.

In November 1917 two of the destroyers from Queenstown forced the surrender of the German submarine *U-58*. In most cases, however, destroyers fired their deck guns and dropped depth charges until they thought their prey was sunk. But there was never any certainty that an enemy sub had been destroyed. Sailors could only search the waves for floating bits of debris or an oil slick, which they optimistically interpreted as another U-boat sent to the bottom of the ocean.

Aerial naval observer comes down from a balloon after a U-boat-scouting tour on the Atlantic Coast. *(National Archives)*

One seaman, William Duke, Jr., described his experience on a cruise in December 1917:

> We were caught in a gale . . . and the seas were breaking over us. We were crawling around on deck . . . looking for a hatch cover that had become unfastened. We suddenly discovered that six depth charges had become unloosed and were lurching about, butting the bulkworks with every roll of the ship.
>
> These depth charges are controlled by the paying out of wire and when a certain amount becomes uncoiled, they automatically explode. As no man knew how much the wire had become unmeshed, we all had to work fast, heaving them overboard. They went 'pop, pop, pop' as quickly as champagne corks at the French Ball. How we ever escaped blowing off our own stern is still regarded as a miracle by us all.

A little later they reached the spot where a U-boat had surfaced and was firing its deck gun at a sailing vessel. As Duke's destroyer approached, the submarine submerged.

> We were soon amid the rushing of turbulent water that is caused by a sub directly after submerging. We let go one [of the remaining depth charges] set to explode at about 80 feet deep . . . We were soon rewarded by seeing the color of the water change [to black] in the immediate vicinity of the explosion.

Duty on convoy destroyers was characterized by days and days of boredom. Such days could be broken at any second by moments of tense, heart-stopping excitement at the appearance of an enemy submarine or torpedo trail.

Yet even the quiet times could be very unpleasant. In rough seas, seamen could sleep only by bracing themselves in their bunks. Men on duty became exhausted from constant holding on to lines or ladders. Then there was the danger of the ship capsizing in the heavy swell.

Wind, rain, and cold added to the sailors' discomfort. The winter of 1917–18 was a particularly bitter one on the North Atlantic. The navy vessels steamed into port looking more like icebergs than ships.

Life ashore at Queenstown was a relief, but not without its troubles. The American sailors were not always on the best of terms with the

Irish at the nearby town of Cork. The assistant secretary of the navy, Franklin Delano Roosevelt, went to visit the base. Years later, when he was president, he recalled:

> The young ladies [of Cork] ... preferred the American boys and, of course, the young gentlemen of Cork didn't like that ... They staged a raid on our seamen. There being about 1,000 civilians, they drove our men back to the train. [The sailors] came back with a good many broken heads. Liberty [off-base passes] ... was suspended until the Mayor of Cork gave assurance that the town people would behave better next time.

Sowing the Seeds of the New Technology
WIRELESS COMMUNICATION

ON THE EVE OF WORLD WAR I, THE AIR WAS CRACKLING with coded messages made possible by the miracle of wireless technology, the invention of Guglielmo Marconi, a young Italian. Marconi had sent the first wireless telegraph message in 1895; in 1901 he had sent the first transatlantic wireless telegraph message.

Naval and military observers were among the first to recognize the potential of wireless communication, and by 1899 Marconi's telegraph system had been installed on three British battleships. Wireless radio followed soon, and the first broadcast of human speech was in 1906. Commercial interests, seeing the potential for broadcasting, soon surfaced, but Congress moved quickly to regulate the new technology, passing a radio licensing law in 1912. One clause stated that "in time of war or public peril or disaster," the president had the authority to seize or close any radio apparatus.

When World War I began, broadcasting was immediately halted and commercial wireless stations were taken over by the army and navy, which promptly ordered mass production of electrical equipment. Radio became the crucial communications link, from ships to the trenches, not only for the Allies but for the Germans. Franklin Delano Roosevelt, then assistant secretary of the navy, recognizing the power of wireless, initiated vast, coordinated development of radio technology serving war needs.

U.S. NAVAL ACTIVITIES IN EUROPEAN WATERS, 1917–1918

Roosevelt also remembered inspecting one of the machine bays aboard the USS *Melville*. He noticed a large canvas covering something. Beneath the canvas Secretary Roosevelt found "the finest assortment of brass knuckles and pieces of lead pipe that you ever saw." He turned to a large redheaded chief petty officer by the name of Flanagan and asked him what they were for. Flanagan saluted and said: "Sir, that's for the next liberty trip to Cork, damn these Irish."

THE BATTLE OF THE ATLANTIC

Not all navy ships were on convoy duty. There were a number of battleships that joined the British blockade against the German fleet. For American seamen, life on the huge battleships not only was considerably more comfortable, it offered less opportunity for excitement. There was little chance that the German warships, now outnumbered two to one, would appear.

Another sort of duty was aboard minelaying ships operating out of Scotland. Their mission was to lay a field of mines from Scotland all the way across the North Sea to Norway (about the same distance as from New York City to Washington, D.C.). This was to be strictly an American project. In all, the navy laid 70,000 mines (each with 300 pounds of TNT), which blew up at least eight submarines.

Minelaying also had little excitement or glory, but it was hard work. There were dangers, too. In rough weather there was the risk of hitting a mine already laid. A ship might suffer, as one seaman put it, "some of our own particular brand of punishment."

Life on a submarine chaser was no less hazardous, but somewhat more exciting. American submarine chasers mainly patrolled waters in the Mediterranean Sea. They took part in many submarine hunts. According to one skipper, whose boat was stationed at the Greek island of Corfu: "Words cannot express the life on the chasers. . . . They are small but mighty. They ride worse than a horse or a mule and rock and roll like a cradle."

Life was even more uncomfortable aboard the fairly crude and fragile American submarines. They were used for the treacherous and difficult work of counter-submarine warfare.

The navy had many tasks. They all led to one purpose—getting transports and merchant ships past the lurking U-boats to the European harbors. In this way the navy played a vital role in the war effort.

11
CONVOY TO FRANCE

Before America's new army could fight in France, it had to cross an ocean. Troops from training camps across the country funneled into embarkation ports along the east coast. From New York, Boston, Norfolk, Charleston, and others, they set sail. They went on large, fast transports, and sometimes on old, slow tubs. Whatever the ship, it always sailed as part of a convoy, which steamed at the pace of the slowest ship.

Aboard the crowded ships, the men tried to stay above deck as much as they could. They amused themselves by playing cards and organizing wrestling matches. For most of them, it was their first time at sea. Many became seasick and some could hardly eat anything for the whole trip.

In more than one sense, enlisted personnel and their officers were literally in the same boat. As one recruit put it: "It gives the bucks [privates] a guilty joy to know that bars and stripes [of high rank] are no protection against seasickness. Another evidence of the democracy of our army is that it doesn't matter whether an officer or soldier goes overboard—the ship won't stop in either case."

Most trips were happily uneventful for the troops. But they always took precautions. Lifeboat drills were a daily exercise. After dark, no lights were allowed on deck; even smoking was prohibited. In danger zones, everyone slept in their clothes and life preservers.

Most of the troops believed that their passage would be a safe one. They put their trust in the new defensive tactics. The ships moved in a zigzag pattern, which made it harder for U-boats to aim their torpedoes. Ship hulls were painted with camouflage patterns that made them difficult to see clearly from submarine periscopes. Most of all, the men felt confident that the accompanying destroyers would keep them from harm.

CONVOY TO FRANCE

There were many false alarms. Periscope sightings often turned out to be a piece of driftwood or a reflection on the water. But sometimes these "sub scares" were real submarines.

Just after dark, on February 5, 1918, a torpedo struck the troopship *Tuscania*. The 2,500 men on board scrambled to get on deck. Unlike the passengers of the *Lusitania*, these men had rehearsed many times for precisely this emergency. They carefully lowered the lifeboats and evacuated the rapidly sinking vessel in good order. Very few lives were lost.

Fortunately, and to the U.S. Navy's credit, the *Tuscania* was the only Europe-bound troop transport to be sunk. There were, however, a number of very close calls. In June 1918, the *Von Steuben* narrowly missed being sunk. The *Von Steuben* was one of a number of German ships, trapped in American ports since 1914, that the U.S. Navy promptly seized when Congress declared war.

The *Von Steuben*'s lookout spotted the foamy white trail of a torpedo heading directly toward them. Within an instant, he alerted the bridge. The captain gave orders for evasive action. The crew, acting without hesitation or confusion, maneuvered the ship. The men held their breath as the torpedo skimmed by, missing the bow by a bare 20 feet.

The commander of convoy operations, Vice Admiral Albert Gleaves, commented later, "Here was a case where three brains acted quickly and in coordination, the lookout, the captain and the helmsman. The slightest mistake on the part of any one of the three would have resulted in the loss of the ship."

Priority was given to loaded troop transports. After their passengers and cargo were safely landed, convoys sometimes had to return to the United States without destroyer escorts. On May 30, 1918, the German submarine *U-90* sighted an unescorted convoy of four ships sailing back from France. The U-boat attacked. Three of the ships got away. The fourth and largest of the ships, the *President Lincoln*, sank after taking three torpedo hits.

Soon after, *U-90* surfaced and approached the survivors' rafts and lifeboats. The German skipper tried to find the ship's commander, Capt. P. W. Foote, but he had disguised himself as a sailor. The men assured the U-boat commander that Foote had gone down with the ship. Noticing the officer uniform of a Lieutenant Isaacs, the German skipper ordered him aboard, then submerged and sailed away.

The next morning, two U.S. destroyers arrived on the scene. Picking up the survivors was slow and risky work. A U-boat might be waiting nearby, using the lifeboats as bait for new victims. The rescue took four hours to complete. Only 26 men were lost out of the 785 that had been aboard.

Shortly after the last man was pulled out of the water one of the destroyers spotted *U-90*'s periscope. The destroyers headed straight for the submarine at top speed and dropped depth charges where it was spotted.

Lieutenant Isaacs, prisoner aboard *U-90*, learned firsthand what it was like to be attacked by an American destroyer. "We felt depth bombs exploding all about us," he wrote months later, in an official report. "I counted 22 bombs in four minutes; five of them very close." The German skipper barely saved his vessel by quickly diving 200 feet, turning off the engines and "playing dead."

U-90 returned to port in Wilhelmshaven, Germany. Lieutenant Isaacs was sent to a prisoner-of-war camp. After persistent effort he managed to escape and made his way to Switzerland. He was then brought to the British Admiralty in London, where he gave a full report about all that he had learned about the operation of U-boats.

In September 1918, a submarine torpedoed the crowded troop transport *Mount Vernon*. Only one torpedo hit, but it blew a 19-foot hole in the transport's side and flooded half the boiler rooms. The escorting destroyers first laid a massive screen of black smoke to hide the stricken vessel. Then they fanned out and began dropping depth charges.

American troops embark for France, 1917. *(National Archives)*

Meanwhile, the *Mount Vernon* had all it could do to stay afloat. Sailors worked feverishly to stop the flooding and keep the remaining boilers going. The soldiers on board had work, too. They formed a bucket line and bailed out water for the next 18 hours until the ship finally reached port in France.

Experiences like these were exceptional on the seas. Only 71 of the more than 2 million American soldiers transported across the Atlantic in 1,142 troopship sailings were lost. Few troops encountered any hazard worse than seasickness.

The navy had achieved a miracle in the face of ever-present danger from beneath the waves. It assembled a "bridge of ships" that transported not only a huge army to France but also an average of four tons of supplies and equipment for each soldier. It won the Atlantic battle. This was an essential prelude to winning the great battles on the western front.

12
OVER THERE

———◆|ᴄᴏᴏ—————————————————

The first American troops arrived in France on June 28, 1917. To the tired French people, exhausted by three years of attrition, these fresh young men brought promise and new hope.

The "doughboys," the nickname (of disputed origin) of the American soldiers, had come to fight on the side of liberty. Many thought it repayment of the debt owed to France for having helped their forebears win the American Revolution.

On July 4, 1917, the city of Paris threw a hearty welcome for the doughboys. During the celebration, an American colonel named C. E. Stanton uttered four words that were to stir both the French and American nations: "Lafayette, we are here." (Stanton was referring, of course, to the French general who fought for the United States during the Revolutionary War.)

These first men were the nucleus of what would become a huge army called the American Expeditionary Force (AEF). Gen. John "Black Jack" Pershing, of the Mexican expedition, was the man President Wilson chose to be commander in chief of the AEF.

Pershing was born in Missouri in 1860 into a family whose original German name was Pfoersching. In 1886 he graduated from the United States Military Academy (West Point) at the top of his class. While serving in the U.S. Cavalry, he fought in the last Indian wars of the American West.

In those days, promotions in rank were painfully slow. By his mid-thirties he was still a lieutenant. He considered leaving the army to become a lawyer. His good friend Charles Dawes, future vice president of the United States (1925–29), convinced Pershing to stick with the army a while longer. Neither of them could have dreamed that Pershing's army career would skyrocket him to international fame.

In 1898 Pershing fought in Cuba where he won the Silver Star. Next he went to the Philippines to help put down the Moro rebellion. Still only a captain, Pershing won the admiration of President Theodore Roosevelt, who sent him to act as an observer in the Russo-Japanese War of 1904–05.

Roosevelt rewarded Pershing in 1906 by elevating him four ranks to brigadier general. Pershing, only 46 years old, had been promoted ahead of 862 senior officers, creating considerable bitterness among his fellow officers for many years.

Pershing's devotion to duty helped him to weather personal hardship. The day he arrived in Texas to lead the Mexican expedition, he received the news that his wife and three small daughters had burned to death in a fire at the Presidio army base in San Francisco. Pershing went on with his mission and proved himself an able leader. When he returned, President Wilson made him a two-star general.

Wilson probably could not have made a better choice for commander of the AEF. Pershing was no great strategist and often lacked military wisdom. Yet, he had patience, emotional balance, and unshakable fortitude—important qualities if one is to shape an army. Pershing's organization of the AEF from scratch was one of the great feats of World War I.

Pershing was the picture-perfect image of an indomitable high commander. His height and rigid posture seemed tailor-made for monuments. He possessed a strength of character that inspired confidence in his troops as well as his political superiors in Washington.

General Pershing arrives in France. *(Library of Congress)*

Most of all, Pershing had the grit and determination to stand up to the Allied governments and their generals. France and Britain were not interested in an independent and untested U.S. Army. They needed men to bolster their thinned-out lines. They wanted to use American manpower to flesh out their depleted units.

Pershing said no. He was appalled by the callous disregard the Allied generals had for the lives of their troops. Casualties were just numbers to them. Pershing could not bear the thought of his men being dragged into some wasteful trench battle at the whim of foreign generals whom he considered to be incompetent strategists.

They Put Down Their Pens to Serve

IN JULY 1918, THE ALLIES FOUGHT A BITTER FIVE-DAY battle at the Marne River in France. Fighting hard were American soldiers with the Rainbow Division, among them Joyce Kilmer, a poet acclaimed for "Trees." A father of four, he had felt a moral imperative to volunteer to serve his country. Even though he was in the intelligence section and could have remained at regimental headquarters, Kilmer volunteered to work as a combat scout.

During the battle, Kilmer, realizing that a number of machine guns were still in the woods ahead, reported this to the battalion commander. A few hours later, his commander found him with a bullet through his head. Kilmer was widely mourned and praised for "always doing more than his orders called for."

Another American poet, E. E. Cummings, volunteered as an ambulance driver in France, but he got into trouble for becoming friendly with an American whose letters home came under attack by the French censors. They concluded he was criticizing the war effort and threw both men into a detention camp, an ordeal Cummings recounted in *The Enormous Room*.

Still another famed writer who served in the war was Ernest Hemingway. He was rejected by the U.S. Army because he had a defective eye, but he eventually got to Europe as an ambulance driver for the American Red Cross. On July 8, 1918, 13 days before his 19th birthday, he was injured on the Austro-Italian front. Hospitalized in Milan, he received a decoration for heroism. This experience inspired his novel *A Farewell to Arms* (1929), probably the most famous American novel written about the war.

Not only was Pershing going to keep his army intact and independent, he also intended to keep it away from the fighting until he felt it was fully trained. The Allies constantly pressured him to commit his troops, ready or not. They even put severe pressure on the American government to remove Pershing, but Wilson doggedly stuck by his general.

Pershing realized that the stateside training his men had received was inadequate for the kind of war that faced them at the front. New training areas were set up in the rear.

French troops, hardened veterans loaned to Pershing, became professors to the green (inexperienced) Americans. The French instructors could hardly believe how ill-trained the doughboys were. Yet, in time, they were amazed by the speed and dedication with which these same Americans applied their new training and tactics.

In early October, Pershing arranged with General Pétain, commander in chief of the French army, to have small American units go into the French line for 10 days at a time for the sake of experience. Through this rotation system, most doughboys would be initiated into trench warfare.

The line around the city of Toul was the spot Pershing chose for the first rotations. This was one of the so-called quiet sectors. Except for occasional shelling, sniping, and trench raids, there had been no fighting there since 1914. Both sides seemed content to keep it that way.

Pershing chose this sector so his men could gain confidence without the risk of getting caught in a major attack and being mauled or beaten. A few weeks later the Germans discovered that the virgin American troops were now in the line. They decided to send a welcoming committee for the new arrivals.

At midnight on November 2, 1917, German infantrymen staged a well-executed raid on the American trench. After a short barrage, the Germans cut through the wire without being detected and infiltrated the American position. They did their bloody work and got away.

The Germans killed three doughboys and took 11 prisoners. Cpl. Nick Mulhall had the unfortunate distinction of being the first U.S. soldier of the war to be captured. He was never seen or heard from again.

The raid was intended to humiliate the Americans and shake their morale. Far from it, the United States now had three heroes to rally around, and the doughboys were eager to retaliate.

Thereafter, trench raids were frequent on both sides. On one occasion, Pvt. Leslie Lane turned a corner and was confronted by a group of soldiers. Lane ducked down to get a better view of them against the dark night sky.

"I was asked in French if I would consent to become a prisoner," he recalled. "I thought it was one of our French friends fooling around . . . The questioner then asked me in quite fluent English."

Lane stepped forward to see that it was a German sergeant-major with a party of about 15 men. The big German grabbed Lane and tried to silence him. "I then kicked the fellow in a vulnerable spot so furiously," recalled Lane, "that it brought him to his knees."

Lane then shot the sergeant-major before he himself was knocked unconscious. The shot alerted the other Americans and the rest of the raiders scattered back to their line. Lane soon came to, only to feel the German sergeant-major quivering at his feet.

"I reached to get a hold of him so I could get up first, and in doing so, found that he had pulled the pin from a 'potato masher' grenade, which exploded as I grabbed his hand, shattering three fingers on my left hand."

Another soldier, who saw this, reported that Lane had been killed. As Lane struggled to crawl to a first aid station, an American sentry turned the corner.

"Knowing there were Germans around and thinking I was killed, he was taking no chances and made a lunge for me with his bayonet. I saw the gleam of the bayonet aimed at my throat and raised my injured hand to ward off the blow."

The bayonet mangled his hand even more. The sentry then realized it was Lane and apologized profusely. "But I had no time to listen," recalled Lane, "as I was bleeding to death and wanted to get to First Aid before it was too late."

The enthusiasm and vigor of the doughboys was refreshing to the tired Allied soldiers. The patriotic American songwriter George M. Cohan put the spirit of the Americans to music. His most famous tune could be heard in every Allied trench, dugout, and gunpit on the western front. French, British, and American soldiers sang it while cleaning their guns. They whistled it while marching. They hummed it between bites of their hard biscuits and creamed beef.

Over there, over there,
Spread the word, send the word, over there,
That the Yanks are coming, the Yanks are coming,
The drums drum drumming everywhere.
So prepare, say a prayer.
Send the word, spread the word to beware,
We'll be over, we're coming over,
And we won't come back till it's over over there.

By the end of 1917, the AEF was becoming a sizable, well-trained force. (Pershing was promoted to four-star general, the first one since the Civil War.) The Allies began to feel that they were past the danger zone and that now it was just a matter of time until the war was won.

The Germans, however, had some deadly surprises left in store for the Allied armies.

13

THE NEW STORM

The first two months of 1918 were calm ones on the western front. They were too calm. The Allies began to wonder what the German army was up to. By mid-March, Allied intelligence confirmed that something big was going on. With remarkable secrecy, the Germans were massing incredible amounts of troops, artillery, ammunition, and other equipment in preparation for a lightning offensive that would stun the world.

The German High Command reasoned that an all-out push in the west might knock the Allies out of the war before Pershing could fully organize the AEF into an independent fighting force. With tens of thousands of Americans arriving in France every week, the Germans knew that the time for attack was now or never. It was a desperate gamble, Germany's last hope for victory.

The British Fifth Army held a 41-mile line that started south of Arras and ran down to Soissons, where the British and French lines joined. The German plan was to crush the Fifth Army and drive a wedge into this sector. They believed that the British would fall back toward their supply bases on the English Channel—away from Paris. The French, the Germans assumed, would pull back to protect their capital. Thus a gap would exist, through which German troops could pour.

The commander of the British Fifth Army, Gen. Sir Hubert Gough, had seen the blow coming and made what preparations he could. General Pershing had loaned him three U.S. Engineer Regiments to help him with his defenses. Afterwards, the engineers fought with the Fifth Army as infantry, the first Americans to see full-scale warfare since the Civil War.

The German High Command: Kaiser Wilhelm II, with Hindenburg and Ludendorff at either side, each with one hand in pocket, as was customary in the presence of the Kaiser, whose left arm was paralyzed from birth. *(National Archives)*

Gough had summoned his division leaders earlier that week for a pep talk. Interestingly, the British general ended by quoting Abraham Lincoln: "We accept this war for one object, a worthy object, and the war will end when that object is attained. Under God, I hope it will never end until that time."

Although Germany had been slow to build tanks, its generals had found another answer to trench warfare. They used specially trained shock units called *Sturmtruppen* (in English, "storm troopers"). They would filter forward under artillery cover and pierce the enemy's line of defense at a number of selected weak points. The strongest points would then be cut off and surrounded and could be dealt with later by other troops coming up behind.

Operation Michael, as the Germans called it, began at 4:50 A.M. on March 21, 1918, with a massive bombardment. The British waited for the attack that they knew would follow. They expected solid lines of men walking into the slaughter as was usually done. Instead, the storm troopers dashed forward, concealed by gas and fog, and slashed into the

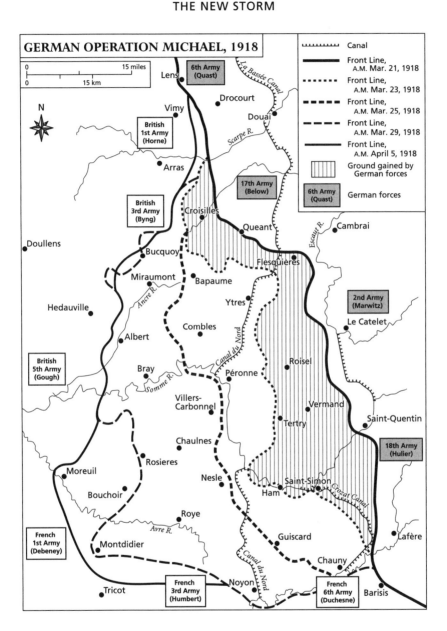

GERMAN OPERATION MICHAEL, 1918

British line. The new tactics caught the British by surprise. The Fifth Army collapsed. All British reserves had to be rushed in to plug the gap.

The German army struck again around Ypres on April 9. Here the British were better prepared. The Germans made only modest gains, at great cost. After 20 days of hard fighting, they gave up the attack. The German army's next blow, however, fell on the French in the hilly region between Soissons and Rheims, on May 27. It smashed through their defenses.

This sector had been considered safe by the French high command. Only the most battered units, some less than half strength, had been stationed there. They had been sent there from more active parts of the front to rest and recuperate.

In just eight days, the Germans advanced 35 miles, more than all the Allied offensives of the previous three years put together. Along the way, the Germans captured much equipment and 65,000 prisoners.

Not since 1914 had the Allied situation been so precarious. The enemy was on the Marne River again, only 37 miles from Paris. The capital was gripped with panic. The French government had packed up and was ready to move to Bordeaux in southwest France.

Gen. Ferdinand Foch of France, who had just been made Supreme Allied Commander, had committed almost all remaining reserves to the sector under attack, but was unable to stem the German advance. The overwhelmed reinforcements, said Foch, "evaporated immediately like drops of rain on a red hot iron." Not since 1914 had Allied hopes of victory seemed so remote.

On May 30, Foch sent General Pétain, commander in chief of the French army, to General Pershing, to ask in person that American troops be sent to the danger point. Pétain had reviewed the situation in detail. He told Pershing that it was doubtful that France could survive the loss of Paris. It was not only the spiritual heart of the nation but also an important industrial center and the focal point of all the major railroad systems.

Pershing listened respectfully to the French general, but was reluctant to comply with his request. Of the half-million American soldiers then in Europe, only four divisions were ready for combat. Two of these had already been pushed into the French line and had seen limited action. If he loaned France more troops it would delay for weeks the plan for an independent U.S. Army.

He also knew the situation was critical. There was no choice. He agreed to put the U.S. Second and Third divisions at Pétain's disposal.

The Second Division, which included a brigade of U.S. Marines, had been stationed in a quiet region northwest of Paris. Commanded by Lt. Col. Frederick Wise, this was the only marine brigade on the western front. Now they headed out for the front as fast as they could along clogged roads. In the last week, these roads had become a tangle of wounded troops, supply trucks, animals, and civilian refugees fleeing the advancing Germans.

Vietnamese drivers (from French Indochina) were assigned to transport the Second Division, and had been on the road almost nonstop for 72 hours. Exhausted, several fell asleep at the wheel, killing and injuring their passengers.

It was dusk by the time the first battalions of doughboys arrived at the French Sixth Army headquarters. The French commanding officer did not know what to do with them. The front was in such flux that danger came from a dozen points at once. Where was the main German blow going to fall? French intelligence had broken down, unable to cope with the rapid movements of open warfare.

The French decided to rush the Americans into the line piecemeal, by companies, as had been done with France's own reinforcements. Col. Preston Brown, Second Division chief of staff, refused to consider this. The Second Division must fight as a unit, he insisted, on a defensive line supporting the French. First, stop the German spearhead, then counterattack. That was the only sensible plan.

Sixth Army headquarters was uneasy about entrusting a section of the line to the raw, inexperienced troops. How could they stand up against tough, disciplined German storm troopers? Colonel Brown indignantly replied, "These are American regulars. In 150 years they've never been beaten. They will hold."

Despite orders to the contrary, French units continued to give ground. They filtered back across fields waist-high in bright-green winter wheat, past deserted farms and villages. Many tried to retreat in orderly fashion, fighting as they went. Others fled in panic, leaving a trail of discarded equipment for the enemy to gather and distribute among its own troops.

By noon on June 2, Lieutenant Colonel Wise's battalion of marines had moved into position and was digging in. Because entrenching equipment had not yet arrived, the men had to dig with bayonets, mess kits, and spoons. Although there were still a few French units between them and the enemy, they wasted no time. The Germans were already shelling their position with artillery.

The marines waited in their pits. They were hungry. The mobile field kitchens were still far behind. The only food around was French rations,

Journalists Drawn to War

BY THE TIME OF WORLD WAR II, WAR CORRESPONDENTS were recognized by most military leaders as important, if sometimes annoying, cogs in the machinery of war. However, the situation was different during World War I. War correspondents were actually held in contempt by Britain's Field Marshal Horatio Herbert Kitchener. He was determined not to have them around and did his best to prevent them from getting accredited. In 1914, when a freelance writer named Granville Fortesque, visiting Brussels, filed a story with London's *Daily Telegraph* about German scout troops inside Belgium territory, Kitchener put out an order: Any correspondent found in the war zone faced arrest and the loss of his passport, plus expulsion. As a few managed to slip through his net and file some stories, he got tougher, putting out orders to actually arrest a number of correspondents in France.

With newspapers and readers hungry for news, the British military came under pressure to stop this persecution and arrest of journalists. By June 1915, a first group of 10 correspondents was given a qualified welcome, but were also told they were expected to be "loyal." They would be visible, dressed in officer's uniforms with a green band on their right arm, provided with cars, conducting officers, and censors.

After the United States entered the war, a press base was established in Paris for the AEF, and the rules for accreditation as a war correspondent—only men, since the U.S. Army refused women—mirrored those that had crippled the British reporters. A correspondent had to swear, in front of the secretary of war or his representative, that he would accept the restrictions set by the military, provide a detailed résumé, and get $1,000 from his paper for his equipment and maintenance and another $10,000 for a bond, to be forfeited if he did not obey the rules.

Gen. John J. Pershing made it clear that American correspondents were guests of the U.S. Army and were expected to be a credit to that institution. One correspondent, Heywood Broun, balked, maintaining he was a reporter, not a flag-waving propaganda mouthpiece. Broun, who later organized the American Newspaper Guild, broke the rules, writing critical pieces on Pershing and the army, which gave the War Department the grounds they needed to revoke his credentials.

Many war correspondents later made a lasting name for themselves, including Damon Runyon, who wrote the book *Guys and Dolls;*

Floyd Gibbons, journalist *(Library of Congress)*

Richard Harding Davis, who wrote many novels; Westbrook Pegler, who won a Pulitzer Prize in 1941 for exposing labor racketeering; and Floyd Gibbons, who wrote a biography of the flamboyant German war ace Baron Manfred von Richthofen.

Doughboys take cover from German shelling. *(National Archives)*

mainly cans of Argentine corned beef called "monkey meat" by the troops. But the beef had spoiled before being canned. Famished as they were, the marines could not choke down the putrid meat.

By late afternoon the last French unit marched by. Their commanding officer went up to one of Wise's company commanders and said that there were orders for everyone to retreat. "Retreat, hell!" barked marine Capt. Lloyd Williams. "We just got here!"

Soon after the blue-uniformed Frenchmen disappeared to the rear, the German bombardment grew more intense. From the woods on the marines' right front, German machine guns opened up. Two columns of enemy infantry fanned out into the field.

Col. Albertus W. Catlin, commanding the Sixth Marine Regiment, recorded an enthusiastic description of what took place in a book he wrote after the war called *With the Help of God and a Few Marines:*

> If the German advance had looked beautiful to me . . . that metal
> curtain that our Marines rang down on the scene was even more
> so. The German lines did not break, they were broken. . . . Three

times they tried to reform and break through that hail of lead, but they had to stop at last. The U.S. Marines had stopped them. Thus repulsed, with heavy losses, they retired, but our fire was relentless; it followed them to their death.

Although it was only a short, small-scale skirmish, Wise's battalion had stopped the Germans at their closest point to Paris since 1914. Back in America the marine corps became the toast of the nation. After the news of this engagement hit the papers, Marine enlistments rose 100 percent in two days.

Defending a dug-in position was one thing, however. It remained to be seen how well the Americans would do when the order came to counterattack.

Idealized marine graces James Montgomery Flagg poster. *(National Archives)*

14
DEVIL DOGS OF BELLEAU WOOD

The French Sixth Army now planned a major counter-attack to begin the morning of June 6. The point of the German spearhead was a quarter-mile east of the marine position in a kidney-shaped patch of trees called Belleau Wood.

The marine brigade was ordered to take control of Belleau Wood while the 167th French Division seized an expanse of wheat fields on the high ground northwest of the wood. French intelligence assured the American commander that it was "lightly held and you should have no trouble capturing it."

The Germans assigned Hans Otto Bischoff, a 46-year-old major, to direct the defense of Belleau Wood. He spent three days carefully preparing his positions. Major Bischoff had turned it into a huge machine-gun nest. The marines soon called it "Hellwood."

In all, Bischoff had carefully positioned 200 machine guns. He arranged the machine-gun nests in such a way that if one was captured, it would be exposed to flanking fire by two others. There were also three elaborate lines of trenches, protected by barbed wire, mortar teams, and sharpshooters in rifle pits.

Bischoff had done his job well, but his troops were not in the best shape. For months they had been surviving on a diet of black bread, barley, and dried vegetables. Many were ill with the flu and dysentery. Nevertheless, he believed his Germans would stop anything the Americans could throw against them.

Soldiers in the debris of Belleau Wood *(Library of Congress)*

The French 167th Division attacked on schedule. The troops advanced well and drove the Germans from several entrenched positions. However, the French artillery did not lengthen its range fast enough. Its barrage fell on its own advancing troops and caused many casualties. Getting hit from behind by their own guns and in front by the enemy proved too much for the French infantry. The shaken, confused Frenchmen retreated to their start line.

The marines had difficulties of their own. A company under Capt. Orland Crowther was ordered to take Hill 142, north of the wood, to protect the left flank. They were pinned down for hours by heavy machine-gun fire. Finally, they rushed forward along with another company and took the north slope just in time to repulse a series of German counterattacks.

The last of these counterattacks was stopped singlehandedly by Gunnery Sgt. Charles Hoffman. He spotted a dozen enemy soldiers crawling through the bushes with several light machine guns. He charged down the slope with a yell, bayoneted two Germans, and drove off the rest. Though badly wounded, he survived and received the Medal of Honor, America's highest award for bravery in combat. It was the first awarded to the Second Division.

Captain Crowther himself caught a bullet in the throat and was killed. His company, however, took Hill 142 as ordered. The cost was heavy. Ninety percent of the officers and 50 percent of the men were killed or wounded. It was a forecast of things to come.

At 3:45 P.M. Colonel Catlin, commander of the Sixth Marine Regiment, looked through his binoculars to watch one of his battalions, under Maj. Benjamin Berry, move out into the wheat fields. Four hundred yards beyond loomed the dark mass of Belleau Wood. "It was a moment fit to shake nerves of steel," wrote Catlin, "like entering a dark room filled with assassins."

Berry's men faced an almost impossible task. They crossed the field, the sun gleaming off their bayonets, the air sweet with the smell of trampled wheat. They were soon being cut down by Major Bischoff's veteran gunners. There were many acts of valor, but the marines were pinned down until nightfall when they crawled back to the trench. With 60 percent casualties, including Major Berry, not one of them had reached the wood.

Colonel Catlin's second battalion, under Maj. Berton Sibley, fared somewhat better. Some were pinned by heavy fire, but the rest moved steadfastly forward and plunged into the wood.

Raising his binoculars again, Catlin grinned as the first wave of marines disappeared among the trees. At that moment a bullet pierced his right lung and came out beneath his shoulder blade. Later, while recovering in Paris, Catlin told a visitor: "It's my own fault. I shouldn't have been so close to the front in a first-class war."

In the wood, Major Bischoff's machine guns covered every section with a gauntlet of fire. The marines learned that the only effective tactic was to work around behind a nest and bomb it with hand grenades. Then they would rush forward and kill or capture the crew.

Bischoff's clever deployment made this deadly strategy work. Every time Sibley's men took a machine-gun nest, they were pinned down by flanking fire from another.

One squad of marines took a German nest only to get fired on by another nest. The marines took cover behind some boulders, where they brought the surviving crew, then left one man behind to guard the captured Germans. The rest of the squad sneaked around the flank of the second nest. They captured its whole crew. Meanwhile, the prisoners at the first nest had killed the guard and started firing at the second nest. The marines bayoneted the crew of the second nest, then recaptured the first nest and killed its crew too.

Between attacks Red Cross volunteers on both sides helped the wounded. No one fired on them at first. Then some marines spotted a German first aid team carrying a machine gun and some ammo boxes on a stretcher. "It looked like a wounded man with his legs drawn up," recalled an officer, "until a gust of wind flipped back the blanket covering the stretcher."

After that, it was hard on the medics and the wounded; it was hard on everyone. An unmailed letter, found later on the body of a German corporal and addressed to the corporal's father, told of the horror from the German perspective. "The Americans are savages," it said. "They kill everything that moves." This brutal fighting made the Germans call the marines *Teufel Hunden*—"Devil Dogs"—a nickname that sticks to this day.

The *New York Times* reported that on that first day the marines charged forward, crying "Remember the *Lusitania*." This seems an unlikely battle cry. No eyewitness accounts confirm it. Several accounts do mention a salty marine sergeant yelling "Come on! Do you want to live forever?"

Darkness fell and the scene became a nightmare of yells, groans, cries for help, machine-gun bursts, and rifle fire. By 9 P.M. Sibley had lost half his command, and the rest were held up at German strong points. He passed the word to dig in and wait for daybreak.

The commanding officer of the marine brigade, Brig. Gen. James G. Harbord, reflected on the day's events. The marines had suffered 1,100 casualties and captured only the southern lobe of the wood. The Germans still firmly held the northern and central parts. Yet Harbord's troops had fought bravely and well, and at least they had a toehold.

It was apparent to Harbord that, as he later wrote, "More than Belleau Wood was at stake, more than standing between the invader and Paris. It was a struggle for psychological mastery.... The stage was small, but the audience was the world of 1918."

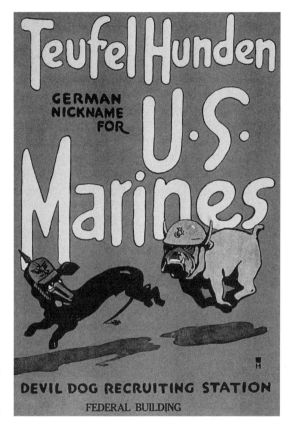

The "Devil Dogs" of Belleau Wood provided rich poster material and attracted a surge of recruits. *(National Archives)*

The German High Command had similar thoughts and was paying close attention to the marines. To abandon Belleau Wood would mean to give the Americans a "cheap success." International newspapers trumpeted that *one* brigade of Yanks was enough to stop the German attack. The German High Command felt that this might have serious consequences on the morale of the Central Powers and on the continuation of the war. They sent a crack division of Prussian Guard Infantry to reinforce the sector.

Thus both sides put more importance on the battle than the on the disputed territory. Prestige was involved, a pivot on which great events can turn.

The next morning, June 8, Sibley's men renewed the advance. Losses were heavy. One company lost all its officers. General Harbord decided they had taken all the punishment they could stand. He ordered Sibley to pull out and take cover in a gully at the south edge of the wood.

Army artillery took over now. The plan was to pulverize the enemy defenses with an intense barrage, then send in fresh marine reserves to sweep the wood clean. On June 9, the artillery laid down 34,000 high-explosive shells. Most of the shells, however, had contact fuses that exploded when they hit the tops of the trees. The trenches beneath them were showered with branches and shrapnel, but the barrage caused relatively few casualties. When it was over, the Germans popped up behind their guns once more.

The marines advanced. A private wrote: "We moved into the tree line. I saw blood-stained bodies everywhere, some missing an arm or leg. My knees felt weak and I wanted to sit down. . . . I guessed we were in Belleau Wood."

Three days of hard fighting gained some ground, but the enemy could not be dislodged from the wood. On June 13, the Germans counterattacked along the whole sector. In Belleau Wood, their main assault fell on Colonel Wise's battalion, the one that had first halted the Germans on the Paris highway 10 days earlier.

The battalion endured murderous attacks, but held on. Wise himself had a narrow escape while giving instructions to two of his officers. A shell burst overhead. It killed the officer on his right and incapacitated the one on his left. The shell fragments ripped through Wise's jacket but did not touch him.

That night, General Harbord sent another battalion, under Maj. Thomas Halcomb, to relieve Wise's hard-pressed men. It was unfortunate timing. As Halcomb's men started into the southern part of the wood, the Germans dropped 7,000 mustard gas bombs and many high explosive shells that also contained a vomiting gas.

Gas masks compounded the darkness and fog so that the men could not see anything. They stumbled through the blackness, bounding off trees and falling into shell holes.

Of Halcomb's 800 men, only 300 survivors drifted in to relieve Colonel Wise. "I did not consider that they were sufficient to relieve me," reported Wise, "and remained in position."

On June 15, the U.S. Army took over the fight. Harbord's marine brigade was relieved by the Seventh Infantry Brigade of the Third U.S. Division, which had not yet seen action. The marine brigade had been cut down to less than half its original strength.

The next morning Colonel Wise reviewed his tattered battalion. He wrote: "It was enough to break your heart. I had left . . . on May 31 with 965 men and 26 officers. Now before me stood 350 men and six officers."

This painting by Marine Corps artist Tom Lovell was an attempt to capture the horror of combat in Belleau Wood. *(U.S. Marine Corps)*

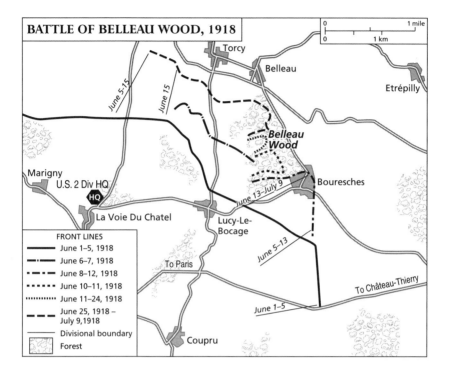

The French High Command was pleased and impressed with the performance of the Second Division (to which the marines belonged). They were not the only ones. On June 17, a copy of a German intelligence report (from a few days earlier) was captured. It contained this excerpt:

> The American 2nd Division may be rated as a very good division. [In particular] the various attacks by both of the Marine regiments were carried out with vigor and regardless of losses. The effect of our firearms did not . . . check the advance of their infantry. The nerves of the Americans are still unshaken. . . . The personnel may be considered excellent. They are healthy, strong and physically well-developed men. The spirit of the American troops is fresh and one of careless confidence.

Belleau Wood stood as the first testing ordeal between Germans and Americans on an otherwise insignificant wood patch. Without roads or rail lines, it was a springboard to nowhere, ground that neither side needed.

The Germans were foolish to let things happen the way they did. They placed the highest stakes on a local cockfight, and had taken on the wrong men. The marine brigade was one of the most determined and aggressive units on the western front.

The Germans were not licked yet. The Seventh U.S. Infantry launched two assaults against Major Bischoff's men. Both were repulsed. On June 22, the army gave Belleau Wood back to the marines. A final assault on June 25 (led by Major Berry's old battalion) at last broke the enemy line. The marines cleared the wood completely, bagging 500 German prisoners in the process.

The marines had not won the war, but they had stopped the Germans in their tracks. For nearly four years the French army had been solely responsible for the Allies' right flank. At last, the French were not alone. The Yanks were in action.

15
TURNING THE TIDE

General Pershing knew how important it had been to help the French in their urgent hour of need. Yet, as the suspense eased, he grew impatient with General Foch, the Supreme Allied Commander. Although American troops were fighting together as units, Pershing felt it was time for an independent U.S. Army under one command. Pershing urged Foch to give him an exclusively American sector of the front.

Foch preferred to attach American divisions piecemeal to large Allied army units commanded by French or British generals, but finally agreed. This plan, however, would have to be put on hold because the next German offensive came so fast.

Germany's generals had one last card to play. They planned a two-pronged attack, east and west of Rheims, hoping to surround and capture this key city, some 50 miles east of Paris. If successful, a drive on Paris might still be possible.

The German generals, it seemed, had failed to fully appreciate the mathematics of change on the western front. The numerical superiority of the Germans had made possible the slashing gains of early spring. By midsummer the constant flow of fresh, fit Americans had overcome that advantage and permanently reversed the whole situation.

This thought was a comfort to Allied commanders. Yet to the Allied soldiers the thought of another German offensive was as terrifying as ever. On July 15, 1918, the German stormtroopers struck hard.

The most notable American actions were along the south bank of the Marne River. At Château-Thierry the Germans made a ferocious assault against the Third U.S. Division, but the Yanks refused to yield.

At one point the Thirty-eighth U.S. Infantry Regiment (part of the Third Division) was squeezed on three sides until it resembled a horseshoe. Despite the danger of encirclement, the Thirty-eighth held firm, inflicting three times as many casualties as they took. In one spot a dead American soldier was found with a rifle in one hand and a pistol in the other. Surrounding him lay 12 dead Germans. For its steadfast defense, the Thirty-eighth was given the nickname "Rock of the Marne."

East of Château-Thierry the Twenty-eighth Pennsylvania National Guard Division also clung to every foot of ground. Four of its companies were surrounded, but continued to resist. When their ammunition ran out, they grappled with the enemy in hand-to-hand combat. The Pennsylvanians won praise from Pershing, who said "They fought like iron men." From this the Twenty-eighth got its name, "the Iron Division."

Unable to penetrate the Allied line, the German offensive petered out on July 17. Along with it died Germany's last hope for victory. Now it was the German army that was in peril.

On July 18 the Allies began their counterattack. By mid-August they had taken back all the territory the Germans had gained in their spring offensives. As summer ended, a total of 310,000 Americans had seen action, with 67,000 killed or wounded.

"Last night I witnessed a truly pitiful sight," one doughboy, Leo Cuthbertson, wrote home, "the burying of our boys. It makes one's blood run cold and increases a passionate desire to deal out misery to the enemy—and I believe before this war is over, he will have more misery than he bargained for."

If the Americans had come to France to fight for democracy, to this purpose they now added revenge and hatred. Watching their buddies get blown away, day after day, turned innocent youths into hardened killers. Gary Roberts of the 167th Infantry wrote home from a hospital:

> I got two of the rascals and finished killing a wounded one with my bayonnet that might have gotten well had I not finished him. . . . I made the first two men holler "mercy, comrade, mercy."But how could I have mercy on such low-lifed rascals as they are. Why, I just couldn't kill them dead enough it didn't seem like. . . . The first one I got was for momma and the other one for myself.

For the Allies, the danger had passed. The summer of 1918 had been the climax of the story of the western front. The grand finale was yet to come. For the soldiers on both sides, many frightful days still lay ahead.

By September, Pershing's dream of a self-sufficient American force of a million men had become a reality. He now sought to launch an offensive that was strictly American from beginning to end. Foch, a marshal by now, protested strongly. He still wanted to scatter American divisions among the French.

Pershing was furious. Even his divisional commanders were tired of having their troops thrown into areas they described as "meat grinders" while French units performed the mopping-up operations. Perhaps Marshal Foch thought this was fair since the French army had suffered years of fighting, but Pershing saw it as no more than a means to get the most glory at the Americans' expense.

Pershing would no longer argue the issue. He threatened to withdraw all American units to their training areas until the dispute was resolved. Foch gave in. He knew Pershing was not bluffing.

American gunners firing a French 75 against German troops in the Saint-Mihiel Salient, 1918. After a long artillery barrage, the attack was launched. *(National Archives)*

For four years the Germans had held a bulge around the city of Saint-Mihiel that jutted like a dagger into the Allied line. Pershing drew up careful plans to flatten that bulge. On September 12, the dough-boys of the U.S. First Army attacked.

The operation went more smoothly than anyone had imagined. Pershing's timing could not have been better. The Germans, having caught wind of the plan, decided to pull out of the bulge. They were caught in the middle of their withdrawal when the Americans attacked.

Taken by surprise, many German strongholds surrendered. In one instance, a sergeant captured 300 prisoners with an empty pistol. By the next day, the American pincers had surrounded the German force in Saint-Mihiel. Some 15,000 Germans were captured, and many artillery pieces as well. It was September 13, Pershing's 58th birthday. He said it was the happiest one he had had for a long time.

There was not much time to celebrate. The Allies were planning a massive push along the entire front. Pershing had less than two weeks to maneuver his army into position.

American casualties in the Saint-Mihiel offensive had been amazingly light. The operation was described as "a stroll." Indeed, it had been a picnic compared to what the doughboys were about to face in the Argonne Forest.

German prisoners are conducted out of a shattered town in the Saint-Mihiel Salient. *(National Archives)*

16

KNIGHTS OF
THE AIR

An important factor in the success of the Saint-Mihiel operation was the superiority of Allied air power. An unprecedented force of 1,500 Allied planes gave General Pershing control of the skies. Although all the aircraft were of French or British make, many of the pilots were American.

This armada of combat airplanes would have been unimaginable four years earlier. When the war began, the total number of military aircraft in the world was only around 1,000.

Military thinkers had always understood the importance of knowing the enemy's whereabouts. By 1914 stationary gas-filled balloons were the primary craft for aerial reconnaissance. Raised and lowered from the ground by cables, they provided the observer with a stable platform from which to chart enemy artillery positions and troop movements.

When the war started, military planners were uncertain about the usefulness of airplanes. Planes at that time were very fragile and could carry only small payloads. On the other hand, they were able to cover more area and had greater freedom of movement than balloons. They could also fly behind enemy lines.

As the armies marched to war in August 1914, airplanes flew ahead of them to gather information on the enemy. Aviation was a hazardous profession. Airplanes were made mostly of cloth and wood. They would sometimes rip apart in strong wind or when diving too fast. Their crude gasoline engines were unreliable and gave off choking fumes, including ether. Many early pilots crashed after being rendered unconscious by ether fumes.

The 148th American Aero Squadron field, France. Preparations are being made for a daylight raid on German trenches and cities. *(National Archives)*

At first there was a chivalry between the pilots of both sides. They saw each other as brother adventurers. Opposing pilots would pass each other with a friendly wave or salute.

That soon changed. Pilots, and especially observers (if it was a two-seater plane), began to fill their pockets with objects to fling at enemy aircraft. Chains and bricks were favorite weapons. But even after pistols replaced these, little damage was done.

When rifles started replacing pistols, aerial shooting became serious, although the difficulty of loading and aiming a rifle in the narrow confines of a cockpit kept the weapon from being more deadly. Shooting at a moving target through a maze of wires, struts and whirling propeller blades was tricky business. The firer often hit parts of his own plane.

Then one day a British observer took a machine gun into the air. The extra weight of the weapon made his plane unable to climb more than 3,500 feet. The observer spotted his prey, a German plane cruising at 5,000 feet. Firing the machine gun made a lot of noise and vibration, but had no effect on the enemy plane. Nonetheless, it was a significant milestone in aerial combat.

New Weapons of War in the Air

FEW MILITARY LEADERS COULD HAVE FORESEEN THE crucial role that aircraft would take in this war. Demonstrated only 10 years earlier by its inventors, Orville and Wilbur Wright, the airplane had led to the launching of a new industry, aviation, which quickly took off at home and overseas.

Prior to the 1914 hostilities, most of the aircraft being built in all the major countries were two-seater biplanes—aircraft with two parallel sets of wings. These planes could reach only about 60 miles per hour at an altitude of no more than 5,000 feet. But as the rumble of war got louder, designers and engineers, particularly in France and Germany, began developing aircraft specifically for military use. In August 1914, as war broke out, the combatants on both sides had a total of 767 aircraft ready for use. Germany also had its zeppelin, a hydrogen-filled, overly large and slow aircraft, used only briefly as a bomber.

The first combat pilot was France's Roland Garros, who, in April 1915, experimented with firing a mounted machine gun through the propeller of his plane and shot down five German planes. The jubilant French called him the "ace of all flyers." After that it became the custom to call every flyer who downed five planes an "ace."

Garros's design was copied and perfected by Germany's Anthony Fokker, who found a way to prevent bullets from hitting the propeller, thus revolutionizing aerial warfare and giving the Germans command of the air. A Romanian inventor, George Constancesco working for the British, then developed a synchronization system for shooting, giving Britain the edge. With ever stronger technology, designers on both sides turned planes into more effective weapons, and a new kind of warfare evolved, with battles fought fiercely in the skies as well as on the ground and at sea.

The rapid development of more powerful airplanes solved the problem of lifting a heavy machine gun into the air. There was still the problem of locating the gun where the pilot or observer could reach it, aim it and fire it—without hitting his own plane.

On many biplanes, the machine gun would be mounted on the top wing so that it could fire over the propeller. Firing it was easy enough, but reloading and in-flight repairs were impossible. The ideal was to have a machine gun directly in front of the cockpit. This way the pilot could easily reach the weapon. Aiming would just be a matter of pointing his plane toward the enemy.

The French led the way by attaching a metal wedge to the propeller, which deflected the bullets that would otherwise shoot the blades off. At first this seemed a promising solution, but it was found the striking bullets created too much stress on the propeller blades. The French air service abandoned the invention.

The big breakthrough came in the spring of 1915 when Germany developed a mechanism that synchronized the spin of the propeller with the stream of bullets. A device was hooked up to the machine gun so that it would not fire whenever the blade was in the way. By the end of May, Germany's new forward-firing guns were shooting Allied planes out of the sky.

The synchronization device gave German pilots a distinct advantage in aerial combat. It was a year before the Allies developed their own mechanism for forward-firing.

To the soldiers wallowing in the mud below, battles between airplanes, called dogfights, were gripping spectacles that broke the monotony of trench life. In a war where millions of soldiers had become faceless numbers to be manipulated by generals, the solo nature of the dogfights had tremendous romantic appeal.

Combat pilots became bigger-than-life heroes. These airborne warriors were a special breed, fighting their own individual battles high above the mud. The media depicted them as modern-day knights, jousting for the skies.

Combat aviation may have been more glamorous than being in the infantry, but it was no less deadly. In a dogfight the slightest mistake could cost the pilot his life. The life expectancy of a combat pilot was only 40 to 60 hours of flight time.

For the aviator, death usually came in two of its most terrible forms— by fire or falling from a great height. There were no parachutes for pilots yet, but many preferred to leap from their flaming planes rather than burn to death in their cockpits. No wonder that pilots called their machines "flying coffins." Yet aviators agreed that ascending, well-groomed and well-fed, to be killed in an airplane was better than going over the top from some filthy trench, to be mashed up in no-man's-land amid rotting corpses.

On April 18, 1916, seven Americans formed a fighter plane squadron (*escadrille* in French) that was to become one of the most famous and romanticized of all air units. They called themselves the Escadrille Americaine. Later they changed the name to Escadrille Lafayette in honor of the French general and hero of the American Revolution.

France provided the squadron with planes and other necessary equipment. All the pilots were American volunteers serving under the French flag. Needless to say, the Escadrille Lafayette added to the growing tension between Germany and the supposedly neutral United States.

In a short time the squadron captured America's heart. On May 18, 1916, it downed its first enemy aircraft. Soon, other Americans already serving in France were transferred to the Escadrille Lafayette. Raoul Lufbery, who had been among the Americans who enlisted as infantrymen in the French Foreign Legion in 1914, reported for duty on May 24, 1916.

Lufbery had been a well-known aviator before the war. Now he was to become the most skillful and successful fighter pilot of the Escadrille Lafayette. In August, Lufbery became America's first ace.

Lufbery became a hero. French and American newspapers were full of his picture and stories of his airborne exploits. He received bundles of fan mail. Children were named after him.

Lufbery was officially credited with 17 kills. No one will know for sure how many enemy aircraft he knocked out, since many went down behind German lines, without witnesses, and were not counted. The French and American nations mourned after Maj. Raoul Lufbery was killed in a dogfight on May 19, 1918.

At the time of Lufbery's death, the United States had been in the war for more than a year but was just forming its own independent air service. Three months earlier, the Escadrille Lafayette had been disbanded. Its pilots had earned the squadron 57 confirmed victories. Nine of the pilots had been killed in action. (Of the original seven men who formed the squadron, only one survived the war unscathed.)

In the United States, aircraft production was slow to get off the ground. In fact, the war ended before any American planes were sent to France. All the aircraft in the new U.S. Air Service were French-built, but the planes now had American insignia and markings.

The first American combat air unit was the Ninety-fifth Aero Squadron. The planes the French had sent to the unit had no machine guns. Undaunted by the lack of weapons, the bold American aviators flew unarmed reconnaissance missions over hostile territory.

After several weeks, the Allies started to criticize the Americans. Allied Command had received reports of aerial engagements by the squadron,

Lt. Raoul Lufbery,
Escadrille Lafayette
(Library of Congress)

with one American pilot lost but so far no enemy planes shot down by the Ninety-fifth.

The American squadron commander returned a report saying that the Ninety-fifth would be most happy to shoot down enemy planes if the Allied command would see fit to supply it with machine guns. After this report, the squadron was immediately pulled from the line and fitted with machine guns.

Leading American ace of the air war—Capt. Eddie Rickenbacker
(Library of Congress)

No pilot did more to enhance the reputation of the Ninety-fifth than Eddie Rickenbacker. A world-famous race car driver and, for a time, General Pershing's personal chauffeur, Rickenbacker put his skill and talent into flying. With 26 confirmed kills to his credit, Captain Rickenbacker was America's leading ace of the First World War.

No American pilot had more of a mystique than 2d Lt. Frank "Balloon Buster" Luke of the U.S. Twenty-seventh Aero Squadron. An

audacious and talented pilot, Luke became, in less than three weeks' time, America's second greatest ace. A loner, Luke preferred to perform missions on his own. Because his reckless behavior in the air made him dangerous to fly with, Luke's commander gave him permission to operate alone.

One important function of fighter planes was to shoot down enemy observation balloons. Because of antiaircraft fire from the ground and enemy fighters assigned to protect these observers, "balloon busting" was a treacherous task. When Luke was told that it was the most difficult and dangerous job a pilot could undertake, he decided to be the best.

Luke's war on balloons began on September 12, 1918, when he sent one down in flames. He shot down two balloons on September 14, three more the next day and another three on September 16. On September 18, he shot down two balloons and three enemy fighters. As a reward Luke was granted leave in Paris, but he came back early. On September 26, he downed a German plane, and on September 27, another balloon.

Luke was an excellent pilot, but not the most disciplined soldier. When ordered to do something, he was often defiant, as well as repeatedly AWOL, or absent without leave. On September 29 Luke was placed under arrest and, at the same time, awarded the Distinguished Service Cross for valor.

Luke was grounded, but managed to take off in his plane before he could be apprehended. As he flew over the American trenches, he

Frank "Balloon Buster" Luke *(National Archives)*

dropped a note to the doughboys below that read: "Watch for three Hun balloons on the Meuse."

American observers looked on as three enemy balloons became earth-bound fireballs. While he was downing his third victim, antiaircraft shrapnel ripped into Luke's plane. Unable to gain altitude, Luke was forced to crash-land in a nearby meadow behind enemy lines.

Luke climbed out of his cockpit without a scratch. He was, however, surrounded by German soldiers. They shouted at him to surrender, but Frank Luke refused. He stood defiantly in the meadow, shooting his pistol at them until he was killed.

More than 650 American aviators saw action during the war. Although they lost 316 aircraft to the enemy, they took down 927 German airplanes and balloons—an impressive kill ratio of almost three-to-one.

By mid-September 1918, the Allies had achieved supremacy in the air. Yet the soldiers on the ground still had a long way to go.

17

INTO THE ARGONNE

After the mop-up at Saint-Mihiel, only 12 days remained for General Pershing to get his forces on the starting line for the huge Allied push to begin September 26. American troops would take part all along the line. The U.S. Ninety-first Division would fight with the Belgian army in the Ypres sector under the command of King Albert. Two more U.S. divisions would be part of a huge British effort on the Somme and another two (including the Second Division) would participate under the French army.

The big show for Pershing and the newly formed First American Army would be in the Meuse-Argonne region, a few miles north of Verdun. The jump-off line extended 24 miles from the Meuse River across to and through the Argonne Forest.

The movement of tremendous amounts of men and equipment had to be made in secrecy. This meant shifting more than 800,000 troops, all under the cover of darkness so as not to be detected. Marshal Foch doubted that the Americans would be able to pull it off.

There were only three main roads, all with deep ruts. Down these mud roads, a seemingly endless convoy of French trucks, driven by sleep-deprived Vietnamese, crawled along by night—without lights. The cramped Americans they carried were tormented by cold, rain, mosquitoes, and exhaust fumes. The men were so closely packed they could not sleep.

Despite the difficulties, the Americans kept on schedule. The U.S. Army even managed to get in place a day before the earliest date that Foch thought possible. Evidence suggests that the Germans were not aware of the move.

American troops boarding trucks bound for the Argonne battlefront
(National Archives)

Yet Pershing was worried. In order to meet Foch's deadline, he had put untried divisions on the primary points of attack. So limited was the experience of these green troops that they could hardly be classified as soldiers. Winston Churchill would later write that the Americans were "half trained, half organized, with only their courage, their numbers and their magnificent youth behind their weapons."

Of the nine divisions taking part in the opening assault, only two had combat experience (one was the veteran Twenty-eighth "Iron" Division). Along this Argonne section was the Seventy-seventh Division, made up of draftees from New York City.

Each doughboy carried 200 rounds of ammunition, two cans of corned beef, six boxes of hardtack (Army biscuits), and a one-quart canteen. Many of the novice troops put wine in their canteens instead of water. They had no veterans around to warn them that in the heat of battle wine was likely to turn a man's stomach as well as increase his dehydration. Later, men who should have been busy fighting the Germans would be busy throwing up.

On September 25, the eve of battle, the Americans waited silently in their positions. It rained softly. According to one infantry private from Mississippi, it was "as though the heavens were weeping over the sacrifice of so many lives that was so soon to be made."

The Americans could not have faced a more challenging obstacle. For hundreds of years, the Meuse-Argonne region had stood as a natural barrier between French kings and German princes. It was a tangle of ravines, woods, dominating heights, and rock-bound citadels. It was ideal for defense.

For four years, the Germans had been improving what nature started. They built a thick belt of defensive earthworks strengthened by wire, steel, and concrete. Its three main trench lines—named after three fabled witches of a Wagnerian opera—were deep and elaborate. The German trenches even had wooden beds and electric lights.

It was Belleau Wood all over again, but on a much larger scale. One American general said that it made the Virginia forest where Civil War generals Grant and Lee fought the Battle of the Wilderness look like a

Ammunition and supplies move forward, while caissons and ambulances stream back from the Argonne battlefront. *(National Archives)*

park. Pershing, however, commanded 12 times as many troops as Grant did at that battle in 1864, used 10 times as many cannon and had more ammunition than the Union army used during the whole Civil War.

Following a three-hour bombardment by 2,700 guns, at 5:30 A.M. on September 26, 1918, the Americans began their assault. Despite an eight-to-one numerical superiority, the advance began to bog down after about a mile. Evening fell with the troops five miles short of the first day's target. The offensive turned into stagnation the second day, and as September ended the advance ground to a halt. By this time, however, more veteran divisions were available to hurl into the attack.

Foot by foot the attack continued. Through rain and sleet, the soldiers inched their way up the treacherous landscape under constant enemy fire. They crawled through the clinging wire on whose rusty barbs pieces of cloth and flesh would remain. They fell into pits and were impaled on spikes that the Germans had cleverly set up for that purpose.

Keeping the troops supplied was also becoming a problem. As the soldiers advanced past the Germans' first line of defense, they left behind them a four-year-old no-man's-land (the same field the battle of Verdun had been fought on). It was a veritable lunar landscape over which serviceable roads would have to be built before supplies could be brought up.

Along with the mud and entanglements, there were mine craters 100 feet wide and 40 feet deep. One soldier described them as "wounds where the very bowels of the earth had been torn out . . . Imagine the ocean at its roughest and then imagine it instantly turned to clay." The time it took to reestablish supply lines gave the Germans the chance to reinforce the sector with more troops.

Meanwhile, the Manhattan men of the Seventy-seventh Division were learning that the Argonne was a long way from Central Park. Yet they pressed on through the forest, meeting fierce resistance every step of the way. Leading the way was the First Battalion of the 308th Infantry Regiment, commanded by Maj. Charles Wittlesey.

On October 1 the battalion made its way into a small valley with steep, wooded banks, about a half-mile in front of the rest of the division. Sensing a trap, Wittlesey ordered his men back across the brook. He was too late. As the men crossed an old footbridge, German machine guns opened up. The battalion was trapped in the valley.

One of Wittlesey's messengers made it to the rear to request assistance. The 307th Regiment was sent, but only one company made it

American soldiers face an enemy barrage in the Argonne. *(National Archives)*

through. The rest were lost in the dark forest or driven off by enemy fire. By morning (October 2) Wittlesey and more than 600 men were completely surrounded.

Throughout the day German mortars, grenades, and snipers took their toll. There was no way for divisional headquarters to contact the First Battalion. Wittlesey, however, had a few homing pigeons that he could send to let them know he and his men had not surrendered.

The next day, October 3, was spent fending off German assaults. By noon, the last of the food had been eaten. The only source of water, a spring, had a German machine gun trained on it. There were many wounded but there was no medical officer. All the bandages had been used up.

By the morning of October 4, fewer than 500 men were still alive. Unable to get infantry in to relieve the First Battalion, the Seventy-seventh Division Command decided to saturate the German positions with artillery fire. But the American artillery, which had only an approximate idea of the battalion's position, dropped its shells on Wittlesey's men.

Wittlesey released his last homing bird, his only hope. The slate-colored carrier pigeon was named Cher Ami. (*Cher ami* is a common

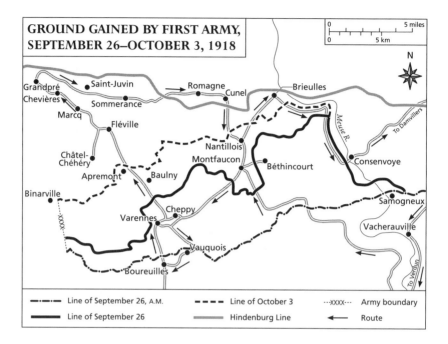

GROUND GAINED BY FIRST ARMY, SEPTEMBER 26–OCTOBER 3, 1918

French opening for a personal letter and means "dear friend.") The pigeon instinctively flew toward the American lines.

Along the way a bullet crashed into Cher Ami's head, tearing out its left eye. Then flaming shrapnel tore into its chest and fractured its breastbone. A third hit ripped away its lower right leg. Yet, miraculously, the pigeon kept flying. Wittlesey's message was still there, hanging from the torn ligaments of Cher Ami's remaining leg. The message finally reached the American artillery. It read: "For heaven's sake, stop it."

The shelling had lasted over an hour and caused at least 30 casualties. It also tore away underbrush that hid the doughboys from enemy snipers. By October 6 only 275 men were left. The Germans urged Wittlesey and his men to surrender. They refused.

Rain at least provided drinking water. The men resorted to eating plant roots and even the bird seed left by the pigeon handler. Allied aircraft dropped food and other supplies, but most of it landed on the German side. German snipers laid out the food packages, killing any American who reached for the bait.

On October 7, weak from hunger and exposure to the cold, and with almost no ammunition left, the men settled into another hopeless night.

Then, a little past 7 P.M., three companies of the 307th Infantry finally cut their way through.

On October 8, the 194 survivors of what became known as the Lost Battalion left the valley. On that same day in another part of the forest, Alvin C. York in just 15 minutes made his reputation as the most famous American hero of World War I.

York was part of a 16-man patrol sent to knock out several enemy machine-gun nests holding a wooded slope. The patrol quietly slipped behind the German lines. In a small clearing it surprised a German

Grist for the Movie Mills

HOLLYWOOD FILMMAKERS HAD TAKEN ON THE TASK of selling war to America as soon as World War I broke out, portraying the Germans as "hideous Huns" in movies with names such as *False Faces, Lest We Forget,* and *Till I Come Back to You.* In the 1920s, a new genre arrived, films depicting the friendship of soldiers and the horror of battle, such as *The Big Parade* and *What Price Glory?*

By the 1930s, movies began to expose the terrible truth of World War I for both sides. In 1930, the United States released *All Quiet on the Western Front,* which conveyed uncompromisingly its message that all war is hideous and wrong. In 1931, *The Last Fight* showed the consequences of war, portraying four flyers who are too damaged mentally and physically to return home. In 1937, the French released the strongly antiwar film, *J'Accuse,* a story of the war's waste seen through the eyes of a French family.

With Hitler on the rise in the late 1930s, patriotism emerged as an important movie theme. In 1940, Hollywood produced *The Fighting 69th* to show the heroism of American men on the battlefield in 1918 France. The exploits of Sgt. Alvin York, one of the most famous American heroes of World War I, made a perfect story for Hollywood. Gary Cooper got his first Oscar for *Sergeant York* (1941), which prepared Americans for an endless series of heroic movies about World War II to sustain patriotism during that war.

It was back to stark realism in 1957, with Stanley Kubrick's *Paths of Glory,* which grimly depicted the troops' despair on the western front. And in 1981, *Gallipoli* brought the futile 1915 battle on the Turkish peninsula to the screen, again exposing this war's waste of human life.

battalion commander and a group of soldiers. Thinking the patrol was part of a large force of Americans, the Germans threw up their hands in surrender.

The German soldiers on the next rise realized the American force was small and opened fire. Six men of the American squad were immediately killed and three more wounded, including the officer in charge.

The captured Germans lay down on the ground while the remaining seven men of the patrol took cover behind some trees. The Germans, now shooting from two sides, created a crossfire, which hit not only the Americans, but also those Germans who had already surrendered and their own troops firing from the opposite side.

The American patrol returned fire and killed several Germans. York then took command of the patrol. He ordered them to watch the prisoners while he moved out to attack the other enemy positions. York had

Sergeant Alvin York, 328th Infantry, in the Argonne Forest, France
(National Archives)

INTO THE ARGONNE

American infantry of the First Army take a rest after capturing territory from the Germans in the battle-scarred Argonne Forest. *(National Archives)*

grown up in the mountains of Tennessee hunting small game and was a crack shot. He now put his marksmanship to work.

One by one York shot the Germans in the first position with his rifle. Then another group charged him from the side with bayonets. Instinctively York pulled out his Colt .45 automatic pistol and aimed. He intentionally fired at the men in the rear of the oncoming squad so that the ones in front would keep charging. He worked his shots forward until he hit the last man.

In all, York shot 17 German soldiers with exactly 17 shots. York and the rest of the patrol then marched the prisoners, including a major, back to the American lines. Along the way, the captured major ordered more Germans to surrender. The seven Americans got back safely with their three wounded comrades and 132 German prisoners. York was awarded the Congressional Medal of Honor.

There were many heroes of the Argonne, but Alvin York was the most famous. Perhaps this was because he symbolized America's citizen soldiers. York was a conscientious objector—that is, he thought all war was bad and had said that fighting in one was against his religious beliefs.

When he was drafted, he entered the army only after "a lot of prayer and soul searching." York did what he had to do. He became a legend, but had no pride in what he had done.

The day after the fight, he wrote in his journal: "I didn't want to kill a whole heap of Germans, I didn't hate them, but I done it just the same." In World War II, York would serve his country again as a counselor for young men who wished to be declared conscientious objectors.

On October 10 the Americans drove the last Germans from the Argonne. The British and French drives farther north had cracked key German defensive lines. It was becoming clear to the Germans that the war was lost. Germany's diplomats began to probe for peace.

18
THE ELEVENTH HOUR

The German army continued to give ground on the western front throughout October 1918. Yet as measured on the map of Europe, Germany's peril was not obvious. In the East, German troops occupied a vast stretch of the Russian empire from the Baltic Sea to the Black Sea. In the West, Germany still had most of Belgium as well as troops firmly entrenched on French soil.

The Allies were anticipating a long, drawn-out fight. The German army was battered and bloody, but not broken. It would surely die hard. Few Allied military or political leaders believed the war would end before mid-1919.

The Germans, however, had lost hope for the future. They knew the French and British were exhausted, but fresh American soldiers were landing in France at the rate of 10,000 every 24 hours. It would only be a matter of time until the United States's enormous resources, production, and manpower overwhelmed Germany.

In early October Berlin began sending notes to President Wilson, from whom the Germans thought they could get the best arrangement for peace. Although Wilson favored some leniency toward Germany, he was not in a position to make decisions without consulting France and Britain.

Wilson's main concern was that Germany become a democracy. "I have no quarrel with the German people," he would say. Then on October 10, 1918, a U-boat sank a British passenger ferry in the English Channel. Hundreds perished, including women, children, and some Americans.

Public outrage, and his own anger, forced Wilson to take a firmer stand. He replied to Berlin that it would be left up to the Allied military leaders to determine the conditions for an armistice. The Allied generals took Germany's peace initiative as a sign of weakness. They resolved to push harder than ever against the German army.

Although the Allies now realized that the end of the war was near, the generals gave orders not to inform the soldiers at the front. They did not want the effort of the troops to slacken while the two sides negotiated. Pershing sent a strong order to his division commanders:

> Now that Germany and the Central Powers are losing, they are begging for an armistice. Their request is an acknowledgement of weakness and clearly means that the Allies are winning the war. That is the best of reasons for our pushing the war more vigorously at this moment. . . . We must strike harder than ever. . . . There can be no conclusion to this war until Germany is brought to her knees.

Meanwhile the Allied armies were making much progress on other fronts. On September 29, 1918, Bulgaria surrendered. The crumbling

German prisoners in a French concentration camp *(National Archives)*

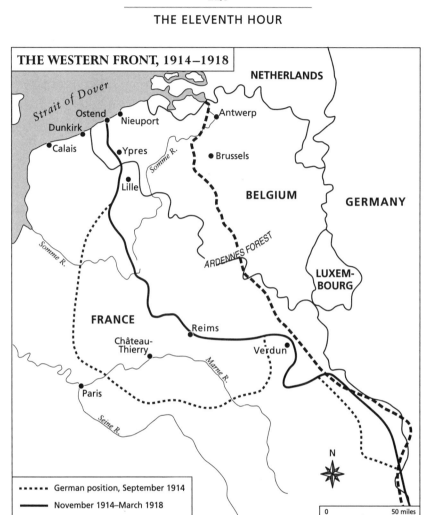

THE WESTERN FRONT, 1914–1918

NETHERLANDS

Strait of Dover

Ostend
Dunkirk
Nieuport
Antwerp

Calais
Ypres
Somme R.
Brussels

Lille
BELGIUM
GERMANY

Somme R.
ARDENNES FOREST

LUXEM-
BOURG

FRANCE
Reims
Château-
Thierry
Verdun
Marne R.

Paris
Seine R.

N

- - - - - German position, September 1914
——— November 1914–March 1918
■ ■ ■ ■ Front line, November 1918

0   50 miles
0   50 km

Ottoman Empire signed an armistice on October 30, and Austria-Hungary did so on November 3.

On November 10, Germany's last monarch gave up his throne, his crown, and his country. Kaiser Wilhelm II abdicated and fled to Holland. There he puttered, gardened, and spoke endless "if onlys" until his death in 1941.

At 5 A.M. on November 11, 1918, Germany signed an armistice with the Allies. Yet the truce did not go into effect that moment. It had been decided by the Allied representatives that, for the sake of historical drama, the war would not end until precisely 11 A.M.—that is, the 11th hour of the 11th day of the 11th month.

This six-hour delay for the sake of a good newspaper headline was an unpardonable gesture. Across the front it was taken by many commanders as a signal for a final bloodbath.

Artillery units everywhere fired frantically, usually without even aiming. Both sides seemed to be trying to shoot every last shell so that none would be left over.

Many American infantry units were ordered to advance right up to 11 A.M. "We thought it was a joke," wrote Lt. Harry C. Rennagel of the U.S. 101st Infantry Regiment. It was no joke. It was the final convulsion of the most horrific and costly war in history.

Lieutenant Rennagel had left the hospital the day before and arrived at his outfit at 10 A.M. on November 11. He was joking and laughing with his men, "waiting for the gong to ring when orders came to go over the top." He and his men moved out as ordered, at 25 minutes to 11. They advanced as slowly and as cautiously as they could.

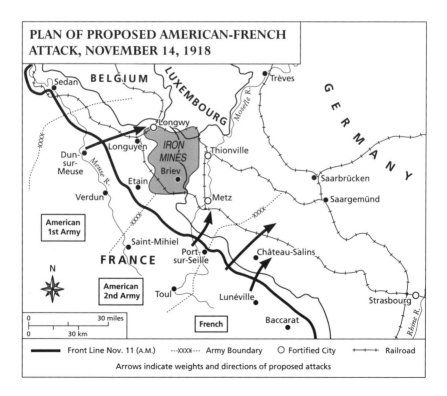

PLAN OF PROPOSED AMERICAN-FRENCH
ATTACK, NOVEMBER 14, 1918

Lost Sons, Grieving Families

DURING ANY WAR, ANY FAMILY WITH A MEMBER IN combat fears a telegram or an officer at the door: "We regret to inform you . . ." If there was one agony that was universal in all the countries fighting in the Great War, it was the anguish of learning that a loved one had died.

Kathe Kollwitz was a prominent German artist of her day. She was also an eloquent advocate for victims of social injustice and inhumanity. She detested war, and when her youngest son, Peter, age 19, was killed in battle in October 1914, Kathe Kollwitz determined to express herself through her art. She began a sculpture of herself and her husband, on their knees, adjacent to their son's grave—eternally begging forgiveness for a war they and the older generation had not prevented. She completed the sculpture in August 1931. It was exhibited at the National Gallery in Berlin and then transported to Belgium, where it rests today.

Some people mourned the loss of their sons by maintaining that the cause was right and exalting the bravery of those lost. Former U.S. president Theodore Roosevelt did so for his son Quentin, and the English author Rudyard Kipling did likewise for his son John. Sir Arthur Conan Doyle, author of the Sherlock Holmes mysteries, was so desperate to contact his deceased son Kingsley that he turned to spiritualism, believing he could reach his son via a medium. He became an advocate of the belief that there is an accessible spirit world, and in 1926 he produced a two-volume work called *History of Spiritualism.*

At 10:55 A.M. Lieutenant Rennagel heard gunfire. "I hurried over and there lay five of my best men." He knelt beside one of the young men who had a hole near his heart.

"Lieutenant," said the fatally injured soldier, "I'm going fast. Don't say I'll get better, you know different and this is a pretty unhappy time for me. You know we all expected things to cease today, so I wrote my girl. We were to be married when I returned, and [I told her and] my folks that I was safe and well and about my plans. And now—by some order— I am not going home."

"I looked away," said Lieutenant Rennagel, "and when I looked back— he had gone . . . I can honestly tell you I cried and so did the rest."

Suddenly, across the entire western front, everything stopped. Mouths wide open, soldiers stared into no-man's-land, dumbstruck by the wonderful quiet that now reigned.

A few minutes later, men began to cry, laugh, shake hands, slap each other on the back, and then cheer wildly. For the first time, they stood up straight in their foxholes. They walked in the open with nothing to fear. They built campfires for the first time. They took off their boots, dried their socks and warmed their chilled fingers.

Within minutes Yanks and Germans got together in the middle ground. Most left their rifles in the trenches. Active bartering sprang up. Doughboys gave the Germans cigarettes, food rations, and soap in exchange for belt buckles, bayonets, and even a few Iron Crosses (German army medals).

Most of the fighting men were too dazed to think much about the future. Relief and joy were all they felt. "No more bombs," said one Yank, "no more mangled, bleeding bodies, no more exposure to terrifying shell fire in the rain and cold and mud! It will be difficult to adjust the mind to the new state of things."

Shouts of joy and tossed helmets are the reaction, after soldier reads terms of Armistice to his friends. *(National Archives)*

Armistice celebration in Alsace-Lorraine, 1918 *(National Archives)*

When the 11th hour struck, it was only 6 A.M. in Washington and New York. There were no radios to spread the news. Yet within hours, a national "yahoo!" had started along the East Coast and spread westward.

In towns and cities throughout France and Britain, people took to the streets in celebration. The crowds became drunk with excitement. In London people smashed shop windows and overturned vehicles. In the end, the London police had to clear the streets and put a few rowdies in jail.

Berlin was even more rowdy, but for another reason. Defeat had caused civil strife and violence to break out. Returning soldiers were horrified to find barricades in the streets of the German capital. They heard the crack of rifle fire and felt the concussion of grenades. Some soldiers had survived the long war only to be shot down in their own city by fellow citizens.

19
THE ROAD HOME

By the morning of November 12, 1918, the frenzy of the previous day was beginning to subside. As the doughboys began to grasp the reality of the armistice, their thoughts turned to how soon they could go home. Unhappily, demobilizing the American Expeditionary Force would be a large and complex task.

British ships and French railroads had been used to help put the U.S. Army in the field. Now they were needed to get the army out of it. The French and British, however, had their own forces to bring home. The Americans would have to wait.

The long wait was hard on the doughboys. Men became irritable. Relations with the locals and each other became strained.

Overseas mail service, which was bad during the war, did not improve in the first months of peace. Food service got even worse. Weary American troops were herded into camps and there forgotten. Most camps were seas of half-frozen mud where the men had to live in tents through the dead of winter. There was almost no fuel to be had and too few blankets.

From these hardships, along with the boredom, grew much bitterness and disillusion among the American troops. Yet their neglect was not deliberate. The AEF had grown too large too quickly. The problem of administration had simply overwhelmed the army's leaders. Before things got better for the troops, there would be one more misery.

Throughout the fall of 1918, a virulent influenza epidemic had raged in the United States. Some 500,000 Americans, four times the number killed overseas during the war, would die from the flu. Some of the last doughboys to arrive in France were already infected.

THE ROAD HOME

The end of "the war to end war," celebrated in Philadelphia, November 11, 1918 *(National Archives)*

The disease spread through the crowded camps faster than bad news. The epidemic increased throughout the AEF by 10,000 cases per week. At one camp the men died at a rate of 250 per day.

Many American units soon found out that they were not going home at all. Rather, they would be a part of the Allied force assigned to occupy the western part of Germany, called the Rhineland. Many complained that they had joined the army to fight, not to be policemen.

Getting to Germany was not easy. Roads had to be built over no-man's-land. Beyond that, rail service was almost nonexistent. Demolition devices had to be removed from bridges and highways.

The weeks after the armistice brought long and punishing marches for the doughboys, in worn-out shoes, stained red from the soldiers' raw and bleeding feet. It was mid-December by the time the occupying American troops reached the German frontier.

The months following the armistice would also be sour ones for the American soldiers stationed in Russia. Back in March 1918, the Germans had forced the Soviet government into signing the harsh treaty of Brest-Litovsk. Under the terms of the treaty, Russia yielded a third of its population, a third of its farmland, half of its industry and 90 percent of its coal mines.

But throughout the summer the German army had continued to push deep into Russian territory. In August the Allies began sending troops into Russia, supposedly to reestablish an eastern front.

Parade in honor of returned soldiers passing the New York Library, 1919
(National Archives)

That month 7,000 U.S. soldiers were sent to the Pacific port of Vladivostok in Siberia to protect 800,000 tons of rusting Allied equipment that had been shipped to help the Russian army when it was still fighting the Germans. American troops were also sent to Russia's arctic ports of Archangel and Murmansk, supposedly to prevent the Germans from establishing submarine bases there.

Yet in the clashes that followed, it was not the German army that the Allies were fighting. It was the communist-led Soviet Red Army. Some Allied leaders secretly wanted the Allied forces in Russia to be used to oppose the Soviet government and help the anticommunist "White" Russians regain power. This fact became more obvious after Germany's surrender ended the military reasons for occupying northern Russia.

The confused American troops had no idea why they were there. They thought that they were headed for the trenches of France. Their first letters home began: "Guess where I am."

In the Battle of Armistice Day (November 11, 1918) 28 U.S. soldiers were killed fighting communist troops. As the furious and merciless Russian Civil War raged, doughboys were sometimes caught in the middle. In all, some 200 Americans died in Russia.

In August 1919, the American Archangel force officially ended its operation and withdrew. An American lieutenant wrote: "Not a soldier knew, no not even vaguely, why he had fought, or why he was going now, or why his comrades were left behind, beneath the wooden crosses." The American expedition in Siberia finally came to an end on April Fools' Day, 1920.

When the summer of 1919 ended, all but five American divisions had been sent home. General Pershing himself sailed in September. The last 2,000 American troops left Europe in 1923. They brought home with them the last of some 1,200 German war brides who married doughboys during the occupation.

20
RECKONING

Although most of the struggle of 1914–18 took place in Europe, it does deserve to be called a world war. Fighting took place on three continents and three oceans. On all six continents there were countries at war. A total of 28 countries (with a combined population of 1.4 billion people) were involved by the end of the war.

The war began with five Allied countries pitted against two for the Central Powers. Within a year, the Ottoman Empire and Bulgaria entered the war. Against these four enemies the number of Allies grew to 24 by war's end. Five more countries broke off diplomatic relations with Germany. Only 16 countries, making up one-sixteenth of the world population, remained neutral.

Even tiny San Marino, a country only 38 square miles in size, joined the Allies and sent 300 men to fight in the Italian army. Although the majority of countries that eventually joined the Allies made only a token contribution to the war effort, the awakening of the world against the Central Powers had a considerable moral effect.

With the war over, the statisticians set about the task of tallying the cost of the war, in lives and money. The staggering figures they came up with broke every record in history to that time.

The direct monetary cost of the war was something like $186 billion, in 1918 dollars—an extraordinary sum, even in today's dollars. To this must be added the indirect cost of the war. When the loss of production, shipping, property, and the economic value of the people killed are figured in, the total cost of the war was at least one-third of a trillion dollars.

For a time, international trade would be disrupted by the shortage of ships caused by the war. Five thousand Allied ships were sunk by U-boats. Another 700 were the victims of mines, airplanes, and surface raiders.

U-BOAT SINKINGS	
Year	*Tons*
1914	310,000
1915	1,301,000
1916	2,322,000
1917	6,270,000
1918	2,659,000

Unlike economically ruined Europe, the U.S. economy emerged stronger than it had been before the war. Yet the war directly cost the United States about $24 billion. In addition, by war's end, America had loaned $10 billion to various countries.

Most important was the loss of life. There was hardly a family in France, Germany, and Britain that did not lose a loved one. Newspaper items like this one from Britain were typical: "Private Thomas Pestorisk . . . has been so badly wounded that he has been invalided out of the service. . . . He is the youngest of nine brothers who joined the Army and he has lost eight brothers in the war."

One historian suggests that the machine gun was the great killer of World War I. It was a relatively new weapon, and military planners failed to realize the machine gun's potential as a defensive weapon. It greatly multiplied the killing power of the soldier who operated it. One squeeze of the trigger could mow down whole ranks.

Another historian suggests that artillery was the great killer. Cannon had been much improved in the previous half-century. They became capable of delivering torrents of explosive shells. At Verdun, for example, 40 million shells were fired during a six-month period. (All the artillery rounds fired by the Union army during all four years of the Civil War totaled only about 5 million.)

Yet most historians agree that the great killer of World War I was the arrogance, stupidity, and stubbornness of the generals and politicians on both sides. They stripped their nations of manpower and led them into an upward spiral of mass slaughter. As the bloodbath dragged on year after year, the generals and politicians made cold-blooded calculations of how

long they could continue to fight before the entire manhood of their nations was wiped out.

Yet what kept the soldiers and the civilian masses going was the hope that their horrible suffering was not in vain. They clung to the belief that this war would be the last one. Some called it Armageddon—the final contest between good and evil referred to in the Bible. The most widespread motto of the war sought to justify the struggle by calling it "the war to end war."

Whatever the reasons for continuing the war, continue it did. The casualty rates were staggering. For example, the British army lost an average of 19,000 soldiers each month in 1915, 44,000 soldiers per month in 1916, 56,000 per month in 1917, and 75,000 per month in 1918.

Warfare had never been fought on such a scale. The major battles often engaged more than 1 million troops. Compare that to, say, the American Revolution, which rarely saw more than 10,000 men engaged. In 1814 the British captured Washington, D.C., with only 3,500 men. In all, more than 60 million men were pressed into military service. Russia mobilized the most men, followed by Germany, the British Empire, then France.

Yet France mobilized the highest percentage of its population and the French army suffered the highest percentage of casualties. One of every five French citizens was inducted into the armed forces. More than 90 percent of France's able-bodied males of military age served in the army, of which more than 70 percent were casualties.

No one will ever know how many lives were lost in the war. It has been estimated that

A shattered church in the ruins of Neuvilly, close to the Argonne Forest, served as a hospital for the wounded as the battle was waged. *(National Archives)*

The Quaker Businessman Who Saved Millions from Starvation

THE WAR IN EUROPE HAD NOT RAGED LONG BEFORE the people, particularly in battered Belgium and France, faced severe hunger. Since men had to leave the farms to fight, fields were barren. Women and children especially were the victims.

The news of this disaster reached an American businessman, a Quaker humanist named Herbert Hoover, who felt moved to ease civilian suffering brought on by war. Acting quickly, organizing like-minded citizens, he launched the Commission for Relief in Belgium in 1914. By war's end, Hoover had supervised shipment of 2.5 million tons of food, valued at $300 million, to feed more than 9 million people in Belgium and France.

Hoover, as head of the U.S. Food Administration, returned to Europe at the end of the war and conducted a relief program that continued to save millions of lives during the postwar period. When Hoover became the 31st U.S. president in 1929, the country was on the verge of a severe economic depression that Hoover was not able to deal with competently. But although he has often been criticized for the failures of his presidency, his achievements in the human services should not be forgotten.

11,000,000 soldiers died. About double that number were wounded, many incapacitated for life. The war was also responsible, directly or indirectly, for the death of perhaps 10,000,000 civilians.

One of the grimmest scenes of modern history took place in what is now eastern Turkey, where a large number of Christian Armenians lived. Isolated cases of collaboration between local Armenians and Russian forces had convinced the government of the Ottoman Turks that the whole Armenian population was disloyal. The Turks decided to massacre them with a calculated program of systematic genocide. Some 1.5 million Armenians perished in this little-known genocide.

The war decimated a generation of Europe's youth. By comparison, the loss of American life seems slight. Yet in only five months of active fighting, some 37,926 doughboys were killed in action. Another 13,628 died of wounds received in action. Disease claimed the lives of 23,853 men overseas and 38,815 men in the United States. Other causes brought the U.S. Army's total dead to 120,144.

Aisne-Marne American Cemetery, Belleau, France *(National Archives)*

In addition, 198,059 American soldiers were wounded. Of these, 700 had hands or feet amputated, 600 had lost arms, and 1,700 went home missing a leg or two. Many were blinded by gas.

To put this human price tag in perspective, consider the cost of the American Revolution. Between 1775 and 1783, 6,800 American soldiers were killed. More men died in a week's fighting in the Argonne Forest.

For veterans of trench warfare, life would never be the same. Many had disfiguring wounds. Prolonged exposure to the constant dampness gave some men a rasping cough that they would never lose. Others found their hands would occasionally shake uncontrollably.

Many veterans suffered from psychological or nervous disorders, ranging from nightmares and bed-wetting to depression and suicide. There were shell-shocked victims, men whose minds snapped under the strain of fear from constant bombardment. Some of these men kept their faces constantly covered with their hands to protect themselves from red-hot shell splinters, even though the splinters had long since stopped flying.

Whatever their problems, the doughboys were glad to be home. A returning soldier, elated to see the Statue of Liberty as his troopship at last entered New York harbor, yelled at the monument: "Old girl, if you ever want to look me in the face again, you'll have to turn around on your pedestal."

21
THE WAR
TO END WAR

The armistice had ended the fighting, but not the war. World War I would not be over until a peace treaty was signed. In January 1919, thousands of Allied delegates went to Versailles, France, where a peace conference was held. German delegates were not invited.

In fact, as far as the Allies were concerned, they were still at war. The half-starved German population would stay that way, for the Allies refused to lift the naval blockade. This cruel and inhumane decision resulted in a terrible famine in Germany. German children starved to death while diplomats in Versailles dickered for months over the terms of the treaty.

President Wilson sailed for Europe in December 1918. He was the first president to leave the country while in office. Wherever he went, the populace gave him a tumultuous reception. Many people throughout the continent believed that their hopes for a better world were in Wilson's hands.

The President's proposal for a democratic and progressive world peace was called the "Fourteen Points." They included plans for arms reduction, abolition of secret treaties, rights for colonial subjects, a halt to interference in Russian affairs, and self-determination of peoples based on ethnic boundaries, not political ones.

The Allies were not overly enthusiastic about the Fourteen Points. Each Allied government found a few provisions it did not like. Britain, for example, opposed the point that called for freedom of the seas.

The Allies had won the war and wanted to dictate their own terms and redraw the map of Europe as they saw fit. Allied representatives at Versailles were becoming very tired of Wilson's high ideals. The venerable

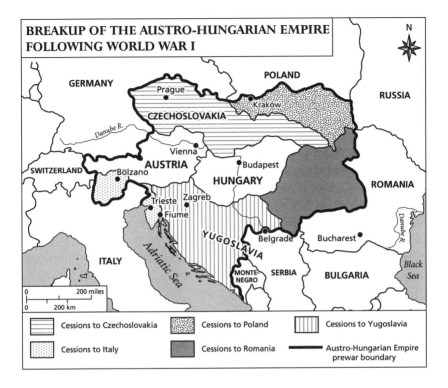

BREAKUP OF THE AUSTRO-HUNGARIAN EMPIRE FOLLOWING WORLD WAR I

Georges Clemenceau, the French premier and chairman of the peace conference, said: "Wilson bores me with his Fourteen Points. Why, God Almighty only had ten."

Wilson's 14th point called for the establishment of the League of Nations. He believed that a strong international coalition was needed to ensure a safe and peaceful future for the world.

No provision was more dear to Wilson, and the Allied diplomats knew it. They threatened to remove the 14th point if he did not make other concessions to their liking. One by one, Wilson sacrificed his principles for a just and lasting peace in order to save the League of Nations.

On June 28, 1919, the Treaty of Versailles was signed amid much pomp and pageantry. It was five years to the day after the assassination of Franz Ferdinand.

The terms of the treaty were harsh. Germany lost some of its territory, all of its colonies, its whole air force, and most of its navy. The German army was to be permanently reduced to 100,000 men.

"Council of Four" at the Peace Conference: President Woodrow Wilson
(far right), Premier Clemenceau, Premier Orlando, and Prime Minister
Lloyd George, May 27, 1919. *(Library of Congress)*

Most humiliating of all, the Germans were told they would have to
pay for much of the cost of the war. Not only would Germany have to
struggle to repair the damage to its own war-ravaged economy, it was
also expected to compensate the Allies financially, right down to pensions for French soldiers. Economists predicted that it would take more
than half a century for Germany to pay this debt, known as a war
indemnity.

The German people were outraged. Citizens had begun to move
toward democratic government, but the anger, fear, and economic hardship caused by the treaty helped extremist groups gain power. Within
a few years, right-wing militarist factions would again control the government. In this way, the Treaty of Versailles sowed the seeds of World
War II.

President Wilson returned to the United States in July 1919. Except for one brief return, he had been overseas more than six months. The America he came back to was not the same nation he had led to war.

The public mood had changed. Most people no longer cared about the rest of the world. They wanted things to be the way they had been before the war. They were tired of "foreign entanglements" and favored America's return to isolation. Citizens began to rally under the slogan "Back to Normalcy."

Americans were feeling the stress of social changes that the war had caused. Before 1914, American industry's ever-growing hunger for cheap labor was fed by millions of immigrants, mainly from Europe. Then the war came and the valve was shut tight. The United States faced a labor shortage at the very moment its industry was about to boom. Where were new workers going to come from?

One source was the African-American population. Most blacks lived in the rural South. Most of America's industry was in the North. Labor

Women work the assembly lines in industrial war effort.
(National Archives)

agents for large companies traveled through the South looking for black workers to do the unskilled jobs formerly done by immigrants.

Lured by promises of higher wages and better treatment, hundreds of thousands of blacks moved to northern cities. Most settled in Detroit, Chicago, Pittsburgh, Philadelphia, and New York. Racial prejudice, coupled with rapidly increasing populations, sometimes led to race riots. In 1918, when African-American soldiers were fighting and dying on the western front, dozens of African-American citizens were being lynched in the states.

Another source was women. Across the country women worked in shipyards, steel mills, coal mines, and on farms, filling in for their absent husbands, fathers, brothers, and sons.

More than 4 million men had served in the armed forces, half of them overseas. After being released from the service, they wanted their jobs back. Women were expected to become docile housewives again, but they had other ideas. They had helped win the war and felt that they should no longer be treated as second-class citizens. They formed political activist groups to demand the same privileges as men, including the right to vote. American women earned this right in 1920.

Thus, the First World War released social forces in America from which there was no turning back. Faced with social change, Americans lost interest in making the world safe for democracy.

During Wilson's long absence, his political opponents waged a persistent "Back to Normalcy" campaign on Capitol Hill. They ripped the president's peace plans to pieces. Wilson decided to take his message to the people. On September 3, 1919, still worn and tired from Versailles, he set off to make speeches across the nation. Wilson's journey took him 8,000 miles in 22 days, during which he made 37 addresses. Exhaustion finally overcame him. On September 26, Wilson suffered a stroke and was partially paralyzed.

Congress did not ratify the Treaty of Versailles. The United States would never join the League of Nations. So strong was the political pressure to return to isolationist policies that Congress even repealed the Declaration of War against the Central Powers.

Without the United States, the League of Nations, led by Britain and France, was hopelessly impotent. Germany rebuilt its war machine. In 1933 a new military dictator came to power. A former German army corporal who had fought doughboys in the Argonne, his name was Adolf Hitler.

A woman boring out a cannon at a New England arsenal. *(National Archives)*

The U.S. economy boomed in the Roaring Twenties, then collapsed in the depression of the Thirties. Then, in the 1940s, the United States would once again go to war. Many historians believe that World War II was basically the second installment of the Great War of 1914–18.

Few people in 1919 could have imagined that the treaty that ended the "war to end war" would keep the peace for only two decades. Yet there were some who saw the storm clouds looming on the distant horizon. U.S. Gen. Tasker H. Bliss, who was at Versailles, wrote in his diary:

"We are in for a high period, followed by a low period. Then there will be the devil to pay all around the world."

Glossary

ace A flyer who shoots down five planes in aerial combat.

Allies In World War I, the 24 nations that opposed the Central Powers. Only 12 provided troops: Belgium, the British Empire, France, Greece, Italy, Japan, Montenegro, Portugal, Romania, Russia, Serbia, and the United States.

armistice A truce or agreement by warring parties to cease hostilities, at least temporarily but usually with the intention of negotiating a permanent peace. The best known armistice of modern times is the one signed by the Allies and Central Powers that brought World War I to an end at 11 A.M. on November 11, 1918.

attrition The calculated goal of the leaders in charge of the battles not primarily to take ground but to kill as many of their opponent's men as possible. World War I became a war of attrition.

balloon busting The goal of fighter planes to shoot down enemy observation balloons.

bayonet A sharp, slashing steel blade attached to the muzzle of a rifle for killing enemy soldiers in hand-to-hand combat.

Big Bertha A gigantic German gun, designed to shoot heavy shells up to a range of 75 miles. There were only two, transported into France to fire on Paris. They were named after a daughter of the Krupp family, the munitions manufacturer of these guns. (In fact, the German nickname was *dicke Bertha*, meaning "fat Bertha.")

blockade Isolating a port, city, region, or nation by surrounding it with ships or troops to prevent the passage of traffic or supplies.

Central Powers In World War I, the four nations that opposed the Allies: Austria-Hungary, Bulgaria, Germany, and Turkey.

convoy   A formation of ships in which the most important vessels—often loaded troop transports—are surrounded by smaller, faster-moving combat ships.

destroyers, combat   Ships designed and equipped to attack submerged submarines.

Devil Dogs   the name given to the U.S. Marines by the Germans in World War I because of the fierceness of their fighting.

doughboys   A name given to U.S. Army fighters. Although the origin of this term is not known, legend says it was linked to soldiers in the Civil War who had big, round brass buttons on their uniforms, reminiscent of "doughboys," which were dumplings or fried dough.

escadrille   The French name for a fighter plane squadron, usually composed of six planes. The Escadrille Lafayette, a U.S. squadron, become one of the most famous and romanticized of all air units.

flame-thrower   From the German *Flammenwerfer,* a weapon with a long nozzle through which oil from an attached container could be discharged by the pressure of compressed air, spraying the enemy with fire.

Fourteen Points   Proposal by President Woodrow Wilson offering 14 points that he believed would bring about a democratic, progressive world peace.

go over the top   The military expression for when soldiers were ordered to leave their trenches and venture into no-man's-land to resume fighting.

howitzer   Cannons for long-range firing of heavy shells that could drop them in a plunging curve, thus reaching troops behind cover.

Iron Cross   A German army medal signifying the highest honor.

Iron Division   Nickname of the Twenty-eighth Pennsylvania National Guard Division. They were praised by General Pershing, who said "they fight like iron men."

kaiser   The German emperor, a name derived from the Roman *caesar.* During World War I, Kaiser Wilhelm II reigned.

KP (kitchen police)   The name given to menial chores done by soldiers in the kitchens or mess units.

League of Nations   An international coalition of nations, proposed by President Wilson, who believed it would ensure a safe and peaceful future for the world. Although the league was established in 1920, the United States never joined the League of Nations, and this left it essentially powerless.

lifeboat   A small boat that can be lowered quickly when a damaged ship has to be abandoned.

minelaying   The duty of specific ships to lay a field of explosive devices (mines) underwater with the intent of blowing up submarines.

mortar   A relatively small thus portable cannon, loaded in the muzzle, that fires its shells at a low speed and short range but with a high, arching trajectory.

nest   A well-prepared position from which soldiers can fire weapons such as machine guns.

no-man's-land   The strip of land between enemy trenches that is held by neither side. In World War I, it was usually cratered by shell holes, often muddy, and laced with deadly barbed wire.

periscope   An optical instrument with specially arranged prisms and mirrors that makes it possible for a submarine crew to view the surface of the water when the submarine is submerged.

shell shock   A nervous condition or mental disorder found in military personnel and brought on by the constant strain and fears of combat conditions in warfare.

storm troopers   Translation of the German *Sturmtruppen,* specially trained German soldiers who could pierce the enemy's line of defense by finding its weakest points.

submarine   A vessel that can be navigated under water, especially effective in war for the discharge of torpedoes.

tank   A self-propelled, heavily armored combat vehicle armed with cannon and machine guns that moves on caterpillar treads.

tent cities   In World War I, the name given to camps located in the South that were poorly constructed and lacking in wooden barracks; they were used primarily to house black men drafted into the U.S. Army.

torpedo   A self-propelled underwater projectile launched from a submarine, ship, or airplane and designed to detonate on contact or in the vicinity of the target, usually a ship.

trench   A long, narrow, deep excavation in the ground serving as a shelter for soldiers to protect them from enemy fire.

GLOSSARY

U-boat   A familiar name for a German submarine, derived from the German word for such a vessel, *Unterseeboot* ("undersea boat").

victory gardens   With the slogan "Food Will Win the War" popularized in the United States, patriotic people took on the planting of their own vegetable gardens so that commercially grown food could be shipped to the soldiers. The nation's Boy Scouts also planted victory gardens under the slogan, "Every Scout to Feed a Soldier."

war bonds   U.S. treasury bonds sold to the public to raise the money needed to fund the war.

Yank   The popular name given to U.S. soldiers by their British allies. It is derived from "Yankee," a name for Americans that appeared in the American Revolutionary War days. The exact origin of the name is unknown.

zeppelins   Germany's cumbersome, slow-moving, lighter-than-air balloon ships, powered by gasoline engines, intended to be used for bombing missions. Designed by Count Ferdinand von Zeppelin, a German general and airship builder, these balloons were highly flammable.

Further Reading

NONFICTION

Addams, Jane. *Peace and Bread in Time of War.* New York: Macmillan, 1922.

Axelrod, Alan. *The Complete Idiot's Guide to World War I.* Indianapolis, Ind.: Alpha Books, 2000.

Barton, Hendrick. *The Life and Letters of Walter H. Page.* Garden City, N.Y.: Doubleday, Page & Co., Volume II, 1922, Volume III, 1925.

Batchelor, John, and Bryan Cooper. *Fighter: A History of Fighter Aircraft.* New York: Scribner, 1973.

Batchelor, John, and Ian Hogg. *Artillery.* New York: Scribner, 1972.

Buckley, Gail. *American Patriots: The Story of Blacks in the Military from the Revolution to Desert Storm.* New York: Random House, 2001.

Burner, David. *Herbert Hoover, A Public Life.* New York: Alfred Knopf, 1979.

Butler, Daniel Alan. *The Lusitania.* Harrisburg, Pennsylvania: Stockpole Books, 2000.

Carey, John, ed. *Eyewitness to History.* New York: Avon Books, 1987.

Clark, George B. *Devil Dogs, Fighting Marines of World War I.* Novato, Calif.: Presidio, 2000.

Cooper, John Milton, Jr. *Breaking the Heart of the World: Woodrow Wilson and the Fight for the League of Nations.* New York: Cambridge University Press, 2001.

Dallas, Gregor. *1918: War and Peace.* New York: Overlook Press, 2001.

Dudley, William, ed. *World War I: Opposing Viewpoints.* San Diego, Calif.: Greenhaven Press, 1998.

Eisenhower, John S. D. *Yanks: The Epic Story of the American Army in World War I.* New York: Free Press, 2001.

Ellis, John. *Eye-Deep in Hell: Trench Warfare in World War I.* Baltimore, Md.: Johns Hopkins University Press, 1989.

Ellis, Mark. *Race, War and Surveillance: African Americans and the United States Government During World War I.* Bloomington: Indiana University Press, 2001.

Ferguson, Niall. *The Pity of War.* New York: Basic Books, 1998.

Ferrell, Robert. *Woodrow Wilson and World War I.* New York: Harper and Row, 1985.

151

FURTHER READING

Feuer, A. B. *The U.S. Navy in World War I: Combat at Sea and in the Air.* Westport, Conn.: Praeger, 1999.
Fussell, Paul. *The Great War and Modern Memory.* New York: Oxford University Press, 1975.
Geis, Joseph. *Crisis 1918.* New York: W. W. Norton, 1974.
Gilbert, Adrian, and Mark Bergin. *Going to War in World War I.* Danbury, Conn.: Franklin Watts, 2001.
The Grolier Encyclopedia of World War I. Danbury, Conn.: Grolier, 1997.
Gilbert, Martin. *The First World War.* New York: Henry Holt, 1994.
Gurney, Gene. *Flying Aces of World War I.* New York: Scholastic Book Services, 1965.
Hall, James Norman, and Charles Nordhoff, eds. *The Lafayette Flying Corps.* Boston, Mass.: Houghton Mifflin, 1920.
Hanson, William L. *World War I, I Was There. A Memoir.* Tucson, Ariz.: Patrice Press, 1982.
Heyman, Neil M. *Daily Life During World War I.* Westport, Conn.: Greenwood Publishing Group, 2002.
———. *World War I.* Westport, Conn.: Greenwood Press, 1997.
Higonet, Margaret R., ed. *Lines of Fire: Women Writers of World War I.* New York: Plume/Penguin, 1999.
Holden, Matthew. *War in the Trenches.* Hove, England: Wayland Publishers Ltd. 1973.
Holmes, Richard. *The Western Front: Ordinary Men and the Defining Battles of World War I.* New York: TV Books, 2000.
Horne, Alistaire. *The Price of Glory: Verdun 1916.* New York: Penguin, 1993.
Johnson, Herbert Alan. *Wingless Eagle: U.S. Army Aviation through World War I.* Chapel Hill: University of North Carolina Press, 2001.
Keane, Jennifer D. *The U.S. and World War I.* White Plains, N.Y.: Longmans, 2000.
Keegan, John. *The First World War.* New York: Knopf, 1998.
———. *An Illustrated History of the First World War.* New York: Random House, 2001.
Knightley, Philip. *The First Casualty.* New York: Harcourt Brace Jovanovich, 1975.
Lafore, Lawrence. *The Long Fuse: An Interpretation of the Origins of World War I.* New York: J. B. Lippincott, 1971.
Lawrence, T. E. *Revolt in the Desert.* New York: George H. Doran, Co., 1927.
Lebow, Eileen. *A Grandstand Seat: The American Balloon Service in World War I.* Westport, Conn.: Praeger, 1998.
MacDonald, Lyn. *1915: The Death of Innocence.* Baltimore, Md.: Johns Hopkins University Press, 2000.
———. *To the Last Man: Spring 1918.* New York: Carroll and Graf, 1999.

Marshall, S. Z. L. *World War I*. Boston, Mass.: Houghton Mifflin, 2001.

Massie, Robert K. *Dreadnought: Britain, Germany and the Coming of the Great War*. New York: Ballantine Books, 1992.

Mead, Gary. *The Doughboys: America and the First World War*. New York: Overlook Press, 2000.

Morton, Frederic. *Thunder at Twilight: Vienna 1913–1914*. New York: Scribner, 1989.

O'Shea, Stephen. *Back to the Front: An Accidental Historian Walks the Trenches of World War I*. New York: Walker & Co., 1997.

Palmer, Alan. *Victory 1918*. New York: Atlantic Monthly Press, 1998.

Pendergast, Tom, and Sara Pendergast, and Christine Slovey, eds. *World War I: Almanac*. Detroit, Mich.: UXL, 2001.

———. *World War I: Biographies*. Detroit, Mich.: UXL, 2001.

———. *World War I: Primary Sources*. Detroit, Mich.: UXL, 2001.

Perret, Geoffrey. *A Country Made by War*. New York: Random House, 1989.

Prior, Robin, and Trevor Wilson. *Passchendaele: The Untold Story*. New Haven, Conn.: Yale University Press, 1998.

Robbins, Keith. *The First World War*. New York and London: Oxford University Press, 1984.

Shay, Michael E. *A Grateful Heart: The History of a World War I Field Hospital*. Westport, Conn.: Greenwood Publishing Group, 2001.

Simpson, Colin. *The Lusitania*. Boston, Mass.: Little, Brown, 1972.

Strachan, Hew. *The First World War: To Arms*. New York: Oxford University Press, 2001.

———. *The Oxford Illustrated History of the First World War*. New York: Oxford University Press, 1998.

Sulzberger, C. L. *The Fall of Eagles*. New York: Crown, 1977.

Suskind, Richard. *The Battle of Belleau Wood*. Toronto, Ont.: Macmillan, 1969.

Toland, John. *No Man's Land*. New York: Doubleday, 1980.

Tuchman, Barbara. *The Guns of August*. New York: Macmillan, 1962.

———. *The Zimmerman Telegram*. New York: Ballantine Books, 1985.

Weintraub, Stanley. *Silent Night: The Story of the World War I Christmas Truce*. New York: The Free Press, 2001.

Westwell, Ian. *World War I: Day by Day*. Osceola, Wisc.: MBI Publishing Co., 2000.

Winter, Denis. *Death's Men: Soldiers of the Great War*. New York: Penguin, 1993.

Winter, Jay, and Blaine Baggett. *The Great War and the Shaping of the 20th Century*. New York: Penguin, 1996.

Wolff, Leon. *In Flanders Fields*. Westport, Conn.: Greenwood, 1984.

World War I: Reference Library. Detroit, Mich.: Gale, 2001.

FICTION

Cummings, E. E. *The Enormous Room.* New York: Boni and Liveright, 1922. Reprint, New York: Penguin Books, 1999.

Dos Passos, John. *Three Soldiers.* New York: George H. Doran, 1921. Reprint, New York: Bantam Books, 1997.

Hemingway, Ernest. *A Farewell to Arms.* New York: Scribner, 1929. Reprint, New York: Scribner, 1995.

Remarque, Erich Maria. *All Quiet on the Western Front.* Boston, Mass.: Little, Brown, 1929. Reprint, Trans. by A. W. Wheen. New York: Fawcett Books, 1995.

Wharton, Edith. *A Son at the Front.* New York: Scribner, 1923. Reprint, De Kalb: Northern Illinois University Press, 1995.

POETRY

Hart-Davis, Rupert, ed. *Siegfried Sassoon: The War Poems.* London, England: Faber and Faber, 1983.

Kilmer, Joyce. *Memoir and Poems.* New York, George H. Doran Co., 1918.

Lewis, Cecil Day, ed. *Collected Poems of Wilfred Owen.* Rev. ed. New York: W. W. Norton, 1965.

Seeger, Alan. *The Collected Poems of Alan Seeger.* Murrieta, Calif.: Classic Books, 2000.

Sitwell, Edith. *The Collected Poems of Edith Sitwell.* New York: Vanguard, 1987.

WEBSITES

The Great War. Available online. URL: http://www.pbs.org/greatwar/. Downloaded on March 27, 2002.

Photos of the Great War. Available online. URL: http://www.ukans.edu/~kansite/ww_one/photos/greatwar.htm. Downloaded on March 27, 2002.

Trenches on the Web Library. Available online. URL: http://www.worldwar1.com/reflib.htm. Downloaded on March 27, 2002.

World War I Document Archive. Available online. URL: http://www.lib.byu.edu/~rdh/wwi/. Downloaded on March 27, 2002.

World War I. "In the Trenches—The Soldier's Experience in the World War I." Available online. URL: http://www.people.virginia.edu/~eglar/wwi.html. Downloaded on March 27, 2002.

Index

Page numbers in *italics* indicate a photograph. Page numbers followed by *m* indicate maps. Page numbers followed by *g* indicate glossary entries. Page numbers in **boldface** indicate box features.

INDEX

INDEX

INDEX

INDEX

STILL LIFE

ALSO BY REBECCA PACHECO

Do Your Om Thing

STILL
LIFE

The Myths and Magic of Mindful Living

REBECCA PACHECO

HARPER WAVE
An Imprint of HarperCollins*Publishers*

HarperCollins books may be purchased for educational, business, or sales promotional use. For information, please email the Special Markets Department at SPsales@harpercollins.com.

FIRST EDITION

Designed by Bonni Leon-Berman

Library of Congress Cataloging-in-Publication Data has been applied for.

ISBN 978-0-06-293728-5

21 22 23 24 25   LSC   10 9 8 7 6 5 4 3 2 1

for dan and edie

who are both in perpetual motion but bring

stillness to my heart

myth:

1. A traditional story, especially one concerning the early history of a people or explaining some natural or social phenomenon, and typically involving supernatural beings or events.

2. A widely held but false belief or idea.

There is nothing particularly unusual or mystical about meditating or being mindful. All it involves is paying attention to your experience from moment to moment. This leads directly to new ways of seeing and being in your life because the present moment, whenever it is recognized and honored, reveals a very special, indeed magical power:

it is the only time that any of us ever has.

—*Jon Kabat-Zinn*, Full Catastrophe Living

contents

x · contents

author's note

For more than two decades, I've taught people how to move their bodies for the purpose of finding stillness. This tranquility is the essence of yoga, one of the most beloved mindfulness practices in the world. The word *yoga* means "to yoke" or "join together," most notably the body, mind, and spirit. There are countless other ways to practice mindfulness, with meditation being at the heart of them all. Life is the ultimate practice, of course, though you may have noticed it has a knack for getting in the way, too.

Moving and bending the body is one way to do yoga (known as *asana*). Yet, in popular consciousness, it constitutes how people largely think about the practice altogether. In truth, yoga is mostly meditation. Consider the following equation, for example: the philosophical origins of yoga map an eight-limbed path, like a family tree; only a single branch is comprised of the postural practice (downward dog, upward dog, all the dogs we know and perhaps love). Meanwhile, the other seven branches intentionally evoke mindfulness in one form or another; four refer directly to meditation. Mindful living, it should be noted, is comprised of both: formal meditation and how to pay attention to life as it's happening in the moment.

Sometimes, we need to move our bodies to find stillness within them. Other times, we must still ourselves wholly and completely for minutes at a time with as few distractions as possible. We must throw our smartphones in the ocean! (Kidding.) One technique is not better than another; mindfulness practices can be personalized to the individual—a system of knowing and using the right tools when we need them.

In 2015, I wrote my first book, *Do Your Om Thing*, in which I explored yoga's meaning beyond the poses and how its ancient philosophical underpinnings apply to real, modern, often-messy life. (Though back then few of us could conceive of just how messy life would become.) *Yoga: Meet Life*, the inside book jacket said. The best thing about putting a book into the world is releasing it from your small, tight grip and watching it belong to other people.

I traveled, taught, and spoke to yogis and non-yogis of all ages. I taught yoga to firefighters in a hazmat facility; led meditations in bookstores, boisterous college lecture halls, and hotel ballrooms at business conferences; I even taught my kooky breathing exercises at a bar (it was a fundraising event). I gave copies to NBA players and staff. I think some of them read it. I hope it made a nice coaster for others.

This is not a yoga book. Nor is it precisely a meditation book either—though you will learn how to meditate and what to do when you *can't* meditate, when life gets in the way, goes off the rails, or has other plans. It's a life book. Since that's why we do mindfulness practice. Not to be (artificially) chill all the time or exuding "good vibes only." We do it to cope with and be present for reality, which is a daring and unpredictable enterprise. We do it to find stillness in the midst of chaos.

Might you have any experience with this?

I've dedicated the majority of my professional life (and much of my personal life) to studying and teaching mindfulness practices such as yoga and meditation, among others. I know unreservedly how healing, empowering, transformative, and life-affirming they can be. And I understand their limits. Technically, there is just one—you guessed it—*life*.

We can be devout and limber yogis, and still, life knocks us down sometimes. You can meditate daily, breathe deeply, and sit quiet as a monk. You can drink all the green juice, burn incense, or adorn your home with crystals. Still, life happens. We cultivate mindfulness for this exact reason. Even in the midst of our hardest times, we can find peace and self-possession. Indeed, we *must* do this as a means of tending and mending what matters most. The stories and practices that follow serve the purpose of connecting you—mind, body, and spirit—with a sense of inner stillness, courage, clarity, wisdom, and love. Steadiness. And readiness. Mindfulness is the training for whatever life brings.

In art, a still life portrait illuminates familiar objects in a new way. "Indeed, that is the essence of still life's seductive appeal," says *The Art of American Still Life: Audubon to Warhol*, "it invites us to see what we know most intimately—but frequently take for granted—in a new and very different light." A plate of fruit on a sunny table. An unoccupied teacup. Books or sheet music on old parchment. A vase of not-too-perfect flowers, they have lived. Or the vase is empty. Life is art. Seeing it with fresh awareness is the magic of mindful living.

PART I

where to begin:
start in the present

1

Meditation

what it is and why we need it

"Meditation is the discovery that the point of life is
always arrived at in the immediate moment."

—ALAN WATTS

What I want to tell you about meditation is this: it never hurts. It always helps. It costs nothing, and it can change everything. There are
some exceptions; they are rare. We can quibble with words like *always*
and *never.* But the essence of these audacious claims has been explored,
discovered, and shared over centuries, across spiritual traditions, and
around the world. Recently, a growing body of scientific evidence supports them. Teachers and gurus, past and present, offer similar versions
of the same ideas. Then again, none of the teachers, data, or glowing
praise for something as simple as sitting still will matter until it works

for you, in your life, as it is right now. This is where we begin. The present is the best place to start.

The problem is never what meditation is capable of. No one misunderstands the mechanics: you sit and watch the breath. It's quite simple. Few people are unaware of the benefits or mystified by the positive impact it might have on our lives, from less stress and anxiety, to better sleep, improved memory, decreased depression, more happiness and compassion, and less feeling like your head is about to explode. That list is wildly incomplete. The miscomprehension, the thing that keeps people from doing something so simple yet powerful, is myths (implicit or explicit) about how the actual experience should look or feel, how it functions in our lives. The myths make things harder, and they get in the way of the magic.

Our stories about things can subvert reality. We think meditation should look and feel a certain way, and when it doesn't, we presume we did something wrong or that it doesn't "work." These are two of the more pervasive myths. All of them similarly undermine the magic of mindful living. Even with caveats for semantics—It (almost) always helps. It (rarely) hurts. It (can) cost nothing, and it might change everything—there are so few things on earth of which this can be said.

Meditation generally makes people feel calmer and more grounded. We are less agitated, mentally cluttered, and emotionally stretched-thin. With regular practice, we create space for creativity and clear decision-making. The head quiets. The heart expands. *The heart expands.* We discover an internal reserve of goodness, which existed all along. Rarely does meditation make people feel worse, though it doesn't eliminate bad days altogether. That's magical thinking. But, beyond the occasional pins and needles in one's foot, beyond feeling bored or fidgety, people typically report feeling some degree better in the short and long terms. We may experience uncomfortable emotions or dark thoughts while meditating, particularly if we've experienced trauma or are going through a difficult time. If meditation makes this worse, we should stop. More often, we grow to befriend the part of ourselves that is hurting. We learn to sit with her/him/them in loving awareness, listening nonjudgmentally, and eventually—this is the breakthrough—eventually, we recognize that the dark thought, like all thought, is fleeting. It's here. It's gone. But it's not actually *what's happening* in the moment. Nor is it who we really are.

Meditation is not what you think. (I love nerdy meditation humor, nerdy humor generally.) All emotions arise and dissipate. We begin to realize that we are not our thoughts. Cultivating mindfulness helps regulate emotions. Consider, psychological studies estimate that the lifespan of any emotion is roughly ninety seconds. What lingers much longer are the stories we tell ourselves about the experience. The way we interrupt this relentless impulse with mindfulness practice is by choosing where to place our attention from moment to moment. In formal meditation, it might be the breath. In yoga, it might be the physical sensations of the body in a pose. While taking a nature walk, it might be the sounds of twigs snapping beneath our feet or the smell of the air before it snows. Our attention is the strongest determinant of how we experience our thoughts and emotions and, by extension, life itself. "The interior life is a real life," James Baldwin wrote. "The intangible dreams of people have a tangible effect on the world." Said more plainly, thoughts influence feelings; our feelings lead us to act. Our actions create reality.

You can pay for mindfulness products and services. Perhaps you bought this book. *Thank you!* But you can also spend just about nothing on paying careful attention to what is happening. Observe how periods of careful and nonjudgmental awareness change your experiences. The practices—whether formal meditation or everyday mindfulness activities (e.g., writing in a journal, drinking a cup of tea without distraction, or walking the dog)—are humble. Exquisitely so. Which can feel reassuring in contrast to aspects of the wellness world, and the world writ large, that are often exclusive. This exclusivity occurs both by design, through the most arduous barrier of high costs or whether a community authentically prioritizes inclusivity, or by default, with health and well-being unjustly and inextricably linked to income, race, location, and other factors historically dictated by biased power structures. Meanwhile, here is a no-frills form of mental, physical, and emotional support that's widely available and often free.

Does this mean that the mindfulness community can rest easy because we've solved the accessibility problem? Definitely not. Taking a nature walk to restore our mind-body may not cost anything—until you consider that living in proximity to parks and forests can. To be truly mindful means we acknowledge and work to change such inequities. Still, I believe that meditation and mindfulness—which require few resources or tools and offer potentially vast benefits—provide a promising path toward healing and well-being for many people.

Meditation contains few discernible drawbacks and delivers seemingly infinite benefits. You sit. You breathe. You watch the emotions come. You watch the emotions go. Where you once may have been in a tiny boat at sea rocked by a storm, taking on water, you are now an onshore observer. Maybe the storm still rages, but you are not in danger of sinking. You observe how you speak to yourself inside your mind. Is that even *your* voice speaking? It's highly possible it's not. Whose voice is it? You notice small details of ordinary moments. You discover a new voice. How you relate to the world begins to change. Your quality of attention becomes both more expansive and more granular. Bigger and smaller, both. It contains more empathy. It sorts distractions. Buried beneath layers of fear or anger or boredom or grief rests wisdom, intuition, and steadiness.

Some of the most practical advice I ever received came from Buddhist chaplain and yoga teacher Cyndi Lee on a retreat in the days immediately following the 2016 election. "You do not have to be happy," she said. "But you do have to be steady." This struck me as deeply honest and compassionate guidance in a time of inner or outer turmoil.

With practice, we make our minds hospitable places to live. Indeed, we are quarantined within our heads 24/7. You practice and practice and practice, and many days not a whole lot happens. Until a time when hope lights a match in the dark and asks if it can sit vigil with you. Courage shows up with some provisions. Sandwiches on good bread. Coffee, maybe. Anyway, it's not something I can tell you. You have to experience it. Your magic, like your life, is a customizable experience.

THE TERM *MINDFULNESS* means different things to different people. It's defined and redefined all the time. Sometimes it's exploited, made glossy, marketed questionably, or wrapped in too many too-lofty ego-tickling promises. Mindfulness will help you achieve financial success. Find the perfect partner. Lose weight. Forget for a moment that these things may happen anyway. (More on that later.) First, we must understand that mindfulness is not self-improvement. That voice—the one imploring you to weigh less, make more money, or seek someone or something outside yourself as the path to happiness—is not the voice of living mindfully. It's a combination, sometimes a cacophony, of insidious voices of social pressure and systemic constructs like capitalism, patriarchy, and white supremacy. You are not good enough: do this. Buy this. Download this app. Eat this not that. Drink this not that. What's radical and magical about paying attention is that it teaches us to politely ask that voice to quiet down. Mindfulness says, *You are already enough as you are, right now.*

You have to marvel at how personal meditation is while revealing how similar the voices in all our heads are. It's almost as if they are not our own. Guess what? They are not our own! They are deeply conditioned thoughts and beliefs we've picked up through past, lived experience. Meanwhile, meditation and mindfulness, a two-pronged approach of formal practice and how we move through life, teach us to pay attention to the present.

The awareness that arises from paying attention on purpose in the present moment, nonjudgmentally is how Dr. Jon Kabat-Zinn defines mindfulness meditation. Kabat-Zinn is often referred to as "the father of the modern mindfulness movement," and I should add that he is also the actual father of one of my dearest friends. As the author of fourteen books and founder of the Mindfulness-Based Stress Reduction Clinic and Professor of Medicine emeritus at the University of Massachusetts Medical School, Dr. Kabat-Zinn pioneered the way people meditate in the West and is most responsible for shepherding the word *mindfulness* and practice of meditation into mainstream consciousness. Beginning with his days as a scientist at MIT, Kabat-Zinn's approach focused on the efficacy of mindfulness by researching its mental, physical, and psychological benefits. This approach to managing chronic pain, specifically, was groundbreaking at the time of its inception in the 1970s and now exists in more than seven hundred hospitals worldwide. Upon defining mindfulness in countless talks and interviews, he always goes on to clarify that this does not mean you won't have judgments, especially when you try to become still. You will have *many* judgments. Banal. Insightful. Petty. Profound. Self-loathing. Self-congratulatory. Benign. Benevolent. Incessant. There will be no shortage. *This feels good. This is boring. How long do I have to sit here? I'm hungry. I'm not good at this. This isn't working.* You will experience these judgments and countless others, in the span of seconds and on loop some days. But with practice, they'll untangle and soften. You'll learn to observe the judgments and criticisms, likes and dislikes, without reacting. It will be a welcome break from frittering your attention into simultaneous multidirectional oblivion all day long. The grip of your judgments *will* loosen, after a lifetime of conditioning. You will notice a deeper, kinder, and truer presence beneath all the conditioning. This is your awareness. Say hello. Acquaint yourself. She comes in peace.

There's a higher stakes, more poetic, less formal definition that Kabat-Zinn also gives. In this version, he doesn't hold back. "Living your life as if it really mattered," he says.

Consider a typical day: it whooshes past, often in a blur. *Life is what happens when we are busy making other plans* people jest. A day is littered with throwaway moments, beleaguered by tasks to be gotten through, endured. Waiting at a stoplight, standing in line at the grocery store, doing the dishes, vacuuming the rug, putting away the toys (again), waiting for the WiFi to connect . . . we presume these seconds and minutes don't matter. Why pay attention? We'd rather bend the moment to our will. Have you ever eaten a meal so quickly and mindlessly that you looked down at your empty plate and genuinely wondered where the food went? It becomes not even remarkable. That's maybe a typical day.

Most of us, most of the time, engage in a pervasive, individual, and collective daily dodging of the present moment. We inhabit a self-imposed virtual reality. We can live whole life chapters pining for a different moment other than the one we're in. We can half-live our whole lives if we're not careful. "This business of becoming conscious," writes Anne Lamott in *Bird by Bird: Some Instructions on Writing and Life*, ". . . is ultimately about asking yourself, How alive am I willing to be?" She was speaking about the consciousness of becoming a writer, but meditation is the same, all a question of awareness. How alive are we willing to be?

The trance of what's next and what's next and what's next is compelling. Surely the next thing will be more interesting, important, or pleasurable than the current thing. We do this in mundane moments (understandably), but we do it when the moment is safe, pleasurable, or delicious, too. We are eating a beautiful meal but already focused on dessert. At graduation, we are obsessed with getting the job. It's unsettling and often anxiety provoking not to know what the future holds, so we construct our own mental artifices of knowing things we cannot know. The guessing (or worrying) provides little solace, but that doesn't stop us from doing it anyway. *To worry*, as a bone or piece of wood, the word derives from the act of gnawing or turning something over and over without progress.

Our avoidance of the present manifests not only as fast-forwarding into the future, but also as a constant reliving of the past. You've probably had at least one conversation with yourself today about something that happened years ago. We want to know what happened, and why. How we felt about it and who was to blame, how great it was and how to re-create it, or how terrible it was and what we can do to avoid it happening again. These are deeply human, adaptive responses. We all experience them because they are hardwired into our operating systems from a time when we wandered into the wrong cave and unintentionally roused a bear. It would behoove us *not* to do that again. One prominent benefit of mindfulness is that it strengthens the parts of our brain that have the capacity to reason beyond this fear-based fight-or-flight response. If we didn't feel stressed by past conditioning or future speculation and panic, we wouldn't need a way to step out of the frantic and artificial pace of what happened in the past or *might* happen in the future. We wouldn't need a way to help us think more logically in the present moment.

It comes down to this: mindfulness allows us to recognize what is real and what is not real. The present moment is the only one that is real. It's all we really have. It's not distorted by memory or guesswork. It's characterized by power and choice—by agency. It carries clarity and nurtures compassion. It is sacred, even when forgettable, still sacred. Potential lives in the present moment. Love lives here. It's the moment that matters. Paying attention to what matters in the moment, compounded over our days and years on earth, is the basis for a meaningful and mindful life. We accept the offhand commentary that time flies because it does, but it's a myth that we must resign ourselves to look upon it in a daze. When we live in a state of autopilot, we lose touch with our humanness. It is possible to look back and think *I was there. I didn't miss it.*

Technology, which has radically changed the way we live, work, connect, and think, exacerbates this reality. We feel an urgent need to go somewhere else while also feeling like we never arrive. Well, we *were* urgently going places, until a global pandemic struck and exposed how unsustainable that pace of life was, how chronically overcommitted we were to *un*-reality, and how distorted our perceptions of what mattered most were.

The coronavirus pandemic, which is ongoing as I write, immediately revealed two things: that we needed to slow down and we are profoundly interconnected. The first was painfully obvious. We had been hurtling at an untenable pace for a long time. One small example that has large ramifications: today we are confronted with more information in a single week than someone one hundred years ago processed in his/her/their lifetime. Meanwhile, the human brain—let's revisit the analogy of an operating system—has not been upgraded in that time. It's an organ after all and reserves the right to maintain a low-tech existence because, um, it keeps us alive! We are not robots. Praise be, we are not robots. Furthermore, life all around sped up and boxed out anything resembling spare or leisure time. This has been doubly true for women who earn less than men, work longer hours, and shoulder a disproportionate amount of work at home. Of course, this worsened catastrophically in the pandemic, especially for women of color, the results of which will be felt for years if not generations to come.

One positive way that some people coped during this time was through meditation. After years of convincing my students to meditate, I suddenly didn't need to convince anyone. For one, many people had more time. They were stuck at home. Stuck with themselves in the most obvious and inescapable of ways. A Buddhist friend of mine joked that we were all suddenly on a meditation retreat that nobody signed up for. Of course, we were always stuck with ourselves, but now, we had fewer distractions at our disposal.

Loneliness had been declared a public health crisis before the pandemic entered our collective consciousness, and it would likely worsen and splinter into myriad other forms of mental health crises as the pandemic wore on. And yet, on the other side of that loneliness, an understanding emerged that while we were longing for each other and life as we knew it, we were also more inextricably connected than most of us previously acknowledged. One daily example of this realization I noticed was that we seemed to abandon small talk. *Are you OK?* we asked and needed to know the honest answer. Professional correspondence relinquished its veneer of compartmentalization, and our breakneck devotion to the trance of productivity finally collapsed. I needed you to be OK because we share a stairwell and doorknobs, and you being well impacts whether I might remain well. I need you to be OK because you are a human being like I am a human being, and it's precarious to pretend that things are more complex than that. It became customary to see infographics depicting one person's level of exposure to the virus with circles and pods that overlapped and expanded so that one infection rapidly became dozens more and soon hundreds or thousands. I kept thinking about the fundamental lesson in Buddhism of interconnectedness.

We have no control over the past. We have some agency over the future. That agency depends, first, on seeing the present clearly. So, the question becomes not only how alive are we willing to be, but also how willing are we to let go of our personal and collective commitments to unreality? I have no interest in hyping meditation to anyone who doesn't want or need it. I am only here to say that meditation works. It can heal or, at least, process past wounds. It can help us recompose ourselves. We can envision new and better selves, communities, and societies. In this way, the future begins now. The future *is* now.

WHILE THE EMERGENCE of mindfulness in the West is fairly recent, its origins, of course, are ancient, dating back to the Buddha, who lived in the sixth century BCE in present-day Nepal. Yoga's earliest mentions date back earlier, to Hindu tradition. And ancient wisdom traditions of all kinds share contemplative practices for paying attention and coping with life. Suffice to say, life today is radically different from the sixth century. It's radically different from a year ago, and we face new and different challenges. Nevertheless, human beings have endured, and we've sought and created ways of making that endurance less fraught. Meditation, prayer, silence, walking, and chanting— all forms of mindfulness—have soothed and strengthened us along the way.

Today mindfulness feels like a necessity for survival. You know those small, internal pockets in winter coats? They're typically for smartphones and barely keep pace with changing technology. One winter your phone fits, the next it feels wildly outdated. Our inner environments reflect a similar struggle. As the gulf widens between real and digital life, between what we see of the world when carefully curated and shared for our consumption versus how things are, we need help anchoring ourselves in reality. We tell the stories of our lives with increasingly innovative imagery, but we still feel the vicissitudes of those lives in ways that remain unfiltered, analog, complex, and human.

What I mean to say is that the mind is not a device and our bodies cannot be hacked. The mind needs quiet. A spirit revitalizes in stillness. The heart craves ease and gentleness. Peace cannot be artificially induced. At different times and for different people, the gifts of mindfulness bear a striking resemblance to those of spiritual practice or yoga practice or taking a walk on a crisp fall day when the air is a companion. Strip away the mechanics of where you do it and what it's called, and the same essence remains. Resting in awareness. Being in the moment. Noticing life as it happens. Communing. Listening. Becoming. Remembering. The purpose of this book and any mindfulness practice is in remembering. To breathe. To return to the moment, to our senses, to what is actually happening, to return yourself *to* yourself. To remember that we belong to each other. To remember how alive we are.

You are here. Now here. And right here.

2

Meditation and Mindfulness

what's the difference?

"Be conscious of yourself as consciousness alone,
watch all the thoughts come and go. Come to the
conclusion, by direct experience, that you are really
consciousness itself, not its ephemeral contents."

—ANNAMALAI SWAMI

The words *meditation* and *mindfulness* are used interchangeably. You
will notice I do this, too. It's shorthand and harmless. However, there
is a distinction between the two concepts that's worth noting. Put
simply: meditation is a practice. It involves focusing the mind on one
object or task, such as observing the breath or feeling the sensations
of your body in the moment. You can do this seated in a chair, on a
meditation cushion (known as a *zafu*), or on the floor, perhaps with

the help of a yoga block, pillow, or folded blanket. There are various types of meditation, but this core is the same.

Before we proceed, I'd like to offer a basic overview of what it means, practically and physically, to meditate. First, find a comfortable position. You don't necessarily have to sit, though that is the most common practice. You can lie down or stand if you prefer. Make sure your spine is long, neutral, and alert; that's the priority of your chosen posture. Your goal is to find a position that evokes wakefulness as well as ease. Become still. Let the fidgeting and wriggling dissipate. Watch it leave your body. Obviously, you can scratch your nose if you have an itch or straighten your legs for a moment to relieve pins and needles in your feet. We are not the meditation police here. Know that the mind, unaccustomed to stillness, will conjure reasons to move and scratch, like a pet pawing the door to go out. You don't need to answer every little itch. Over time, your mind will settle. As best you can, feel your body drop into stillness. That's generally it: the formal practice of meditation.

Mindfulness, on the other hand, is a *state of being*. Which means life offers all the opportunities to practice that we need, as long as we pay attention. Each moment provides lessons to learn—about the nature of our minds, humankind, and the world. No fancy programs or special retreats necessary. It's all here in the moment, literally. You can chop carrots mindfully as you prepare the soup. Sip a cup of tea while watching the steam and smelling the chamomile or bergamot, tasting bitter tannins or sweet honey. You can go for a run. Fold the laundry. Make some art. Take out the trash. Water the garden or a humble houseplant on the sill. You can be a vessel of care and profound tenderness. Have a conversation with someone you love or who drives you crazy—sometimes this is the same person—and really, really listen. These everyday moments are not explicitly meditation, but they represent an array of mindfulness practices, in which you become aware of awareness itself.

The two spiritual traditions of Buddhism and Hinduism and the cultures in which they originated laid the earliest and most lasting foundations for many theories and applications of mindfulness today. As a college student, studying these traditions stoked a youthful obsession with yoga and meditation. Dr. Miranda Shaw, religious studies professor at the University of Richmond, author of *Buddhist Goddesses of India*, and my independent study advisor, assigned lengthy readings from ancient texts, regaled us with tales of living and studying in the Himalayas—on a remote cliff overlooking a monastery—and taught us how to decode the meaning of sacred artifacts. What a statue of the Buddha means when depicted sitting versus reclining, how the hand gestures (i.e. mudras) of various deities conveyed secret messages. *Have no fear*, they said. *You are blessed*, they said. I would look at them and exhale. We learned to distinguish the era of an ancient sculpture or relic by nothing more than a grainy black and white photocopy. Dr. Shaw gave us the exceedingly modern and rudimentary homework of washing the dishes. This assignment was inspired by the teachings and work of the Vietnamese monk and peace activist Thich Nhat Hanh. The objective was to fully experience the act of washing the dishes rather than dash through another portion of our day in the semiconscious slapdash manner with which we typically do the dishes. My roommates loved when I had this assignment. We noticed the weather en route to class without judging it, no matter how hot or cold. This, too, was a genuine assignment. Just to feel.

There are lots of ways to meditate and infinite ways to experience awareness in your daily life. One practice enhances the other. Meditating makes mindfulness in daily life more accessible. Mindfulness while doing anything makes meditation easier and more fulfilling. The two-prong approach reduces stress, stabilizes emotions, boosts immunity, and enhances creativity and compassion, to name just a few benefits.

Perhaps you are already a seasoned meditator, or you were on a roll, meditating regularly for a while, but life happened and you need to revivify your practice. Yourself, too. Maybe you found your meditation sea legs with an app and want to go deeper. Wouldn't it be nice not to need an app every time? Perhaps you've tried it all before and it didn't work, but now you sense something has shifted. Whatever your reason or stage, reinforcements are closer than you think. Obstacles will arise, small and middling or sweeping and devastating. You'll be too busy. It might be boring. You will question whether you're doing it right. You might feel sad or furious or lonely. None of it means you're doing it wrong, it's not working, or you should stop. Bust those myths. Sit with yourself in stillness. Give yourself the gift of finding the ground again.

It's worth it when it's difficult. It's working when you feel sad. It works when it's not working. That's part of the magic. The problem is that we're looking for a rabbit pulled from a hat or shiny gold coins falling from our ears, and this spell is different. Miracles wear mundane disguises all the time. The other way to think about it is that if we're consistently preoccupied with what's next, what feels good, and what serves our personal needs better than what is actually happening, then we will miss our chance to inhabit reality. We become ensconced in illusion. We serve no one but ourselves. We are rarely contented with what is. The cycle continues.

Sometimes illusions are compelling, enjoyable even, but when we fall under their thrall too powerfully for too long, we lose our way. We miss things. Ordinary stuff like birds singing on a bright morning; they are unaware you awoke with worry before dawn. You see, you are not your fear. You have fear. You feel it. But it's not who you *are*. You are part of the moment, which is comprised of much more than fearful, separate thoughts. Vast oceans, whether you can see them or not, are helping you breathe this unremarkable remarkable next breath. Somewhere a baby learned to walk and maybe you are learning finally to be gentle with yourself. Right now, the tireless thrum of your heart beats, and you don't have to *do* anything. A moment can be mundane *and* magical. We know, and we forget, until something reminds us.

The term for mindfulness in Pali (the language spoken by the Buddha) is *sati*. More closely, that word translates to mean "memory of the present." The first time this concept was translated into English was in the late 1800s by a British magistrate in present day Sri Lanka named Thomas William Rhys Davids. In Sanskrit, a similarly ancient language closely linked to Pali and the language of yoga, the word is *smriti*.

So, the concept existed in the English language for a couple of centuries before entering popular consciousness in the late twentieth century. Mindfulness has long since achieved a new stratosphere of usage and relevance in the twenty-first century. The word itself is now everywhere; I'm sure you've noticed. At this very moment, I bet we could all search our inboxes and likely uncover a wide array of references or promotions for everything from core mindfulness practices to mindful eating, parenting, or financial investing.

"What about a word other than mindful?" my friend Chris asked me once.

"You see it everywhere."

She makes a fair point. What about contemplative, intentional, attentive, or awakened?

Although the truth is that what we call it matters less than how it functions in our lives. How do you feel on the days when you meditate, or how do you hope to feel? What happens in your body when you slow down and focus on your breath? Can you feel your heart rate decrease? And your shoulders relax? If you were able to release all the other moments that are not this moment, how would it feel to proceed with this *memory of the present*?

3

The Story of the Buddha

tradition and context

Your worst enemy cannot harm you as much
as your own thoughts, unguarded.

—BUDDHA

There are self-defeating myths that derail meditation practice before it gathers much momentum. We'll further examine those and put them to rest in the chapters ahead. You'll learn to recognize little falsities more easily so that you can focus on the business of staying focused.

And then there are more universal and epic myths, which lift, teach, and inspire us. Many wisdom traditions are based on allegorical stories like these. None is more essential to the origins of mindfulness than the story of the Buddha. The Buddha's enlightenment around 600 BCE is the most formative and vivid tale in mindfulness tradition, and more than two thousand years later, it remains relevant and vital.

You will never guess what the Buddha was doing on the night he became enlightened.

Actually, you will. He was sitting in meditation.

He sat beneath a beautiful, gnarled tree under the moon, and he breathed in and out. He watched his thoughts. He must have felt himself on the precipice of something. But then, a demon showed up.

A demon showing up when you're trying to meditate makes this story very relatable. Who among us doesn't have our own demons—ancient or modern, real or imagined—that show up to stymie our good intentions? While we may continually struggle with ours, the Buddha figured out how to vanquish his demon. And his technique and teachings persisted for more than two millennia.

Before the Buddha became the Buddha, he was just a guy. He wasn't a God or saint or sage. Technically, he was a prince. His name was Siddhartha Gautama. He had no special powers. The palace where he lived was outfitted with every luxury of the time; he had no reason to leave. Servants anticipated and tended his every need. He wore fine clothes. People trailed him all day long solving problems that arose. He never futzed with the printer, for example. He never circled for a parking space or installed an air conditioner window unit, which is a universally precarious and humbling affair. He did not worry about bills. No matter that printers, cars, and AC units didn't exist yet. You get the idea: royalty. Siddhartha's father, the king, took pains to shelter his son from life's larger, harsher realities, too. As the story goes, the prince had never encountered (in any impressionable way) aging, illness, or death.

Time out! How could a grown man not know about aging, illness, or death? Let's focus on the symbolism. Most people can relate to not comprehending the gravity of something until we have to.

Siddhartha started to wake up. He began asking questions. He wanted to see more of the world than his highly sheltered experience allowed. As it's told, this process began with a voice, a palace singer who entertained with songs about wondrous landscapes and faraway cities. What they sparked in Siddhartha was a new and undeniable curiosity. Maybe he heard that life was messier and more thrilling, contained depth and heartache, exposed you to demoralizing defeats and triumphant victories, but he'd never quite seen them. They were urban myths, as far as the not-yet Buddha was concerned. Maybe he heard a small inner voice that said, *Something does not seem right. Something is missing.* He expressed a desire to explore life beyond the palace gates, to which his father obliged and arranged a tour to sate his son's interest. He curated a purposefully sanitized version, containing no poverty, aging, illness, or death. It sounds sort of like Instagram, doesn't it?

Siddhartha was not satisfied with the tour. It felt anemic and maybe phony, so he wandered away, down darkened alleys and under dodgy bridges. As famously told, he came upon beggars who were hungry, people who were miserable with illness, lepers in exile, an old man stooped and frail with age, and a funeral procession—all shocking contrasts to his protected existence. For the first time, he was struck in a real and raw way with the inescapable vulnerability of the human condition. Suffering exists. It was an incontrovertible fact of life.

Later, this realization becomes the central tenet of Buddhism, the first of its Four Noble Truths. Sometimes misrepresented as *life is suffering*, which can be interpreted as dour or macabre; scholars clarify that what is meant is more along the lines of life *contains* suffering. We don't have to be Buddhist to understand that ignoring this basic reality misaligns us with the nature of life. So, this is both the beginning of all Buddhist philosophy and not Buddhism at all. It's just the truth. We will age, become sick, and eventually die. Gallows humor tells us that the death rate still holds steady at 100 percent.

Siddhartha decides to leave his superficial life and depart the palace forever. He absconds in the night and disguises himself as a commoner.

He is in search of enlightenment, but he doesn't know how or where he'll find it. There's no GPS for this kind of journey, then or now. He just knows he needs to figure things out.

A lot happens between this moment and the moment under the beautiful Bodhi tree, so I need to skip ahead. Your thirties are like this—so much to cover! Throw in a mythic journey toward enlightenment and we could be here all day. On the eve of his awakening, Siddhartha is meditating when he runs into some trouble. This happens to all of us, of course. We sit down, close our eyes, breathe deeply, and await peace, wisdom, and equanimity, and instead we get a flood of thoughts, emotions, irritating noises, and visions of that one horrible ex. Terrifying breaking news flashes scroll across the screen inside our foreheads. We radiate worry. We fidget and shift in boredom. The name of the demon that comes for Siddhartha is Mara.

Mara is hell-bent on thwarting Siddhartha, and he summons three formidable obstacles to accomplish his sinister plan. First, he deploys temptation. How easy this will be, the demon must think. Everyone crumbles for temptation. He will seduce Siddhartha into thinking there are better things to do than sit quietly in the present moment focusing on what is real, what is here, and what matters. *Don't be a dullard, Siddhartha.* To achieve this end, he sends a gaggle of gorgeous women to dance and encircle the tree under which Siddhartha sits. Without opening his eyes, he senses their presence, the intoxicating fragrance of flowers woven in their long hair and rich oils on their supple skin. All he has to do is pay attention to them. All he has to do is cave to the desire to be somewhere else, doing something else, other than the moment he's in, doing what he's doing, which is meditating alone in the dark.

Siddhartha is not falling for this ruse. He remains steady. He continues to meditate. The beautiful maidens disperse.

Mara vows to do better. He will up the ante. He is a legitimate demon, after all. The next logical step is violence, in the form of hundreds of troops armed with bows and arrows descending upon the peaceful meditator. The artillery is unsophisticated but menacing nonetheless; guns and explosives do not yet exist. But when you're sitting alone in the woods at night wearing little more than a loincloth, any weapon is troublesome. Siddhartha senses their arrival but doesn't engage, which is a surefire way to tick off people who crave war, seethe vitriol, and identify by separateness. He must have been scared. Did his heart race? Did his skin prickle with heat? But he doesn't flee. He barely moves. He observes. He concludes that he can remain calm in the moment, that *he is not his fear.* He stays still. Does he know what's about to happen?

The soldiers fire at Siddhartha. Hundreds of arrows soar through the air; meanwhile their target sits. He doesn't run or cower. He must know something because his hands don't flinch toward his head. He doesn't reposition his body, doesn't attempt to deflect the arrows from piercing his most defenseless organs. Throat. Underbelly. Heart. It's possible, if we are seeing him right, that he sits a little taller, the crown of his head ascending toward the moon. The trajectory of the arrows passes the apex over his head now. But in the moment when they should curve downward and surely kill him, they transform . . . midair, they turn to flowers, and thousands of petals rain down. They fall upon his head, bounce softly off his shoulders, and cover the ground around him like a blanket.

A triumph! Siddhartha is prevailing over a demon with nothing more than his mind. Or, or, OR—is his mind the source of the battle altogether? Either way, the charade vexes Mara. He counters. *You want to understand the nature of the mind? Buckle up, buddy.* Demons live for this kind of thing. Their anger festers and metastasizes until it consumes everything in sight. Mara reaches for the most daunting obstacle yet. Nobody withstands this one. The alluring temptations failed to seduce. A vicious attack barely registered. What could be worse? What will send Siddhartha running for safety? What will dislodge him from his peace? You can see Mara stroking his chin. It's so obvious, really.

Self-doubt. The most daunting and destructive obstacle that a demon can send on the eve of the enlightenment is self-doubt. Show of hands: anyone have experience with this kind of thing? *Likewise.*

In depictions of this moment in scholarly texts, ancient art, and cinematography, we see the Buddha presented with a mirror image of himself. In the film *Kundun*, directed by Martin Scorsese, Keanu Reeves stars as Buddha. I managed to incorporate the movie into my independent study on Buddhism in college—my obsession with this story is well established. Buddha sits faced with the reality of himself, every physical, mental, and emotional flaw magnified into grotesque detail and experienced anew. The message is clear. There is no escaping ourselves. Nor is there any easily identifiable "self" that we can see in a mirror. We're changing every second. Our physical form, age, station in life, clothes, job title, they're all impermanent. Beneath it all, what is the consistent thread? Who is this *self*?

By now you know Siddhartha prevails. In this moment of radical self-exposure, he drops one hand from his lap, down to the earth in a gesture of grounding. He asks Mother Earth to bear witness as he becomes enlightened. He recognizes that threats to inner peace take multiple forms, but the source of suffering is the same. It's an attempt to hold or grasp a version of life that isn't real, something other than what is happening in the moment. This attachment includes our egocentric idea of ourselves, which helps us construct a particular image to serve our singular, individual interests. Our suffering stems from not understanding impermanence, that we will lose things, and that we are all interconnected, not separate from each other.

The Buddha's journey eschewed extravagant wealth in favor of near-naked, starving asceticism. He wandered through the forest foraging for food, hoping to free himself from material attachments, only to discover this deprivation wasn't the answer. The answer was somewhere in the middle, not walled off in a palace or isolated in the woods. He called it the Middle Way. Perhaps the revelation suggests that the meaning of life is in the living of it. It raises plenty of questions we still ask, too. Can we recognize our illusions? Can we see through our own demons? How might we emerge kinder and wiser on the other side of our own battles? Are we willing to stop running from the full spectrum of life experiences? What can we do to alleviate suffering, our own and others? The word *buddha* translates to mean "one who is awake." This story belongs to Buddhism; it forms the beginning of the lineage of mindfulness. And yet, it illuminates a familiar battle for all of us: What happens when we are faced with the realities of suffering? What happens when life happens?

Modern mindfulness emerged in the United States around the 1970s, largely led by Kabat-Zinn, originally a practitioner of Zen Buddhism. Other early stewards of meditation and influential teachers included Joseph Goldstein, Jack Kornfield, and Sharon Salzberg, who had recently returned from Asia (Burma, Thailand, and India) and began sharing what they learned. In the case of Kabat-Zinn, Buddhist philosophy was not an explicit part of his teaching. With Goldstein, Kornfield, and Salzberg, Theravada Buddhism remained at the forefront but was not a requirement for students. To make the teachings more accessible, their Buddhist underpinnings became less prominent. This made meditation less mystical and more approachable and palatable to Westerners.

As I mentioned earlier, not only were more people practicing mindfulness; science began to research it. Could its benefits be quantified and proven? Could it heal people, of ailments of all kinds: mental, physical, emotional . . . existential? Could it reduce stress? This last question became the most pressing and popular. The answer to these questions then and now, anecdotally and scientifically, was a resounding yes.

Today, mindfulness practices including meditation, yoga, and many others, are taught everywhere from dedicated studios and retreat centers to health clubs, hospitals, prisons, fire stations, big corporations, and preschool classrooms. And although the Buddha's story doesn't necessarily get mentioned, its essence seems inescapable, and its roots are important. Each time we sit down in an attempt to "wake up," don't we experience a similar onslaught of obstacles, judgments, and temptations? We might feel lost in a forest or alone in the dark. We would rather do anything, *anything*, other than sit still. We could make a sandwich or organize the junk drawer. We could send a text. To whom? Who cares! *Hi. I'm here. Could you please confirm my existence? I don't want to sit with myself.*

"Your worst enemy cannot harm you as much as your own thoughts unguarded," the Buddha said. For the remainder of his life, he taught people how to make their minds less like battlefields and more like flower gardens. All the time we are planting something—consciously and unconsciously. What will we cultivate? And when we neglect the garden of our mind, what else takes root—when we're *not* paying attention? "Sooner or later, the monastery comes to you," former monk and meditation teacher Shinzen Young tells us.

Our stories are a lot like the Buddha's. They're nothing like the Buddha's. Our lives are like living in a monastery. Our lives are nothing like living in a monastery. The details matter less than the quality of attention that holds them.

The way the mindfulness movement unfolded was a product of its tradition, timing, context, and the people who started it. We would be remiss not to acknowledge that they were mostly young, white, male, able-bodied, and of means. They could travel from the United States to Asia, live there, learn for long periods of time, and return. They were on particular journeys. They found something deeply meaningful and wanted to share it. Their experiences were groundbreaking, and their work has radically changed many lives. But their experience is not meant to be conclusive of all of mindfulness, for everyone, for all time.

Everything evolves: teachers, students; the social, cultural, and political moment; who we are and what is required of us. What stresses you out right now might be drastically different from what stressed you out five years ago or what will stress you out five years from now. The practice itself, however, is pretty timeless. We sit like the Buddha sat. We sit like ancient yogi statues carved into the sides of the temples thousands of years ago, legs entwined in lotus pose, eyes closed. We are yogis. We are real-world secular monks whose monastery has arrived. You sit with your breath, doubts, and demons. You wonder if it's working. You do your best. This is both the journey and destination.

4

The Benefits

Meditation is not a means to an end.
It is both the means and the end.

—JIDDU KRISHNAMURTI

Here are some things that can happen when you meditate:

You feel less stressed.
You sleep better.
You walk through the world half-asleep less often.
Your blood pressure decreases.
The part of your brain responsible for making sound decisions gets
   stronger.
The likelihood that you remember someone's name increases.
You remember who *you* are.
You experience less chronic pain in severity or frequency.
You become a better listener, to yourself and others.
You become a better friend, to yourself and others.

You become a more patient parent.

You become a more compassionate child.

You taste your food.

You recognize your connection to all beings and the earth.

You can hold a thought.

You can do just one thing.

You can do the courageous thing.

You pay attention.

The impulsive part of your brain feels triggered and agitated less
often.

You remember to breathe.

You love deeper.

You pay attention.

You remember to breathe.

You live your life rather than life living you.

Big things happen when you meditate, and small things. Life can
improve. Rather, how we feel within life shifts. The shifts are micro-
scopic. The shifts are wholesale. I can't promise which, only that when
we pay attention, things change. Something happens.

The big thing that happens with practice is that you relax. Biologically speaking, you access your relaxation response, also known as the
parasympathetic nervous system, which serves the fundamental purpose of allowing your body to "rest and digest." Activities of the parasympathetic nervous system include stimulating digestion, activating
metabolism, and helping the body relax, heal, and recover.

This function is a necessary balancing component to the sympathetic
nervous system, commonly known as our *fight-or-flight* response, also
referred to as *fight, flight, or freeze*. The problem is that most of us operate in the latter state more than is necessary or beneficial to our mental, physical, and emotional health. Our ability to fight, flee, or freeze
when we are threatened is the brain's built-in survival mechanism. It's

how our ancestors avoided predators in the wilderness, and you can thank it for your suddenly superior reflexes when catching your child before she falls or pulling her out of harm's way on the playground or in the crosswalk. But to be in that hypervigilant state too often wears us down on every conceivable level. Every system in the body can be affected; our health can go haywire in a multitude of ways. Meditation, yoga, and other mindfulness routines rebalance the nervous system, by soothing the fight-or-flight response, turning on the parasympathetic nervous system, and helping us evaluate perceived threats with keener awareness. If a bear is chasing you, running at top speed is paramount. If a bear is not chasing you, wouldn't it make sense to eventually slow down and rest? Less fighting and fleeing—more *being*—that's the basic idea.

The smaller shifts happen cumulatively, but there's a temptation to wish we could special order our desired results.

"If you do it for the benefits, you don't get the benefits," my friend, a longtime meditator, likes to say.

She makes a salient point. It reminds me of athletics or music or just about anything you want to be good at. You have to practice. In school, you can't sit in the classroom and expect to absorb knowledge; you have to engage with the material. You have to concentrate, ask questions, do the readings, and take notes. Everyone wants the benefits of meditation. Who wouldn't? But are we ready to engage with the material? The material being reality itself.

Sometimes the benefits will rain down upon you like the flower petals onto Buddha's shoulders. You will awake from a restful night's sleep and know how it happened. You will sense your immune system strengthening and your creativity revving to life again. You will feel less anxious. The benefits will be obvious and everywhere. More likely, there will be periods when you feel not much at all, you might wonder if it's "working." It may seem like a waste of time. The truth is that it's always working because we are always works in progress. Not to mention, we waste our time in so many ways that are *way* less useful. In other words, you are on a journey and meditation is one of the tools to help you navigate your way. It can't eradicate *all* sleeplessness, stress, or threats to our immune systems and sanity. It's not a cure-all, but it is a balm.

When you distill it, the skill that you practice and refine, over and over again, is the creation of space between a stimulus and your response. Famously, Austrian neurobiologist and Holocaust survivor Viktor Frankl said, "Between stimulus and response there is a space. In that space is our power to choose our response. In our response lies our growth and our freedom." The stimuli happen in myriad forms, of external and internal varieties.

Externally, you will notice distracting sounds, like a passing siren or the neighbor's weed whacker. There's an ancient Zen proverb: *When the meditator is ready, the neighbor shall commence weed whacking*. You might be aware of the temperature and your associations with it: too hot or too cold. I wish it were more of this or less of that. Internally, thoughts arise. They can be spectacularly noisy. They put the weed whacker to shame. You may feel strong emotions tied to those thoughts or notice corresponding physical sensations in your body, represented by areas of tension. This is why we aim for an easy posture when we meditate and how continually checking in with the physical sensations of the body helps bring us back to the present moment.

It's essential to remember that we are never trying to block out certain aspects of the moment. We're not manufacturing blissful thoughts or preventing unpleasant ones. We're experiencing the details of the experience of the moment. We watch. We observe. We breathe. We practice nonjudgmental awareness. This is not a show on Netflix you're meant to form an opinion about. You're not writing a review on the internet. This is your mind. This is your attention. This is the way to peace.

When you practice this skill, the same thing happens as when you practice anything: you improve. Nevertheless, meditation is not self-improvement (more on that in Chapter 6). You watch the thought, hear the sound, or feel the sensation. Rather than judge it or get into an involved mental debate about its value, witness it. Acknowledge its arrival, notice how you're responding—the reactions in your mind or sensations in your body—but then, come back to the breath. Come back to the moment.

Meditation Primer

Find a comfortable seat, feeling your feet on the floor and resting your hands in your lap. You could place your palms downward, ever so slightly pressing into your thighbones. This is called calmness-abiding mudra (see Chapter 14). Note your spine and bring it into a long and neutral position. Start by taking a few deep breaths, and then, let the breath settle into a natural pace. Watch it coming in and going out, as you might see it outside on a cold day. You don't need to manipulate the rhythm of your breath, just observe. If possible, breathe through your nose. When your mind wanders away, notice where it went and gently bring it back to the breath. Your breath is now a meditative anchor, the object of your attention. You are cultivating a simple and remarkable skill. By doing this, you connect to an interior source of stillness, which is only available in the present moment.

Do this for a short while to start. Three to five minutes is a reasonable commitment if you've never formally meditated before. As a general guide, aim for reasonable commitments. Remember, you are building a muscle. Like training for a marathon, you begin by running 5 miles and then 8 miles and then gradually, you build your way up to 26.2 miles. You will struggle and have bad days. You may set out to run 10 miles but only do 4. You didn't fail. You are still getting stronger. You are still on the path. We are always on the path.

5

Mindfulness in Modern Life

changes, challenges, and opportunities

When I collapsed, I was—by our society's definition—
very successful, but by any sane definition of success, I
was not [...] As long as our culture defines success as
money and power, we're stuck on a treadmill of stress,
sleep deprivation, and burnout.

—ARIANNA HUFFINGTON

Not so long ago I turned forty. My arrival into midlife was accompanied by an awareness of my technological limitations. My generation boasts the last known species of non-native cell phone users. After us, no beasts will roam the earth that remember landlines, record players, cassette tapes, or car windows that manually roll. Typewriters, too! At my first summer job, the clacking sound thrilled me for its auditory resemblance to literary greatness. I was Ernest Hemingway! I was Kurt Vonnegut! I was Joan Didion! To be fair, I was typing addresses on envelopes.

It would be crazy to discuss mindfulness in the modern era without acknowledging how dramatically the flow of life and work have changed in recent years. How our ways of being and relating to each other have altered, how that feels in our bodies and minds, and what we can do about it. How can we adapt to our rapidly changing world, cope with its challenges, and make the most of our evolving mindfulness practices, resources, and opportunities? None of us can peer into the future, but our best chance for making it better, kinder, and saner is by paying attention right now.

Changes

For a long time, I was the youngest person in any yoga or meditation gathering I attended. I became accustomed to looking like I wandered into the wrong room. In the mid-1990s when I started, classes seemed largely comprised of the first wave of Americans to bring yoga and meditation en masse from the East to the West. Hippies in the 1960s, my first fellow yogis were now white-haired and kindly, doing an appropriately slow and gentle style of yoga known as hatha. These environments soothed my turbulent teenage soul.

The yoga landscape changed rapidly from that point onward, and the wellness industry as a whole expanded—exploded, really—with it. These two juggernauts, yoga and wellness, formed a symbiotic relationship. Into wellness, yoga injected a force that was at once mystical and ancient while simultaneously thrilling and new. Meanwhile, wellness culture seeped into every aspect of our lives, beyond gyms and health clubs, and into the aisles of department stores, on television commercials for products ranging from yogurt to tampons to prescription drugs, on restaurant menus, and hanging in our closets. No fashion trend has been as pervasive or seemingly permanent as athleisure.

As the turn of the century approached, meditation became more popular, too. But it wasn't nearly as accessible as it is now. This is one extraordinary benefit of the digital age. You could read books . . . I read as many books on the topic as I could find. I investigated Buddhist centers in my area. I attended talks with renowned teachers. When Pema Chodron, a prominent Tibetan Buddhist nun, teacher, and author, gave a public lecture at the Harvard Divinity School, I attended. I was in my early twenties and expected a high level of mystique: pomp and circumstance, rituals and gongs, robes and chanting. And while she did wear her signature monastic robes, there was zero pomp. If anything, she dazzled us with earthbound realness. I started paying attention to that original cohort of mindfulness teachers. Still, there were few places where you could find people and teachings like these on a regular basis. Certainly, there were no podcasts, online courses, or apps. The internet barely existed. And to be fair, in those halcyon days of wellness becoming cool and yoga becoming mainstream and meditation becoming not weird, technology was largely seen as a distraction. Which, hello, it is. It's other remarkable things, too, *and* insanely distracting.

The internet revolutionized our access to everything, including meditation. Whereas it was once possible only to study with a preeminent teacher if you happened to live where they did, could pay to attend remote talks and retreats, or kept a close eye on their travel schedules. Maybe one of them would come through a couple times a year. Now, you can follow beloved teacher Sharon Salzberg on Instagram. You can listen to a talk via podcast with Buddhist psychotherapist Tara Brach. I often do this while scrubbing my bathtub on Sunday nights. You can listen to broadcast journalist turned meditation evangelist Dan Harris tell his story of finding meditation after experiencing a panic attack on live TV, or interview others about their experiences, from scholars to rock stars, to politicians, to celebrity chefs. There are apps like Headspace, Calm, and Insight Timer. Cyndi Lee, Susan Piver, and Roshi Joan Halifax have parlayed decades of wisdom in various traditions into insightful online programming. Oprah teams up with Deepak Chopra from time to time and often talks to Pema Chodron, Jon Kabat-Zinn, and Jack Kornfield, to name a few. Black Buddhist thinkers, teachers, and leaders including Angel Kyodo Williams, Lama Rod Owens, and Sebene Selassie put equality and justice at the forefront of spiritual practice, which is right where they belong. And spaces defined by high traffic and busyness such as airports, hotels, and conference centers now have dedicated areas for yoga or meditation in some cities. His Holiness the Dalai Lama is on Twitter. The internet breeds distraction and social media warps our minds in harmful ways, but it also radically shifted who could meditate, where, and how. The question becomes then, how will we use it?

I floundered for a good decade trying to meditate but not having the right resources or knowledge to pull it off. One myth that was almost my undoing, for instance, was that meditation wasn't worthwhile if it consisted of less than twenty minutes per day. I heard that insight many times from multiple sources. It was a widely held and promoted belief at the time. The guideline was well-meaning, a suggestion not a dictate, but I suspect it derailed more people than just me.

The truth is that twenty minutes is a very long time for a brand-new meditator. Twenty minutes is an interminable sentence in your own head without guidance. If the frenetic pace of life today and flood of new meditation products to the market demonstrates anything, it's that we have to start somewhere, and something is better than nothing. We might start with an app, but we won't always rely on one. Someday, we'll be able to sit for twenty minutes easily. Maybe thirty or more. We can notice and nourish the fractured nature of our attention, its dopamine-seeking thirst for instant gratification, attachment to virtual reality, and unwillingness to face what's happening in the moment.

There's a reason people call this collective commodity our "attention economy." It is infinitely, crucially valuable, especially to marketers, brands, and the algorithms that operate on behalf of big companies with an interest in altering our behavior. But our attention is not infinite, and only we can control how to spend this most precious resource. For many of us now, meditation is an essential way of wresting control of our minds away from the internet, social media, and mass distraction, and directing it back to the things that matter or might recharge us.

Challenges

Technology has allowed modern mindfulness to become more accessible and reflective of real life. And yet, while engaging with healthy content online is a godsend, it still keeps us connected to our devices. Consider, for example, that the most recent data suggests that American adults spend eleven to fourteen hours on average looking at a screen of some kind per day. These estimates are likely conservative given they were calculated before a global pandemic forced businesses, schools, and life as a whole to shut down, leading to a greater need to be online. The answer, of course, is not to forgo enriching online experiences. However, it's worth considering how we might apply our mindfulness skills and sensibilities to how we engage with our devices, as well as the type of content we consume.

In a 2018 Harvard study, researchers explored the ways in which phones, while spectacularly convenient, also breed anxiety and wield extraordinary influence over our thinking and behavior. The study's authors wrote, "Not only do our phones shape our thoughts in deep and complicated ways, but the effects persist even when we aren't using the devices. As the brain grows dependent on technology, the research suggests, the intellect weakens."

One experiment tested the theory by separating students into three groups before taking an exam. The first group was allowed to place their phones on their desks. The second group stowed their phones in their bags. The final group was asked to leave their phones outside the room. Guess who scored highest?

The results were striking. Students whose phones remained in view scored the worst. Meanwhile, subsequent groups posted grades that inversely correlated to the proximity of the phone: the closer the phone, the weaker the brainpower. What's more is that nearly all participants reported that they believed their phones were *not* a distraction.

This is exactly what people say about phones at the top edges of mats in yoga classes, resting faceup on the dinner table, or close at hand in conversation with real people. What's more, the same folks might bemoan that yoga failed to relieve stress, they didn't feel a connection on the dinner date, and most people are bad listeners.

One thing you can do to investigate how you are engaging with mindfulness content online is to pause and notice what's happening in the moment. A key characteristic of mindless or addictive online habits is that we're not in our bodies. We hold our breath. Perhaps you have heard the term *email apnea*? It's true; most of us stop breathing altogether while reading or responding to our email. We use our hands impulsively. We may miss important elements of what is happening around us. We don't hear someone asking a question. We nearly walk into a lamppost. Have you ever misplaced your phone only to notice that it was in your hand? Have you opened a new tab for the same website you were just logged into? Have you ever felt lonely or disconnected while engaging with plenty of people online?

Pause. Slow down. Breathe. Notice the sensations in your body. Take a moment to sit still or notice how you are walking while listening to the podcast. Can you disable social media and other distractions? After the guided meditation, can you challenge yourself to sit in silence for a few minutes? For all the ways devices have opened the world of meditation to us, it's important that we part with them sometimes. All of these wonderful teachers are ultimately trying to guide us back to ourselves, encouraging us not to flee the moment when it gets boring or uncomfortable, and to be present with the people, environments, sounds, and experiences that surround us. Not to mention, if you happen to be taking a test, remember to leave your phone elsewhere.

Maybe we can be even less picky about proper meditation. It seems safe to say that any time spent *not* looking at a screen *and* breathing is a vast improvement from how we spend most of our time. The world has upped its ante on stress significantly. So, maybe you don't need to meditate. Just put down your phone. Leave it in another room. A writer friend, Joanna Rakoff, puts hers in an actual lockbox. Just think: the *key* to more mindful presence might be a *lock*.

The likelihood that we are doing significant damage to our psyches and culture as a whole by being so wired is dangerously high and being born out in real time. My sense is that your awareness of this reality has steered you toward meditation and made you reach for this book. Entire books and studies have been and are being written on the impact of the Internet Age on our minds, bodies, and spirits. This is not my area of expertise. I'm an expert in helping people do the opposite: unplugging.

Disconnect. Tune inward. Breathe deeply. Untether from your devices more often. Unhook from the locked jaws of breaking news and hungry ghosts of social media. Not forever, but at least for a little while each day. Longer when needed. Come back to your senses: the sounds and sights around you, the taste of your food or warmth of your coat. Focus on something that doesn't light up or hijack your attention at every opportunity with a ding or a bing or a buzz. Treat your attention as the powerful resource that it is. It is renewable, but only if you pause to recharge.

Opportunity

In late summer 2020, I attended a weekend retreat with Pema Chodron. This time we gathered online since large gatherings were unsafe. The theme was "How to Welcome the Unwelcome," which was fitting since so much that year felt *unwelcome*—painful, divisive, and terrifying. Why would anyone want to welcome any of it?

According to Pema, the answer was simple. Because it was the reality of what was happening. And what is desperately needed in moments of suffering is compassionate, discerning, loving people who are willing to face reality and take action to make it better. Pema used the word *collaborate* often. How can we *collaborate* with reality rather than avoid or encumber it?

The opportunity for all of us—the work of our time—in every sphere, from mindfulness to wellness to spiritual communities, public service to social justice, education to the environment, is to wake up and show up for one another. I remember the words of my first yoga teacher. *Anyone can meditate in a dark room with their eyes closed.* Then: the challenge. She would always follow with a question. What about at the dentist? Could you meditate there? What about while stuck in traffic? How about when stuck in your home for months on end? In a sense, no matter what the present reveals, it always asks the same thing: What about now? Can we see clearly, breathe deeply, focus on what matters, and extend kindness where it is needed most?

If not, what are we practicing for?

Much has been made recently about engaging with technology in mindful ways, and this is valuable, too. Are we breathing? What is the quality of our attention? What are the sensations in our bodies: fingertips, hands, neck, shoulders, back, and eyes? What emotions arise? What if you set a calendar alert that reminded you to take ten deep breaths or drink a giant glass of water? A smartphone can access information, but what we do with information determines our wisdom.

Digital meditation resources, from apps to articles, classes to podcasts, can be transformative. They can reformulate healthy habits and dramatically improve our mental, physical, and emotional health over time. They also (to some degree) democratize who has access to mindfulness, which is important and necessary. It's antithetical to mindfulness as a whole if the community is only comprised of people in positions of privilege. Innovation has improved diversity and inclusion of teachers and students, but we have a long way to go.

Ideally, we aim to cultivate a sense of inner stillness without needing external accoutrements like a smartphone. Always, the underlying lesson remains that we don't meditate to get really good at sitting in a room with our eyes closed not talking to people. We meditate to feel greater peace and presence in our lives, among people, and in relationship to the world around us. Even when we are far apart—there were five thousand of us gathered with Pema that weekend, all around the globe—we belong to each other. The delivery systems for how and when we access meditation content may change, but the fundamental nature of what we're doing remains.

The purpose of the program was to find solace, comfort, and resilience within a time of fear and uncertainty. "Super challenging times have the greatest potential for growth," she told us. It was a Friday evening. Pema was in Nova Scotia. I was in Boston. People in small thumbnail views sat in their homes around the world. The light streaming in their windows captured a variety of time zones. This astounding new technology had brought us together. But the fact of our togetherness—sharing a human experience and all it contains—is and will always be analog.

The best part of modern mindfulness is that many of the daunting logistics that kept us from previously trying meditation can now be solved easier and faster. Or, as is the language of the internet: now, now, now. I began meditating before apps, so it doesn't make sense for me to incorporate them into an established routine that already works.

One of my personal mindfulness goals is to create fewer reasons to pick up my phone rather than more. But for people trying to establish a routine, apps can be an important element for getting started and finding success. They remove obstacles, generate momentum, and create healthy habits. With any luck, you will meditate for a long time, so keep in mind that how you begin will differ from how you practice over the months and years ahead. You may need more guidance or less at times. Help comes from many sources, some of which have been around for centuries and others yet to be invented. The key to a mindful life is waking up to the possibility of the moment.

PART II

life myths

(What the Ego Tells Us)

6

This Will Fix Me

The ego is who we think we are.
And the soul is really, really who we are.

—RAM DASS

Many of us seek out practices, like yoga or meditation, as a way to improve our lives, ideally ourselves. These are noble desires. Something isn't working with life, and we would like to *fix* it. Make a few tweaks or a total reconstruction. Where do we sign up?

My friend Priscilla Warner tells one of my favorite stories about this impulse. Priscilla is wise and witty, and she dropped the f-bomb about three minutes into our first meeting and endeared herself to me forever. She's in her sixties with wild salt-and-pepper hair that she prefers not to comb. She credits a really great conditioner; I am not sure which one. Our age difference makes our friendship a tad unexpected but also rich and affirming. I have a toddler. She has two adult sons. We're both writers, seekers, and overthinkers. We're often each other's earliest readers and like to joke about how sometimes it feels like all the real writers are in the same room and we're not invited. It's important to have friends who get you. Of course, that feeling of people being in a room to which you're not invited is familiar ego territory. The ego is a bit misunderstood. We all have one. It's not necessarily bad. It's just a voice in your head that tells lots of stories. Part of the beauty of meditation is recognizing the ego, the stories it tells us, and coming back to reality.

Priscilla's first book, *The Faith Club*, was a *New York Times* bestseller. If you studied religion in college, there's a chance it was part of your curriculum. In her next book, *Learning to Breathe*, she details her experience coping with a lifetime of anxiety and severe panic attacks. Growing up, she self-medicated with alcohol, she openly admits. Later, she discovered meditation and other mindfulness practices. The book chronicles many of her healing experiences, including Buddhist meditation retreats, EMDR (eye movement desensitization and reprocessing) therapy (an effective treatment for trauma), Ayurvedic treatments, chanting, painting, ritual baths, and more.

My favorite part of the book is when she shares the story of arriving at a retreat with lofty yet relatable goals.

"I'm a neurotic Jew," she announces to the Buddhist monk who greets her, "but I want to be a peaceful Tibetan monk like you."

The monk responds gently, "But you are not Tibetan and you are not a monk, so why not try to be the most peaceful neurotic Jew you can be?"

This exchange still makes me laugh.

Most of us are Priscilla, especially when we arrive on the doorstep of a new mindfulness practice. I think of Matt Damon's character in *Good Will Hunting* when he first sits down before his therapist played by Robin Williams.

"OK, yeah, let the healing begin!" he says sarcastically, clapping his hands together.

We come to meditation or therapy or yoga or pottery or birding because we hope it will fix some faulty wiring in our heart or mind, or both.

The job stress, parenting burnout, or existential dread have become too much. A shadow of loneliness falls across our inner landscape in the winter months or we are having difficulty keeping the nipping dog of our personality hidden behind a tidy fence so as not to scare the neighbors. Worry. Trauma. Grief. Low self-esteem. Codependency. Something we can't name because it keeps changing. It doesn't go away; it just morphs from solid to liquid to gas. *You can fix this, right, Doc?*

If I'm honest, this is still a seductive thought for me. I have to catch myself. Technically, I have to catch the voice of my ego, which relentlessly aims to convince me that something is wrong, I am wrong, and I must make adjustments.

"The ego is who we think we are. And the soul is really, really who we are," Ram Dass says.

Here's what the soul would say: *I'm here for you anyway.*

Imagine if you told a dear friend, I'm sorry, I can't be with you in your time of need until you organize the closets, lose ten pounds, or earn an advanced degree. What horrible nonsense. And yet, we do this to ourselves all the time. We leave ourselves incrementally, in the moment when we don't want to feel something, when the moment is uncomfortable, or for longer periods, which would be unacceptable to our friends. This negligence would be unacceptable to most goldfish or houseplants. I don't want to name names or point fingers, so I'll speak for myself only. I have, in moments, treated myself with less care than a houseplant.

The soul says, *Whoa, whoa, whoa. A friend is needed, here. Not another story, Ego. No more advice, please.*

You are not an entity to be fixed because you are not a fixed entity. You do not need to be fixed because you are not broken, merely human. And meditation is not self-improvement. It is self-acceptance. It is befriending the self. It heals, resolves, and improves a great many things, which is somewhat ironic. But we don't do it to fix ourselves. Like a friend, meditation is available for you right now, as you are. It cannot be another way. Not only is this what's best for you; it's what's possible. Remember, you are not an immovable, static, permanent *you*.

If we ask, *Will this fix me?* mindfulness might counter by asking, *Who is the "me"?* What can we point to? We all think we know, but this is a fundamental myth of how we see the world and ourselves. It's one of the underlying principles of what mindfulness is and how it works. You, me, we: we are impermanent concepts. We are in process all the time.

A decade ago, you were something different than you are now. You might have identified with your life stage: I'm a student, I'm a new mom, I'm retired. You'd give your job title: teacher, artist, or astrophysicist, or the thing about which you are most passionate. Book lover. Dancer. New Yorker. You're the boss. You're the intern. You may or may not identify the same way now. You could be a different gender. You could be married or divorced. I have a family friend, Jeffrey, who was a staunch vegan for years. We made tofurkey for him at Thanksgiving. He went to Italy to work as a photographer, and when he arrived in Milan, his friends picked him up and they all drove to a famous focaccia place. One friend ordered for the group. He paused and looked at Jeffrey, "Are you cool with whatever?" he asked. Jeffrey doesn't recall the moment as a sea change. The whole scene was a radical shift. He was living in a foreign country. He was chasing a dream. He'd worked at a mattress store all summer to save up and bought a one-way ticket in the fall. "Whatever's best," he told his friend. Being a vegan had been central to his identity, but it wasn't anymore. *Arrivederci*.

What makes you, *you?* What persists across time and life stages and abides when your tastes, behaviors, job, hairstyle, productivity, political party, or address change? Is it your physical body—the confines of your appearance? No. That changes all the time. (Try as we might to stave the inevitable with our serums and workouts.) You were once three feet tall! What about a belief system, an essential or spiritual scaffolding that underpins your worldview? You once believed in Santa. What I mean to say is that you are not your diet. Or job title. You are more than your sexual identity, family history, or religious upbringing. I am not my body—the super tricky yoga poses it could do but no longer wants to or what it can do today but won't when I'm old. You are not your address. They are not their mood. We are not our thoughts.

To need fixing also implies you are broken. You're not. Your essence cannot break. You can break your arm. Our hearts break, gosh, on a daily basis sometimes. You might have bad knees or a cranky uterus, but the *you*est part of you persists. It goes by many names: soul, self, spirit, to name a few. When we speak of stillness, it is this sacred aspect of our being that we nurture.

Sit with yourself quietly and without interruption, in communion and fortification of this essence. In simple terms, know yourself. Befriend yourself. Can you show up for yourself in all forms, moods, and evolutions? The task is not to hold out for a better version of yourself. Instead, aim to be a better friend. Trust that improvement and growth happen. Till then, love this version, this draft.

When our friends do this, their love profoundly shapes us. Without it, our lives would not be the same. A good friend bears witness to all parts of us. They celebrate who we are in the smallest-grandest ways. They sit with us when we are sniveling and hopeless, hold our hand when we hurt, and hold our newborns in the hospital. Only they were allowed entry on that intimate and precious day. They listen to the same pitiful story until we *finally* hear ourselves, and it is not pitiful at all. It is merely the course of things. We recount our latest mortifying gaffe, and suddenly, it feels not so bad because at least it makes great material for their ears. We uncensor and unpolish our thoughts and feelings. They listen. Through this process, something within is polished and brightened, tumbled until the hard edges turn smooth.

A friend who sits with us only when we are shiny and happy and weaving intelligible tales of success is not a friend in the meaningful or enduring sense of the word. True friends are avatars for the selves we want to strengthen. They reflect and by extension protect us just by being themselves. Knowing how to be a good friend is largely intuitive. Listen. Love. Make good-natured fun. Support. Forgive. Can you do this for yourself? I'm not asking about all the time. For a few minutes today, what if you tried?

Two Wolves

There's a Native American story often referenced in mindfulness teaching because it evokes the fundamental power of not fixing but rather befriending ourselves on a deep and practical level.

According to legend, a Cherokee elder sits by the fire telling a young child about a great battle.[1]

"I have two wolves fighting in my heart," says the elder. He then describes them in vivid detail. You can imagine the fight. You can feel it in your chest.

"One wolf is fearful, vengeful, envious, resentful, and deceitful."

This wolf looms and growls and salivates.

"The other wolf is compassionate, loving, generous, truthful, and peaceful."

You can imagine this affable and gentle wolf resting by the fire with the elder and child. Gnawing a bone under the stars maybe, tail thumping the earth.

"Which wolf wins?" asks the child.

"The one I feed," responds the elder.

Inner stillness will never come from further waging battle with our scared or angry wolf. This saps our energy and makes the wolf more hostile. It bares its teeth and readies to bite. We won't succeed in hurting or killing the angry wolf. Why incite a protracted and bloody fight?

---

1 The following version of this oft told story is inspired by a Happify video narrated by Sharon Salzberg. I also referenced Lama Surya Das's book *Buddha Is as Buddha Does*.

Meanwhile, hating the wolf sucks the strength out of us. The practical shift through meditation is that we calmly attend to the angry wolf and let go of believing its stories, wounds, and worries. If we can maintain this attentive and loving awareness, then the wolf will lie down at our feet by the fire, no longer an enemy.

I want to pause to talk a bit more about anger. I fear that if I don't we might move ahead too fast thinking that anger is "bad." It's not. Like any emotion, it's informative, and in the case of anger in the space of mindfulness, this emotion can be generative. Anger spurs action. I am thinking of the Civil Rights movement of the 1960s and unfolding again today. When we see injustice, anger is a logical, compassionate, and deeply sane response. The key is having a loving awareness of your anger so that you can use it wisely. Feel the anger, yes. But unleash love.

We must nourish the gentle and loving wolf. What does it need? Let's investigate a bit. Go ahead, put your hand on your heart right now. Take three deep breaths. How can you feed this wolf? What would make it your peaceful and steady companion?

"It's very powerful to know what we're thinking *as we're thinking it*, know what we feel *as we're feeling it*. Ultimately, mindfulness gives us the choice of what to feed, befriend, and bring into action. We can let go of our old ways of being and patterns. It just takes practice," says mindfulness teacher Sharon Salzberg. She voices an online video retelling of this story meant for kids, but I highly recommend it for grown-ups, too. I have shared the link in the bibliography.

Meditation and mindfulness may make a lot of things better, arguably *most* things, but that's not its focus. The focus is focus itself. When our perspective shifts from old, wounded, and fear-based patterns (prompted by ego) to compassionate awareness and inner listening (the realm of our deeper self or soul), anything can change. The angry wolf still exists as part of our human nature, but it rests. Meanwhile, we have made our kind wolf a constant companion.

Investigating Our Inner Voice

It's regularly said that *wherever you go, there you are.*[2] With practice, we become aware of the voice in our heads. We hear it when we meditate but also when we shop for toothpaste, participate in a Zoom meeting, and, definitely, when we lie down to sleep at night. That voice, "the obnoxious roommate in my head," Arianna Huffington called it in her book *Thrive*, is always home. Mostly, our job is merely to notice it. By doing so, over and over again, we unhook from its grasp, and as a result, experience more quietude. The roommate is no longer blaring dance music at 4 a.m. Maybe it's only a hushed conversation on the other side of the wall. However, there are times when it behooves us to replace or respond to our inner voice. We do this with the utmost kindness.

Tone

We often reserve our snidest, most critical, and demeaning voices for ourselves. There is power in noticing this fact, in pausing and truly listening to this voice. Where did it begin? How did it become so harsh? There is sadness, too, because we learned this dialogue somewhere and turned it inward. Chances are we've been speaking to ourselves this way for a *long* time. The realization can be a little gutting, but then, it contains healing and possibility. We can defang the voice now.

You listen like a good friend, patient and nonjudging. Just holding space for the voice. Eventually, it's less surprising. You start to see it coming, and you can replace the voice with something gentler. Sometimes you have to be a hostage negotiator in your own head. You have to speak slowly, relaxed yet firm; convince yourself to put down your weapons and let everyone walk free. You may need to be your own parent, to a younger self you still carry (of course you do, we all do), who needs unconditional love and acceptance, craves it

---

2   This is also the title of a classic book on mindfulness written by Jon Kabat-Zinn.

desperately. You will probably discover a sense of humor up there. Maybe the voice will start to sound like your piano teacher or Morgan Freeman. A student of mine named Laura described a breakthrough when she noticed she could start speaking to herself in a tone that resembled how she talks to her beloved dog. When the dog wanders away or gets into something he shouldn't—as the mind is wont to do in meditation—she doesn't get angry or snap his leash violently. She just gives it a soft tug and says something like *over here, buddy, we're going this way.* When you pay attention to your thoughts, you become more comfortable directing them away from trouble and toward the good qualities, actions, and inclinations you want to bring forth.

Phrase

It's important to clarify that we're not cultivating lengthy or lively conversations in our heads. We're replacing the critical voice with something healthier—not writing a screenplay. This inward shift can happen by changing the tone, as above, or choosing a nourishing phrase to feed the mind. We'll discuss mantras in depth later, as they represent a specific and effective form of meditation known as *japa.* I'm not quite talking about mantras here. Instead, I'm referring to a quick way to redirect the mind from a negative mental loop. *Over here, buddy. We're going this way.* Formal meditation is the ideal place to practice this technique, but daily life works just as well. Since we're rarely without the voice in our heads, investigating this voice on occasion is important. You can think of your redirect or "friendly phrase" in advance or you may find that one (or several) naturally emerge over time.

Intention

While working on the manuscript for this book, I had a baby and suffered a rare and severe postpartum health complication, which resulted in a chronic autoimmune disorder affecting my physical, mental, and emotional health. As someone who is self-employed, I didn't receive any paid leave. Not a single day for pregnancy appointments or illness, childbirth, recovery, or the postpartum health crisis that followed. I am not unique. According to the U.S. Bureau of Labor Statistics, only 17 percent of civilian workers have access to paid family leave. Many women must return to work almost immediately, jeopardizing their health and sacrificing crucial time for care and bonding with their infants. Naturally, my career felt like it was imploding, and here I was trying to write about peace, balance, and clarity. You guys—clarity! What I'm trying to say is: I was a mess. I needed consoling. I'm reminded of a New Yorker cartoon I once saw in which a mother is holding an infant while reading a book entitled *How to Parent*. The caption reads, "Chapter One: Crying."

Meditation couldn't fix me. I did it anyway because it was a form of refuge. I learned how to soothe myself when my health, career, or confidence were tanking. *There, there*, I would say. Or I'd find myself saying with cheerful and tender resolve, curiously in the second-person, *You're OK . . . you're OK*. I didn't choose these words. If I had, I would have chosen better ones. More inspirational or writerly, a little more nuanced. *There, there* is so cliché, no? Nevertheless, those words arose when needed. Their intention superseded language, and perhaps grander language would have been the voice of someone trying to fix herself rather than offer comfort, which is what was needed.

My deepest, truest, most comforting voice came easily when I spoke to my new baby. It was low, steady, and tender. My daughter recognized it immediately when we met in the delivery room for the first time, the doctor laying her upon my chest. She squawked against the cold foreign air and then nestled beneath my collarbone, goopy and birdlike.

"*Shhhhh*," I whispered, my open palm covering her entire back. She was smaller than a baguette with feathery limbs tucked into her warm body.

And she stopped crying. The room quieted. Comfort and safety as basic and profound as anything in my life enveloped us. *There, there*.

7

I Will Get What I Want

Service to others is the rent you pay
for your room here on earth.

—MUHAMMAD ALI

There's a popular television series centered on themes of greed, extortion, and corruption where even the most cutthroat characters are shown meditating. I haven't watched it yet, but it has some great actors, so maybe I will one day. I'm curious how the image of meditation factors. When a student told me about it in passing, my first thought was *Ugh*, another false advertisement for meditation as a means of getting what we want, like we're ordering a pizza.

We all want things. This is natural and necessary territory of the ego. If meditation can help us get what we want, then we will meditate. That must be its value, right? This premise is a key selling point, and it frames much of the public conversation surrounding modern mindfulness. After a Super Bowl, we hear how the championship team meditated to develop its winning mindset. A famous tech billionaire takes a break from Silicon Valley to attend a silent Vipassana retreat, and media outlets, ranging from the serious to unserious, depict it breathlessly. Rock stars backstage. CEOs at desks varnished to a high shine. You will win. You will gain power and influence. You will find love. You will sleep like a baby. You will become rich. Visualize it in meditation and you make it so. *Manifest it.* This is a sneaky, tantalizing doctrine, one that has undergirded the wellness industry for a long time and shaped American identity for much longer. And while it's true that mindfulness improves performance in most areas of life (because paying attention is vital to doing anything well), the purpose of meditation is not to give us what we want. It teaches us to show up fully and compassionately for what is. It explores how we respond when faced with what we *don't* want.

One succinct description of the ego is "resistance to life itself." We resist life in small (and often relatively harmless) ways, like losing ourselves in a TV show to numb the day's stress, retail therapy, taking comfort in food, or "taking the edge off" with a drink. Still, one can easily see how without awareness or other, more adaptive, resilience-building skills, any of these coping mechanisms could be taken too far and make matters worse over time. Ego alone is not bad. It exists. It demarcates the lines between others and ourselves. It enumerates needs and desires, likes and dislikes, and serves as a source of information. However, things can get dramatically worse when we let our ego take the driver's seat. Here's a brief sampling of behaviors that might crop up:

- Becoming obsessed with getting what we want.
- Making everything about us.
- Continuing down a path even when we are wrong.
- Trying to control other people.
- Denying the reality of others (also known as gaslighting).
- Denying your own reality (i.e., gaslighting ourselves).

- Speaking over or for other people.
- Denigrating others in order to elevate yourself.

If you had an emotional or physical reaction in your body when you read that list—if something felt uncomfortable, your stomach dropped, you felt hot, angry, or defensive—well then, congratulations: you are a conscious person. Only when we are aware of what we're doing and feeling can we give ourselves space to choose our thoughts and actions more wisely.

The ego may not be altogether bad, but neither is it known for having the firmest grasp on reality. This is why it's sometimes referred to as a "trance." It tells stories and makes assumptions largely in an effort to keep us safe, but it tends to be driven by reactivity and impulsivity. All of this can be an exhausting and menacing mindset to inhabit *all the time*. Left unchecked, it creates undue suffering for the world and us. Remember the scared wolf at our feet? We don't pretend it doesn't exist. We teach ourselves to recognize its presence and, instead, nourish the wise wolf, and more evolved part of our brains.

It's inevitable in life that we don't get what we want. Sometimes, we feel powerless. We take our knocks. Love leaves. We fall ill or someone we care about does. Sleep eludes us. Bills loom. Our friend who was here just last week is now gone forever; it blows the mind. It makes absolutely no sense. A child, a *child* gets a terminal diagnosis. Meditation cannot stave, reverse, or inoculate us from any of it, and the gravity of this vulnerability is sobering. Does that mean meditation *isn't* for us? If it doesn't give us what we want, does that mean it failed? The inverted logic sounds silly. Of course, meditation is for us. It "works" if you do it. Of course, it can't eradicate all suffering. Still, its grace and usefulness are baked into the practice; they are not performance-based rewards. They reveal themselves in our living and relating—in who and how we are *being*. What it feels like to be alive, and how alive are we willing to be? None of this equates to tallying results based only on what serves us. In fact, what often makes us feel most alive is what we do for others.

But one could also make the case that it doesn't matter. Isn't anything that motivates someone to become more mindful a positive force, in the end?

Even if the motivations are initially ego-driven, it's unlikely most people will persist for purely selfish motives. Meditation was designed for life's hard times, and hard times befall everyone, no matter how selfish or enlightened. One chief hallmark of meditation is an increased capacity to regulate our emotions. The more we are able to develop that space between thought and reaction, the less we are alarmed by stress or failure. Attempting escape from difficult feelings and experiences, on the other hand, only delays or exacerbates the pain, and in the process, robs us of the wisdom contained within it. Not to mention, from a psychological standpoint, it's well documented that we can't selectively numb emotions. If we numb unwanted feelings, we inevitably numb our joys and triumphs. Thankfully, we're not alone in this struggle. All of humanity struggles. It's part of what bonds us.

Compassion Practice

One hallmark of Buddhism, yoga philosophy, and countless other wisdom traditions is the cultivation of compassion. Later, you will learn how to do lovingkindness meditation. *Compassion* and *lovingkindness* are two words for the same guiding principle of care, understanding, and acceptance of ourselves and others. Both formal meditation and mindfulness in daily life, relationships specifically, help us to cultivate compassion by paying attention to what is truly going on, rather than staying attached to the stories our minds create and retell about our experiences. We begin by paying attention, maybe concentrating on the breath for a few minutes at first. We build up to meditating for longer periods and extending awareness into other activities. Over time, paying careful attention gives rise to a greater capacity for care itself. This teaching is not hokey, overstated, or soft—compassion is one of the most powerful and sustaining forces of humankind.

When cultural anthropologist Margaret Mead was asked about the first signs of civilization, she gave a surprising answer. People expected that she would likely make a reference to tools, cave paintings, or certain human-made creations. Instead, she focused on a bone broken fifteen thousand years ago. The femur bone, which is the largest in our bodies, running through the thigh attaching to the hip joint, had fractured and then healed. This discovery meant one revelatory thing. That a human being, living in the wilderness, was able to rest, largely motionless to aid healing, for several months while the bone fused back together. In other words, someone else had tended to this wounded person—brought food and water, provided protection from predators and the elements, and prioritized the well-being of another. Put this way, compassion is basic to our evolutionary nature and was the fundamental key to the establishment of our species.

Broken bones and hearts. Lost income or health. Death, grief, pain, and depression. The worst cold of your life. The point at which your toddler stops napping. A flooded basement. A sty in your eye! No one *wants* any of it. Obviously, I'm not suggesting parity among these types of suffering. Only that they are largely beyond our control. We don't have to compare our personal suffering or rank it on the scale of human experience. We don't need to make it any more or less than it is. We do need to feel and observe it as it is, so that we can mindfully choose what to do next. Be wary of any program, mindfulness or otherwise, that suggests some ability to stave reality or blames hardship on user error. Perhaps that mended bone was the earliest sign of civilized society, but it was definitely a sign of compassion. Today, it's an apt reminder of how people heal: by having the space and safety to let the bone fuse—to feel solid once more.

Compassionate awareness in difficult times is not the same thing as toxic positivity, blithely telling people in a devastating moment of their lives that everything happens for a reason or offering unsolicited advice that an unfathomably painful, unjust, or life-threatening event is actually a blessing, for example. Compassion is not Pollyanna-ish delusion. It's hard-won wisdom within the entirety of the human experience. Nor does it condone or overlook harmful behavior. "In some situations, strong compassion may give rise to an equally strong sense of outrage—that is anger about an injustice," says His Holiness the Dalai Lama. Compassion is not toothless.

No matter what we feel, we are not alone. Someone somewhere has felt something similar. In any given moment, any number of people might be feeling similar emotions or having similar thoughts, fears, hopes, or dreams as you. There is comfort, healing, and solace in this fact. Further, people around us are likely dealing with some amount of untold suffering. Everyone. We have no idea. Merely by acknowledging what we do not know about someone's experience, we hold space and grace for him, her, or them.

Sometimes dashed hopes work out for the better; other times they leave a trail of emotional, physical, or psychological wreckage in their wake. First, we open ourselves to what is so that we can consciously choose what to do next. Along the way we develop greater compassion for others who have suffered similarly. I doubt this is how it ends up on the greed and corruption TV show, but it's how it *can* unfold in reality with earnest practice and real empathy.

Creating What We Want While Accepting What Is

Being resilient when things go awry doesn't mean we can't or shouldn't have a clear understanding of what we want. Having goals is a valuable and meaningful part of life. Knowing how we feel and what we want are crucial to inner wisdom, and meditation helps sharpen our clarity in this process, as well as cope with setbacks along the way. A popular form of meditation features the visualization of an ideal outcome you wish to create. I do this activity often with athletes and artists in particular. It's a useful way to know our minds, hone our attention, and summon qualities within ourselves that support our success. To be clear, we're not meditating to get a reward. Rather, we're preparing the mind and purposefully aligning it with healthy and positive intentions. Anytime we meditate, we prepare the mind for the whole experience of life, which naturally includes both hardships and successes.

Visualization Exercise

Most of us are highly adept at visualizing worst-case scenarios. I count myself among the extra talented in this arena. (I wish this were a good thing.) Perhaps that's why I love this visualization exercise so much. It wires our minds in the direction of success. It teaches us to think about our intentions and focus on what truly matters to us. What would the most positive outcome be, for us or for someone else? Of course, it goes without saying that if things don't work out, it's not because we didn't meditate or manifest enough. It means we're human, and life often isn't fair.

Become still and take a few deep breaths. If you'd like, bring your hand to your heart center. Feel your breath rise and fall in your chest. Perhaps notice your heartbeat, the temperature of your skin, and any sensations in your body. Pay particular attention to the area of your heart. Imagine going into your heart as if it were a room or natural environment to which you feel profoundly connected. Maybe you imagine the space of your heart as more of a feeling. Now, go into your heart, and pick a dream. Begin to visualize your dream in detail. Where are you? Who is nearby? What are you wearing? Are you dressed formally or casually? What sounds do you hear? Is it a natural environment with few people or a room filled with friends and family?

Continue to focus on your breath as you welcome these images in your mind. If you get stuck on an element of your visualization, don't worry. You don't need to force anything or overly control what you see. Notice what moves you and where your attention wants to go. Now, *pause*. I want you to imagine that your dream *just happened*. It just came true. How does it feel? Note the sensations in your body. Feel the expression on your face. Practicing this feeling is powerful because every dream that was ever accomplished, whether modest and individual or collective and historic, began here, first, as a thought.

MOMENTS OF DIFFICULTY are precisely the times when we need mindfulness the most *and* when it is at its best. It's counterproductive to use it merely as a way to reinforce the whims of the ego. Instead, we aim to use it as the training ground to see the ego more clearly. Notice how frequently the mind darts from one desire to the next, judges one person, emotion, or idea as unpleasant or less worthy than the next. See if you can watch this pattern without reactivity. Go to the heart of what's happening with the same readiness. Hold your heart, relationships, and all of life with a sense of equanimity and tenderness when things are going well as when they're not. Look into the losses. All of it is life. All of it is yours. All of it is worthy of attention.

8

Everything Will Be OK

When the crowded Vietnamese refugee boats met
with storms or pirates, if everyone panicked all would
be lost. But if even one person on the boat remained
calm and centered, it was enough. It showed the way
for everyone to survive.

—THICH NHAT HANH

Here's the thing: these myths are not revolutionary. None of the bargains our ego wagers are *that* creative. Further, we're not trying to eradicate the ego or kid ourselves by thinking we can change the basic nature of life, which is that things change, often beyond our control. We're attempting instead to respond, cope, and heal, to feel sturdier on our feet and clearer in our heads. We want things to be OK. Of course we do! You do. I do. But (you knew there was a *but*) . . . at any given moment, things may not be OK. Even when they are for us (perhaps better than OK), for someone else they're not. Intellectually, we understand this. However, emotionally, psychologically, spiritually—

impulsively—we look for a workaround. A magic pill or secret password. The right SPF. A new diet or religion or hairstyle. Something to scroll or scrutinize; eat, drink, or buy.

I admire the pragmatism of Buddhism in this regard. Years ago, I joined my devoted Tibetan Buddhist friends, Wendy and Nick, at a lecture with a venerable lama named Ling Rinpoche, said to be the reincarnation of the Dalai Lama's senior tutor in his past life. I was newly pregnant and terribly nauseous. The lecture hall at MIT where we gathered was impressive, with stadium seating and soaring glass windows. Still, I felt cloistered and queasy. Before the program began, a translator took to the stage and outlined some logistics, first in Tibetan and then in English. He identified the bathrooms and fire exits. He invited people to silence their phones.

"If you have a baby or small child . . ." he began.

I didn't have either yet, but my consciousness was preemptively attuned to the advice that would follow.

"If the baby begins to cry . . . because this is what babies do . . . please step out of the room, calm the child, and then come back."

I smiled at the pragmatism. *This is what babies do.* The lecture had not yet started, but already we were asked to cultivate this generous, compassionate, and unflinching attention to reality.

We want things to be OK and to go according to plan, but the planet is melting, with coral bleaching from vivid to colorless, forests burning from lush to ash, and sea levels rising, rising, rising. Systemic racism is a public health crisis. Food insecurity affects one in five households with school-age children as I write this. The healthcare system is so inequitable that falling ill can bankrupt a person or family. Life can be lonely and short. Wildly unjust. Dangerous or devastating. It is still life.

What can we do about it?

First, we must acknowledge reality and allow ourselves our feelings without making them bad, broken, or wrong. Next, we must attempt to deal with what is happening in a compassionate and useful way, beginning with the present. We can also hold enough space for more than one feeling. Finally, begin again. This last point is the essential teaching of meditation mechanics. Each time our attention drifts, we start over. We *come back*. It's a spectacularly convenient and simple practice (sometimes maddeningly so). And it's applicable throughout life. Even when the big picture is disheartening, we know what to do with this one breath.

Some spiritual communities are vulnerable to losing their footing when it comes to how we can be OK in a moment of suffering. Part of this incongruence has to do with an inability to decipher between these meaningful practices and the wellness industrial complex with which they overlap. For instance, in trying to sell a product or service it behooves a brand to suggest that it is the magic pill we need. If we use it, all will be well. If all is not well—the logic goes—it must be user error. Another risk is when spiritual ideas or practices are used "to sidestep personal, emotional 'unfinished business,' to shore up a shaky sense of self, or to belittle basic needs, feelings, and developmental tasks," according to John Welwood, a prominent psychotherapist who coined the term *spiritual bypassing*, which is in plainer terms a defense mechanism and, when directed at others, a form of gaslighting.

Some signs of spiritual bypassing include[1]:

- Not focusing on the here and now, living in a spiritual realm much of the time.
- Overemphasizing the positive and avoiding the negative.
- Being self-righteous about the concept of enlightenment.
- Being overly detached.
- Being overly idealistic.
- Pretending that everything is OK when it's not.

---

1 "What Is Spiritual Bypassing?", *Psychology Today* article by Diana Raab Ph.D.

With mindfulness we are not trying to bypass any aspect of the moment. In fact, the basic theory is that best way to pragmatically address reality is to practice. We can use any aspect of the here and now to do this. One opportunity is, first, to consider when in your day are you most mindful? You might quickly jot a list. When are you most present in the moment and focused on what is actually happening rather than how you'd like things to be different? In contrast, when are you least present? What do you rush through, ignore, dash off, wish away, or worry ahead at the cost of experiencing the moment?

I always pose this question when I teach a course called Meditation Academy as our opening exercise. It's a fascinating way to create a sense of connection that can lead to some surprising discoveries. Here are some of the most popular answers.

MOST

- Art
- Cleaning
- Commuting
- Cooking (chopping vegetables comes up often)
- Dancing
- Exercising
- Jewelry making
- Singing
- Spending time with babies and young children
- Spending time with seniors
- Stacking firewood
- Walking (walking the dog ranks high for dog owners)
- Washing the dishes
- Yoga

LEAST

- Commuting (especially via public transit)
- Drinking alcohol
- Driving
- Eating
- Reading or responding to email
- Scrolling the internet/social media
- Washing the dishes
- Watching TV
- Working

You probably notice that some activities appear in *both* columns. This phenomenon happens a lot, far more often than depicted here. Take coffee, for example. I don't drink it, but I appreciate the concept. I'm an admittedly obsessive tea drinker, which doesn't command the same cultural respect. I have to know you to suggest that we grab tea together.

People often share how their morning coffee rituals can be habitual impulses possessing minimal awareness or the complete opposite: deeply grounding routines that place them in the present moment with full, almost holy attention—to the aroma of the grinds, the feel of the mug in hand, and the sensory impressions throughout the house as the world wakes up around you. The sound of the coffeemaker! Even I love that sound.

If you don't have time to meditate or you need to find a small respite in your day, choose anything you do regularly and turn it into practice. Here's how.

- Choose a daily routine, preferably something you do mindlessly and automatically most of the time.

- Make sure it's small and finite. Some examples: brushing your teeth, taking out the trash, washing your face or hands, locking or unlocking a door, logging in to your phone or computer, eating a meal, cooking a meal, or washing the dishes.
- For one week, do this small task with total, unbroken attention. Take three deep breaths before you open the door or enter your password. Feel the physical experience of your body in the moment: how tightly you hold the toothbrush, the cold air on your skin when you step outside holding the weight of the trash bag in your hand, the sound of the gravel beneath your feet as you walk, the temperature of the water as you soak the pan from dinner.
- Notice any changes in your attitude before, during, and after performing this everyday activity.
- Become inquisitive about what it reveals about the way you perform other everyday tasks. What can you learn about yourself through this small task or as it reflects larger actions?

This mindfulness practice through everyday activities doesn't require altering a daily routine or adding time to an already full schedule. It merely requires a shift in awareness. We're paying attention to life *as it's happening*, the tiny, trivial stuff as well as the momentous and meaningful. Of course, we can't operate this way all the time. But it's powerful and instructive to step out of autopilot and into awareness whenever we can.

On the way out the door following one of my meditation workshops, a woman paused to say thank you. Her husband had been the one interested in learning about meditation, and she had come to support him.

"You made me realize why I used to make jewelry," she told me with a big smile, as we paused in the doorway.

Then, she confided that she'd gotten caught up in considering the quality of her designs and whether she should sell them online.

Her grandson had suggested as much. Somewhere along the way she stopped making jewelry. It was such a small thing, but it heartened us both. We realized how valuable it is, not necessarily to "do" anything different or new but to pay attention to what is already there, to work with the materials we have, whether tucked away in a craft closet or right before us in the here and now.

PART III

meditation myths

(What to Remember about Practice)

9

Stopping Thoughts

If it weren't for my mind,
my meditation would be excellent.

—PEMA CHODRON

So far, we've discussed myths about mindfulness as they relate to life in general, specifically the sneaky assumptions the ego tells us about how things should operate to serve its interests. Once we see these thought patterns within ourselves, we can respond more effectively to what's happening in reality. Remember, the ego can be an unreliable narrator and is often consumed by past memories and future speculations. Its chief concern is the story it tells and how it's perceived. For example, it likes to suggest that we're doing something wrong when we have thoughts in meditation. Like weather systems, we can't stop the mind's fluctuations. We can only dress appropriately: wear the sturdier coat, remember mittens, or perhaps secure the outdoor furniture against a gale.

Next, we'll break down myths about meditation specifically. The most pervasive of which is the pesky idea that meditation requires stopping thoughts.

The Meditation Academy course that I mentioned outlines key concepts of practice, how to do them, and what to do in daily life when you can't meditate. It's like this book but in classroom form. Befitting its name, I open with a pop quiz. Let's see how you do.

Meditation is . . .
  a. The ability to stop all thoughts so that we can experience peace.
  b. An ancient and mysterious practice into which one must be indoctrinated by a guru.
  c. Escaping reality.
  d. Paying attention, on purpose, without judgment.

If you answered "d," you are correct! But if the option "a"—stopping thoughts—gave you pause, then you are also in good company. The idea that meditation causes all thoughts to vanish is a particularly ubiquitous misunderstanding. Even though we intellectually know it's impossible to stop thinking, the mythic pull is strong, and it can lead to further unhelpful judgments such as evaluating meditation as "good" or "bad." Our performance-based impulses are never too far away. It is helpful to free ourselves of these judgments from the start. Meditation is not a performance-based activity.

The purpose of this book is to help you spot implicit or explicit misconceptions before they derail your mindfulness practice. Stopping thought as a goal is a losing, untenable battle. If you try to meditate with the intention of quieting your mind entirely or experiencing a kind of majestic serenity, then you would probably feel like a failure. You might decide that meditation is not for you. You're unsuited for it. I hear this all the time. *My mind is too busy. I just can't stop thinking of all the things I have to do.*

Thinking is what the mind does. Thinking, planning, ruminating, list-making, worrying, figuring out what's for dinner, drafting your Oscar acceptance speech . . . it's all standard stuff. The truly magical breakthrough is learning you are not your thoughts and can, therefore, experience freedom and space from them. Ironically, this distinction often results in the thinking mind feeling quieter. There will be spaces between your thoughts. Greater silence and stillness. This quietude is a side effect rather than the purpose. If you make it your purpose, it can drive you nuts.

One simple yet essential technique while we practice is to notice our thoughts as being *just thoughts* rather than definitive of who we are and needing an immediate, impulsive response from us all the time.

For example:

Become still and take a few deep breaths. Notice how you feel. Perhaps ask yourself, as a friend might, *How am I feeling? What am I feeling in this moment?* Don't edit or exaggerate your answers. Just notice them nonjudgmentally. When we are overwhelmed by thoughts, especially negative ones, the tendency is to let them color our entire experience. Our language suggests as much. *I am scared. I am angry. I am anxious. I am so sad,* the inner voice might say. A gentler alternative is to notice that you are not your fear. You *have* fear. You can practice this distinction by saying *I have fear* or *I am feeling fearful in this moment. I have anxiety/I am feeling anxious in this moment. I am experiencing sadness/I have sadness.* This technique of checking in with ourselves teaches us to be able to experience "bad" feelings without making ourselves bad, to be OK when we don't feel OK, and to experience our thoughts without letting them have their way with us. We also experience multiple feelings at once or thoughts in rapid and disjointed succession. Seeing each thought or emotion clearly and offering it a little space without critique, allows room for discernment. Things start to slow down.

You have surely heard that meditation is beneficial for the brain. A popular analogy is that it strengthens the prefrontal cortex the way a bicep curl at the gym strengthens the muscle in your upper arm. The comparison is apt. As we'll discuss soon, scientific studies have shown that gray matter in the brain increases through regular meditation practice. Meanwhile, we have to wonder how we've somehow conflated strengthening our minds with deactivating their ability to think? Given the current and complex challenges facing society, it's preposterous that we might benefit from more unthinking people. We need more and clearer thinkers. All of which is to say that meditation makes the mind stronger, clearer, wired more often toward kindness and patience and away from impulsivity and anger, and better capable of nuance and wisdom. It can provide space and quiet from the perpetual onslaught of thoughts and stories, but it doesn't accomplish this by somehow minimizing the brain's capacity. On the contrary, it wires the brain for a more expansive and perceptive response. Thoughts come; thoughts go. They're not interrupting meditation; they are part of it.

If there is a pivotal scientific study to validate what mindfulness does for the brain to reference (and there are *many*), Harvard neuroscientist Sara Lazar's work is an excellent place to start. Following a running injury, Dr. Lazar started to do yoga. By definition, a yoga practice contains a significant amount of meditation. So, in one fell swoop, Lazar became a yogi and a meditator. She also became accustomed to hearing all kinds of lofty claims about what these mindfulness practices can do, and while she had to admit that her personal experience seemed to support these claims, she wanted proof that what she felt was real.

Had others studied the effects of mindfulness? Indeed, many people had, and several had validated the effects Dr. Lazar experienced: decreased stress, fewer symptoms of depression and anxiety, reduced pain, better quality sleep, an improved ability to pay attention, and an increased quality of life. Other researchers had found that people who meditated reported being happier—the data existed. Nevertheless, Lazar wanted to know *why*. What was happening internally, neurobiologically, to produce these results?

The answer, she discovered, lies in the concept of *neuroplasticity*, or the brain's ability to change and rewire itself throughout our lifetimes. Neuroplasticity is based on the observation that, as the saying goes, *what fires together wires together*—in other words, when neurons in the brain signal to one another repeatedly, new neural pathways are formed. Over time, these pathways allow for new behaviors or choices to become less effortful. *Practice becomes plastic* is a simple way of saying that repetition and practice of any given activity can rewire the brain.

In Lazar's first study, researchers compared a group of Bostonians who meditated with a control group that didn't. The meditators weren't monks or experts, just average folks who meditated about thirty minutes per day. Scientists observed the groups for three months. Using magnetic resonance imaging (MRI) scans to observe the brains of participants, the researchers found that several regions in the brains of the meditators were more developed than those of the non-meditators. Specifically, the prefrontal cortex—the command center for working memory and executive decision-making—was bigger in the brains of the meditators. The difference was so stark between the groups that fifty-year-old meditators possessed the same amount of gray matter as individuals half their age in the control group. We know that memory fades as we age, but these results suggested that memory decline might be staved or slowed with meditation. It also suggests that we can truly appear twenty to thirty years younger in photos without cosmetic surgery purely by meditating. The fact that the photos will be of the inside of our skulls seems of nominal importance.

This study was promising, but it raised questions, too. You can practically hear them already. Namely, aren't meditators hippies and weirdos and health nuts to begin with?

In comparing a meditating and non-meditating group, scientists couldn't account for a range of lifestyle differences that might exist between the groups. Maybe the meditators were more likely to be vegetarians or have therapeutic relationships with their pets, for example. There could be ample hypotheses for how the same results may have been achieved. So, to resolve any doubts they performed a second study, this time evaluating the same group of people twice: first, before ever having meditated. And second, after an eight-week program of meditating for about thirty to forty minutes per day. Again, the data confirmed what yogis and meditators have said for ages. (Which isn't to say we're right about everything—a lot of yogis got it very wrong about Bikram being a good guy, for example.) Nevertheless, the validation through scientific study and data supported eons of anecdotal evidence and has been a boon to the meditation community.

People were happier. Areas of the brain associated with executive functioning, such as planning, reasoning, and memory, enlarged. Meanwhile, their more primal, lesser-evolved, more impulsive amygdalas shrunk. Think of your amygdala as the smoke detector for your brain. It serves the important function of alerting us to danger, but when it becomes sensitive or overactive, as happens after traumatic experiences, it overrides everything else. It becomes incredibly difficult to perceive things accurately and make logic-based decisions.

As with any scientific study, it's worthwhile to consider what the control factors are and how they compare with our ability to re-create the benefits yielded by the study. On one hand, we want to avoid conflating the benefits of meditation in specific research with *any* amount of meditation anytime. We can't meditate a couple times over the course of a lifetime for five minutes a pop using an app and expect the same results as someone who meditates for a specific amount of time each day, sustained over many weeks, months, or years. On the other hand, it's worth mentioning that if you meditate and find it benefits your life, relationships, work, health, and happiness, then you don't need a study to prove it.

This research helps us understand how meditation is quite literally mind-expanding. Over time and with practice, we become skilled at watching our thoughts without trying to control them or feeling drawn to reacting to them nonstop. The more we practice, the stronger and stiller our minds become. While meditation can be maddening at first, science helps us understand the idea of enlightenment, or at least working toward it. The amygdala will always keep watch and sound the alarm in times of fear. But with consistent practice, we develop the ability to decipher when our inner smoke detector is giving us real information and when it just needs a new battery. Space grows between thoughts, between a stimulus and our response. We expand our capacity to choose.

The goal is not to stop thoughts, and as you approach mindfulness practice, I encourage you to let go of this expectation. It's like thinking someday the laundry will be done. It will never be done. You will finish the laundry, and there will be more dirty clothes. Instead, you can expect that a meditation practice gives you the space and choice to replace harmful thoughts with more productive ones. Rather than wasting energy resisting cyclical or negative thoughts, try offering your mind a grounding, constructive, and restorative substitute, such as one of the examples below.

May I rest in awareness.
May I meet the moment as a friend.
May I feel my mind and body connect.

Above all, when we stop aiming for the cessation of thought, the mind becomes a quieter place to be.

10

Doing It Wrong

Your goal is not to battle with the mind,
but to witness the mind.
—SWAMI MUKTANANDA

The most common question people ask me about meditation is: *How do I know if I'm doing it right?* Doing it wrong isn't a myth exclusive to meditation or mindfulness. It underpins the experience of our lives much of the time. In reality, doing meditation correctly is merely a matter of doing it. Buddhist teacher Allan Lokos says it perfectly: "So what is a good meditator then? The one who meditates."

The goodness is in the doing. *No, but you don't understand; I am really bad* you will try to tell me. You tried but couldn't sit still. Within seconds, you were distracted. Your mind raced; your knees ached, your back hurt; your nose itched. You dreamt of scones and more closet space. It was exhausting. You needed to lie down. It was 9 a.m.

It's OK. This is how it is sometimes.

We get so many messages about our wrongness that it's hard not to believe, internalize, and re-litigate them around the clock. As it relates to meditation, you might think you're doing it wrong if you have anxiety. You're doing it wrong if your mind wanders, your foot falls asleep, you fall asleep, or you get bored and wish you could go to sleep. You are doing it wrong if you daydream about an island you saw in the article you clicked on when you should have been doing something else. You are doing it wrong if you are trying to meditate but keep seeing breaking news flashes behind your eyelids. You're doing it wrong if you don't feel blissful. *Do people really say "blissed out"? I can't say that. I'm not cut out for this.* There are so many potential reasons that you could be doing meditation wrong that one can safely assume you are definitely doing it wrong.

But I promise you are not doing it wrong.

Now, imagine how liberating it is to have a place in your life where you *cannot* do it wrong. A place where all the benefits of meditation live, and your key to the lock works regardless of any scorecard for duration, frequency, form, level of difficulty, or artistic impression. Whenever I say this to a group of people—a place in your life where this holds true—the whole room exhales. The dimension of the space feels like it actually expands; the walls move back three feet and the air lightens. This freedom stands in stark contrast to so many messages we receive throughout the day, whether from within ourselves or society at large.

Wrong before we answer, underqualified before applying, or out of our league before taking the field—most of us are well-acquainted with this feeling. This is especially true for women and BIPOC, who are conditioned to second-guess themselves so that they might be perceived as more likeable and less aggressive or threatening.

For this reason, meditation can be a cultural, social, and political force for positive change. We must see reality before we can change it. We begin with a seat at the table of our own mind. This table offers opportunity, agency, potential, and power. We learn to show up fully for ourselves, here, first. There will be so many outside obstacles; this is one way to control what we can. At this table in our minds, we experience our irrevocable value. We nurture qualities we want to bring forth outwardly: courage, compassion, resilience, or ease, for example. Becoming brave in the face of whatever thoughts, emotions, or naysaying inner voices insist requires a decision to try anyway. It is a decision of presence and, by virtue of presence alone, a decision of courage, too. We will not abandon ourselves. When we meditate, we become more awake and aware, both in the moment and organically and cumulatively in life. When we are conscious in this way, we have more choices for how to direct our attention.

I've come to realize that the myth of wrongness stems not merely from a concern that we're meditating wrong but an underlying fear that *we* are wrong. I am this, but I want to be that. I *should* be that. These are big ideas, so let's address them one at a time. Meditating wrong versus being wrong. Before we do, it's helpful to remember how the interchangeable words for meditation and mindfulness are not technically the same. The former is a practice, the latter a state of being.

If it's impossible to meditate wrong, one might ask why anyone needs instruction in doing it right. Can we all twirl around in circles singing Beyoncé lyrics and accurately call it meditation? Sadly, no. Though that sounds like fun, and broadly speaking, I support it. You may not be able to do meditation *wrong*, but you can do it more or less effectively.

How to meditate effectively is fairly simple. You find a comfortable position, ideally seated with a long, neutral spine, but you could lie down, too. Take a few deep breaths to center yourself. Watch the breath as you would on a cold day outside. Each time a thought, emotion, or urge to make toast or check email or put the laundry in the dryer arises, refocus your attention on your breath. If the breath is not an effective anchor for you, you can choose something else, such as one sensory impression on which to focus (i.e., sight, sound, or the kinesthetic feeling in your physical body). You can use a mantra, which we'll discuss in detail later. You can close your eyes or keep them open.

What is the connection between meditating as described above—this simple thing that we do—and experiencing a change in our way of being? Specifically, how does meditating ease the grating feeling of wrongness, the voice of the incessant inner critic?

Wanting to do something right or to do the right thing are worthy goals. We should all strive to do the right thing as people, citizens, parents, friends, and neighbors. Of course, it's exciting and inspiring to seek aptitude at, say, dribbling a basketball, doing a headstand, baking sourdough, or planting a garden. Meditation, however, is less about aptitude and more about awareness, also known as attention or consciousness. It's an opportunity to rest in awareness for a little time each day rather than further relentlessly striving.

We probably aren't destined to become Tibetan monks, as Priscilla Warner quickly learned on her personal journey to quiet this voice. But aren't we likely to be happier?

Vanquishing our inner wrongness in real time is the magic of meditation. Witness the doubts, stress, and second-guessing for what they are: human emotions. They come; they go. We stay. We watch. They shift. We breathe. We notice the sensations in the body. The embarrassing follies and ugly flaws we replay, incessant chatter and crippling anxiety about the future—so many mistakes! So many dumb things said!—it's all so human. Sometimes I channel the matter-of-fact voice of Buddhist nun and teacher Pema Chodron when she imparts one of her favorite mantras "No big deal." These emotional currents are working on us in unseen and uninvestigated ways all the time. The purpose of meditation and mindfulness is inquiry, as a way of bringing light and understanding. Enlightenment, some say. We offer this light to our unprocessed grief or anger. To our would-be greatness, which maybe we can't face yet because it means rejecting proven safety and comfort, even if the safety stifles and comfort quashes. The seeds of all these thoughts and judgments exist within us all the time. There is no such thing as a mind that is "better" at meditation than another. So often I hear from people who wish they could meditate, they know it would be so good for them, but their mind is "too busy."

When we sit with these thoughts, without calling them wrong, we foster a new reaction. In fact, the skill is in the *not* reacting. Just watching. Just observing. We accept all parts of ourselves in the moment, breathing into the places that pulse with fear or uncertainty. We tend to our breath and minds again and again, until our minds are stronger and calmer places to be. All of which is important because, try as we might, we cannot escape our own minds. A great deal of our unhappiness comes from perpetually trying to escape this reality.

In a society that insists we must constantly measure ourselves against each other, in the form of accomplishments, appearances, accolades, likes, and wealth, to name a few, the subtleties of meditation can be hard to assess. The practice doesn't cater to our desire for immediate gratification and that is precisely its value. Its value is experiential and cumulative, felt not seen. It makes whole by demonstrating the completeness that exists in basic humanness. Which is, at once, no big deal and the biggest possible deal. It's a BFD, you might say.

If you meditate, you will doubt your abilities less and believe in yourself more. You will feel the benefits not just in the five or fifteen or thirty minutes during which you meditate but in the other twenty-three hours and fifty-five, forty-five, or thirty minutes of the day. You will watch the myth of doing it wrong dissolve and feel the power of simply doing it materialize from within, like a gold coin pulled from your ear, a flower blooming from your lapel, a rabbit under your hat. How did this get here? *Magic.*

11

I Don't Have Time

An awake heart is like a sky that pours light.

—HAFIZ

You do.

(I promise.)

You may not have much time to meditate, but you have *something*. We can work with that.

Furthermore, while it's important to dispel the notion that you don't have enough time to meditate or practice mindfulness, I'm also unwilling to perpetuate another, opposing kind of myth. Common in self-improvement arenas and social media memes intending to motivate is the assertion that you have the same number of hours in your day as, say, Taylor Swift or William Shakespeare. Creative forces both, the former released two albums during the first nine months of the coronavirus pandemic, and the latter purportedly wrote *King Lear* while in quarantine during the bubonic plague. Meanwhile, putting on pants represented a Herculean effort for many of us some days. Although conceptually true, as we're each allotted twenty-four hours, such statements overlook a wide variance in our lived experience on a practical level. I bought lines like this one for a while myself. They seem empowering enough. Look what can be accomplished with the same basic temporal materials! All the possibilities!

Implicit, of course, is . . . So, what's your problem? What's your excuse? *Excuses . . . Excuses . . .* Someone is shaking her/his/their head at us disapprovingly because we can't carve time to meditate, Kondo the closet, write a novel, or roast a perfect buttermilk chicken. But there's a colossal flaw in this argument, overlooking a broad range of factors that make the same twenty-four hours vastly different for different people. I am in no way disrespecting the bard or Taylor Swift. Heavens, they're legends and not the ones peddling this notion. I only mean to say that we cannot pretend everyone has the same access to the support systems—both personal and institutional—that allow for this level of accomplishment. The same responsibilities, health concerns, working hours, financial security. The same ability to drive a car without being pulled over or apply for a home loan without being refused.

To presume that people's "choices" are all that keep them from achieving self-actualization is to dismiss or ignore the inequities that permeate society at every level. You truly may not have twenty minutes a day to sit still with your eyes closed, but you *do* have thirty seconds. You might have a one-minute mini meditation window, two minutes for a yoga intervention, or perhaps five minutes to meditate for real. You do have *some* time. Maybe not a lot, but it's a start. There's a reason why this is the shortest chapter in the book.

30-Second Sighing Meditation

You have thirty seconds to spare. Why not try something that might save your life? Apparently, sighing is one such biological feature. It serves the purpose of inflating the alveoli, the balloon-like sacs in our lungs where oxygen enters and carbon dioxide leaves the bloodstream. Sometimes the alveoli collapse; the natural act of sighing can bring in double the oxygen to pop them back up again.[1] It's an emphatic exhalation that we do, on average, once every five minutes. Psychologically, the super-powered exhale helps us relax as well as activate the parasympathetic nervous system. Try three big sighs the next time you feel stressed. Make them as dramatic and audible as you like. (Maybe do this out of earshot of housemates or coworkers, lest they think you're trying on a new exasperated teenager routine.) Notice how you feel. Less exasperated already, right?

1-Minute Mini Meditation

Think of a word that embodies how you want to feel. Something positive that's in your mind's best interest. No need to think too hard. Just choose the first word that resonates. This mini meditation is an ideal tool to use before entering intense circumstances (think: job interviews, sales pitches, wedding toasts, doctor's appointments, etc.). You can do it anytime, anywhere, to quiet and focus the mind. Take a couple breaths and ask yourself: *How or what do I want to feel?* Then, listen for the answer.

Calm.
Clear.
Confident.
Joy.
Love.

---

1 Mary Grace Garis, "Science Says Sighing Is Involuntary Self Care," *Well + Good*, June 7, 2019.

Peace.
Resilient.
Strong.
Trust.

Do you have your word yet?

Now, take a single, deep breath in, counting "1." As you exhale, silently say your word. Inhale, count "2." Exhale, silently say your word again . . . keep going until you get to 10. This will take roughly one minute. Once you get to 10, if you want to keep going, you can begin again at 1, or you can let go of the counting and observe your breath in conventional mindfulness meditation.

2-Minute Yoga Intervention

In terms of the families of yoga poses that people do—backbends, inversions, twists, for example—forward bends are among the most calming and cooling. Think of it: you fold in, toward yourself. You can hear your breath more easily. You can slow the breath down. You will get a nice stretch. Mind you, I wouldn't recommend a yoga interlude in line at the coffee shop, for instance. I definitely wouldn't recommend it on the subway (too jerky) or in an open floor plan workplace (too eyebrow raising). But if you have two minutes and an appropriate level of privacy (or social acceptance), hang down in a standing forward bend known as "rag doll." It looks just the way it sounds.

Stand with your feet hip-width apart. Soften your knees and fold forward so that your torso hangs over your thighs. You can let your arms dangle or clasp opposite elbows. Allow your head to hang down. Relax your neck, jaw, face, and eyes. Maybe shake out your head. Feel the fresh blood go to your brain, the stretch in the backs of your legs, and the lengthening of your spine. Imagine uncapping the top of your head and letting the day's debris empty out. Take long, slow breaths. When you're ready, slowly roll up to standing. Once you're upright, roll your shoulders up to your ears and back three times. No need to roll forward—we hunch that way plenty while sitting at a computer, driving a car, or looking at our phones. Lift your shoulders up as you inhale, then slide them down your back as you exhale, as though you were letting a heavy, cumbersome coat drop to the floor. Let the weight of the moment drop away. Take a moment to notice your posture now, feet grounded, spine long, shoulders soft, chest open. Mind open.

5 Minutes, You Got This

Start with the one-minute mediation above. (It's one of my all-time favorites.) When you complete one round of ten breaths, you can either begin again at "1," or you can sit and enjoy the stillness you've created for a few more minutes. Watch your breath. Be sure to set a timer, so that peeking at the clock does not distract you. Five minutes goes by fast, but it can also be just enough to slow us down. This exercise is an easy way to start meditating as a beginner or pick up whenever you lose connection to your center. Customize the length of your practice based on what you can manage that day, beginning with a one-minute mental refresh, sneaking in a short five-minute meditation, or as the entry point to a longer session.

A LOT CAN happen in twenty-four hours. Fortunately, we all have an innate capacity to ground ourselves in the present moment. I hope the quick fixes here prove helpful for tapping into that capacity for steadiness and presence. No matter who we are, the most important moment of our lives is the one happening right now.

PART IV

the magic

12

Breathing

To them breathing wasn't an unconscious act;
it wasn't something they just did. It was a force, a
medicine, and mechanism through which they could
gain an almost superhuman power.

—JAMES NESTOR

A cartoon depicts two people leaving yoga class, rolled mats beneath their arms;[1] one carries a water bottle. The caption reads: "How is it that we're the most successful species on the planet, but we need to pay people to remind us to drink water and breathe?"

As someone who is, in fact, paid to remind people to breathe (among other things, thankfully), I find this cartoon unforgettably funny and fitting. Breathing is an autonomic function, meaning it happens involuntarily. And thank goodness, because can you imagine if we had to remember to do it on our own, like making dentist appointments? We'd all be goners. The good news is that connecting to our breath

---

1 Cartoon by Hilary B. Price

unlocks the benefits of mindfulness in an accessible yet profoundly transformative way. Your breath is always there, and you can always use it to center yourself. No one masters this skill; it is a continual remembering, and forgetting, and remembering.

We've touched on this idea a little bit already, but this chapter is solely dedicated to respiration, which is both our life force and lifeline to mindfulness practice. "If you have time to breathe, you have time to meditate," said Buddhist monk, teacher, and abbot Ajahn Amaro. "You breathe when you walk. You breathe when you stand. You breathe when you lie down." Put another way, if you *can't* meditate, you can always breathe with attention and intention, and you will, with overwhelming reliability, feel better as a result.

You have been breathing since the day you were born when you took a momentous, here-I-am, earthbound breath upon arrival into this chilly, well-lit world, a stark contrast to your previous dark, warm, and watery environment. You breathed *air* for the first time, inhaling oxygen and exhaling carbon dioxide. Maybe you sputtered or gasped or wailed, emitting a pneumatic squawk or hearty cry. Maybe your mother cried, too, in relief or pain or awesome love, possibly all three. You were here. That breath confirmed it.

We intuitively know how to breathe; no one has to teach us. Infants cannot yet hold up their own heads and their eyes don't work well beyond eight to ten inches from their faces. The world appears as a noisy confusing blur. But we know how to breathe.

Inhale/exhale.
I breathe in/I breathe out.
In/out.

These paired instructions are common, especially in mindfulness environments such as yoga and meditation classes. We hear them so often that you might think we eventually wouldn't need reminding. You would be wrong. I repeat these words countless times a day and still need to remind *myself* all the time. I'm grateful when others remind me, too. One quick way to remind yourself is to use one of the phrases above as a mantra, linking it to the flow of your breath so that you say the first word or phrase on the inhalation and the second on the exhalation.

Each day we take approximately 25,000 inhales and exhales. Checking email isn't the only activity that stymies this process, causing us to hold our breath, though the rest of them may not have such cute names as email apnea. Once we become aware, it's astonishing how frequently we move through our day intermittently depriving ourselves of oxygen. Cumulatively, these mindless moments of shallow breathing negatively impact our health. Our blood pressure elevates. We struggle to focus. We might feel panicky or depleted or both. Even our metabolism is affected by the nature of our breath.

Breathwork, known as *pranayama* to yogis, relaxes the body, calms the mind, and eases stress. It does this incrementally and holistically over time. The more you practice pranayama, the more you will experience its effects. What's exciting about breathwork is that you can use it as needed to shift how you feel throughout the day. Most of these exercises can be done anytime anywhere, though to be fair some are kookier than others. Need to concentrate? An on-the-go energy boost that doesn't cost anything or leave behind a plastic lid in our oceans for eternity? Help falling asleep? There's a breathing exercise for that!

You can integrate breathwork into your life and mindfulness practice in a few key ways:

1. As a stand-alone practice.
2. As a gateway exercise to meditation. For example, you might do a specific breathing exercise to focus your attention. Then, you can sit

in meditation watching the breath (i.e. breath awareness) without any manipulation of it.

3. As a way to regroup or reset during meditation when you start to struggle. Whenever you get lost in thought, a breathing exercise can be an ideal way to catch yourself and re-anchor in the present.

It's fascinating to see how different techniques connect with different people. I once taught a college football team several exercises as part of a talk I gave at their university. A couple weeks later I was heartened to receive a thank you note from a mental health counselor who works with student-athletes. She shared that the players had taken to doing "orchestra breathing" late at night to stay awake and energized while studying instead of chugging sugary or caffeinated drinks nonstop. Technically, the exercise is called *breath of joy*. It's so wild, bordering on dancing, that it's in the section about movement. What follows here are more soothing techniques that pair well with seated or formal meditation. Rest assured there's something for everyone.

It's important to personalize your practice for the life you have right now because that's what mindfulness is. Life training. You can't do it wrong, as long as you are putting forth honest effort. However, it can't help us at all if we don't do it.

The goal is staying present—even to the best ways to cultivate presence. Undoubtedly, we'll meditate differently at various points in our lives, when routines change; while working from home versus commuting to an office; when we live alone or cohabit with others; or in response to fluctuating stressors. We start with noticing the breath. Am I breathing? Where is the breath most dominant in my body right now? Is it possible to slow or deepen the breath in this moment? This basic technique is called *breath awareness*. Here's a quick review of how to practice it, as well as how to direct breath to areas of your physical or subtle body that hold extra stress, pain, tightness, or emotion.

Breath Awareness

Step 1:

Take a few deep breaths. If this feels difficult, note the sensation but don't worry about it too much. Just allow your breath to settle into its natural rhythm. If possible, breathe through your nose. According to James Nestor, whose book *Breath* is a tour de force of how nothing is more essential to our health and well-being than breathing, "Breathing through the nose has immeasurable benefits including more oxygen, lowered heart rate, and protection from pathogens." To help maintain focus, you might link one of the phrases at the start of this chapter, such as I breathe in/I breathe out, to the pace of your breath flow.

Step 2:

Notice where in your body your breath is most dominant. Some key areas include belly, diaphragm, chest, throat, and tip of nose. Rest your awareness on this part of your body and continue to pay attention. Keep your attention light, as a butterfly lands on a leaf or bird touches down on a tree branch. It's not hard focus but soft and easeful. As many times as your attention wanders, gently bring it back to this location of breath awareness.

Breath Direction (or Channeling the Breath)

Say you discover some tightness or agitation. You might be in physical pain, sharp and local or chronic and nagging. You feel the emotion of the day clamping down on your chest or constricting your throat. Your head or your back hurts. You might be so tired your bones ache. In this instance, it can help to direct your breath to a specific area of your body.

In contrast to breath awareness, in which you locate the place where the breath resides most prominently, now you will pinpoint where your energy is stuck, stagnant, or blocked. The word for the presence of energy in the body in yoga is *prana*, synonymous with breath. In Chinese healing modalities, like acupuncture or qi gong for instance, it's called *chi*. No matter what you call it, energy needs to move freely through your body. When it does, you feel more present, less tense, and better able to tend to what is actually happening. Your body has an ability to heal. Your mind is clearer and better able to function.

To practice breath direction, you can alternate between two simple approaches. First, imagine breathing into the area of your body that needs attention. Visualize inflating or ventilating that tense part of your body with breath. See if you experience some expansion or opening. The other technique is to imagine breathing *with* or *from* that part of your body. Your lungs are powerful, but it is not them alone that respire. You can breathe from your fingers and toes. You can breathe into your lower back and under your shoulder blades. You can breathe into your temples. You can definitely breathe with your skin, the largest organ, breathing all the time with you and for you.

Everyday, Any Breath

Your breath is the most portable and efficient mindfulness tool you have, and it costs nothing to use it skillfully. You can practice becoming aware of your breath anytime and anywhere. You can weave this practice into the context of your day, observing your breath as you walk down the street, read your email, or make your bed in the morning. What's valuable about everyday practice is that, like practicing anything, you and your breath will improve. The reason this is so important is that as stress rises, you will have a built-in release valve. If you are already in a moment of elevated stress, it's a bit late to start training.

A firefighter in a mental performance workshop once asked me, "What is the one thing that I can do to steady my nerves in the time between the firehouse alarm sounding and getting on the truck?" This period is preciously short, less than two minutes. Can you imagine if I said, in front of dozens of his fellow firefighters of every rank, *Well, I recommend sitting down, closing your eyes, and taking a few extra minutes to meditate* . . . NO! Wrong answer! Instead, I shared a few ideas for breathing mindfully while getting dressed or selecting a mantra to say to himself before (literally) the heat of the moment. Moreover, training to be more awake and mindful in life is like fire training, in that it's best if it happens in advance. Breathing is "one thing" you can always do in the moment, but remembering to do it, deeply and calmly when it really matters, improves greatly with practice.

The magic of mindful breathing and mindfulness in general is its cumulative benefit. We do it regardless of how it feels or how "good" we think we are at it, so that over time, we accrue the ability to pay attention more often. We develop more presence and clarity in heightened moments of stress, too. Mindfulness resembles a bank account this way. You deposit money into the account as savings and withdraw from it when needed. Breathwork is a great way to make regular deposits into your mindfulness bank, building up stores that will provide for you in the future. You can withdraw from it as needed.

One biological measurement that illustrates this phenomenon is called HRV, or heart rate variability. If you wear a fitness tracker, you might already be familiar with this data point. In short, heart rate variability measures the relative balance between the sympathetic and parasympathetic systems. As you'll recall from Chapter 4, the sympathetic nervous system prepares us for *fight, flight, or freeze* mode; meanwhile, our parasympathetic nervous system helps us to maintain a calm, composed state. In his groundbreaking book *The Body Keeps the*

Score, Dr. Bessel van der Kolk explains that steady, rhythmical fluctuations in heart rate, produced by breathing in and breathing out, are a predictable measure of basic well-being. "As long as we manage to stay calm, we can choose how we want to respond," he writes.

Dr. van der Kolk's work focuses on how to heal the body, brain, and mind from trauma. People with PTSD, he notes, have unusually low HRV. The good news is that you can improve your HRV, which in turn can enhance your well-being and ability to cope with stress. The best way van der Kolk and his team determined how to improve this crucial function? Yoga. Specifically, its breath practices.

Here are some of the best breathing techniques used in yoga practices of all kinds for building your mindfulness reserves, enhancing well-being, and feeling calmer and more capable of choosing your response to the moment. Each has its own distinct quality and effect, which can be used alone or in conjunction with formal meditation.

Diaphragmatic or Belly Breathing

- *Position:* Seated or lying down.
- *Purpose:* To calm down.
- *Practice:* Start with ten breaths and work up to several minutes. This can be used before or during meditation.

Our bodies default to different styles of breathing depending on the physical or emotional demands of the moment. After an all-out sprint, you might hunch over with your hands on your knees, panting vigorously. Your chest heaves and heart pounds. After a short while, you breathe normally again, deeper and lower into your belly. Thoracic breathing, which occurs in the lungs and chest, is useful in shorter spurts of activity but is not sustainable. If you do it too long, you can hyperventilate.

Diaphragmatic or belly breathing is the opposite. It's more sustainable, not to mention more soothing. It evokes spaciousness and ease. You don't have to do anything special to practice it, but you might enjoy the following exercise performed lying down for ideal relaxation.

Lie down comfortably on your back. Your legs can be straight, or you can bend your knees, place your feet on the floor wider than hips-width distance, and lean your knees together. In yoga, this pose is called *ardha shavasana*. It's a great way to neutralize your lower back and refresh a tired spine. You can lie on the floor, on a yoga mat, or in bed.

Begin by taking a few conscious breaths. Notice the sensations in your body as you do this. Imagine your breath dropping down into your body. Feel the floor or mattress rise to hold your body weight. Next, place your hands on your abdomen. As you continue to breathe, feel your belly expand into the palms of your hands while you inhale and retract as you exhale. Do this until you find a rhythm. You don't need to force anything; just breathe and feel how the air travels all the way up to the diaphragm and back down again. Finally, notice the effects of this deeper, slower breathing on your body. What sensations do you feel? Perhaps your body temperature cools slightly. Your heart rate steadies. Does your spine feel longer and more relaxed? Observe your mind. What is its quality now? Do you notice a change?

Equal Breathing

- *Position:* Preferably seated.
- *Purpose:* To ease anxiety and feel a sense of equanimity.
- *Practice:* Match your inhalation and exhalation, beginning with a four-count and working your way up.

Equal breathing, also known as *sama vritti* (*sama* means "same" in Sanskrit and *vritti* is "breath"), involves matching the length of your inhale to that of your exhale. The effect is one of feeling awake but relaxed. It's also particularly helpful for addressing anxiety. Before I explain it, I'd like to share a story related to handling panic.

My friend Kim Vandenberg, who is an Olympic swimmer, made me realize how simple yet effective the tool of counting can be for anyone, whether in water or on land. And she defines panic in an unforgettable and exceedingly useful way.

Kim and I became friends about ten years ago. I was previously a swimmer—also in water, never in the Olympics, so we quickly bonded over our shared love for the sport, as well as other common interests, including yoga. I once visited her while she was in training in the South of France, at a facility that attracts the best swimmers from all over the world. Their routine was grueling: in the pool twice a day, weight room in between, plus running up hilly, cobblestone streets while dodging Vespa scooters. Peppered within this unyielding physical training was the gentler itinerary of crêpes and sunbathing and jumping off jagged rocks into the ocean. We wore striped shirts because are you even in France if you're not wearing a striped shirt?

Hypoxic training caps off the most intense training block prior to major competitions like the Olympic trials. It's a litmus test for how much fitness the swimmers have gained in preparation for the race of their lives. *Hypoxic training* means "without oxygen," as in holding your breath. Each time a swimmer lifts her head out of the water to breathe, however brief, valuable time is lost. When dealing in fractions of seconds, using as little time and energy as possible to breathe can mean the difference between achieving a lifelong dream and boarding a flight home. So, swimmers explore every conceivable advantage: shaving their bodies completely, wearing a specialized suit that requires two friends and twenty minutes of wriggling into, and only breathing when absolutely necessary.

The hypoxic workout before the 2016 Olympics in London was the stuff of nightmares: the athletes swam underwater for fifty meters, *sixteen* times without a single breath.

"It's terrifying," Kim said, recounting the training to me later. "People break down . . . I've seen people cry hysterically."

"Does panicking make it worse?" I asked.

"WAY worse," Kim said, eyes widening.

"Are there any mental tricks you use to get through it?"

"Counting . . . When I swim butterfly, I have a rhythm. 1, 2 . . . 1, 2 . . . 1, 2 . . . So I don't get ahead of myself." At this, she paused. "That's all panic is, really . . . Getting ahead of yourself."

I think about this conversation a lot. Few people in the world know what it's like to train, prepare, push their bodies, wrangle their minds, and sacrifice their personal lives in pursuit of an Olympic medal, but most of us know how it feels to panic. Many people deal with this feeling on a regular basis ranging from manageable to debilitating and everything in between. Anxiety is the most common form of mental illness in the United States, affecting more than forty million people over the age of eighteen. Thankfully, it's highly treatable.

Equal breathing should not be viewed as a cure-all or substitute for qualified mental health care, but it is a helpful tool when you feel overwhelmed or panicky. Its purpose is to put you back in the moment and reestablish a sense of stability. Here's how it works:

Find a comfortable seat, either in a chair or on the floor. If on the floor, you will need a cushion or yoga block on which to sit. The ideal posture for meditation and/or breathwork is one that is as effortless as possible to maintain. Next, match the length of your inhale to that of your exhale. For beginners, a four-count is a good place to start. Meaning, you will inhale for a slow count of four and exhale for a slow count of four. From there, you can work toward five, six, seven, or eight. Notice how your counts lengthen and become easier with practice and when you're calm versus stressed. Like Kim and her teammates, we can all use counting as a mechanism to soothe panic and stay present. This enhances both physical and mental performance, as well as emotional well-being.

The effect of equal breathing is a feeling of concentrated calm. We become relaxed but alert, ready for whatever comes next but not ruled by it. The best thing about this exercise is that you can do it anywhere. And for those of us who thrive on competition, this exercise can be a healthy way to measure your personal progress by increasing the length of your count gradually. Soon, you may have the lungs of an Olympian.

Box Breathing

- *Position:* Preferably seated.
- *Purpose:* To increase concentration.
- *Practice:* A four-part breath including inhalation, hold; exhalation, hold.

Box breathing is another technique that uses counting. It's a lot like equal breathing but a tad more complex. The reason you might choose a breathing technique that is more complex is because your mind benefits from a more involved task in order to focus. You're learning to customize your approach to stillness and balance; find what works for you. If, for example, your mind is overly distracted, distraught, or tending toward boredom, you might need to give it a job that requires extra attention. Box breathing fits this criterion.

Like a square or box that has four equal sides, box breathing is comprised of four equal parts. Here's how to do it:

- *Inhale* for a count of four.
- *Hold* the retention for a count of four.

- *Exhale* for a count of four.
- *Hold* the extension of the breath for a count of four.

Box breathing is a great gateway activity before meditation because of the high level of concentration it requires. Because this technique is so specific, measured, and symmetrical, it evokes a blunt way of saying to the mind, "It's time to pay attention now." Very often, the response from the mind is "Cool. Thank you. I needed some help. I'm ready now."

Breath Retention

- *Position:* Preferably seated.
- *Purpose:* To refresh and reset. To *let go.*
- *Practice:* Take a long slow breath in and hold it. "Sip" a bit more air and hold it. Then, let it all go. Repeat one or two times. (Note: Please do not try this if you are pregnant.)

Breath retention (or *kumbhaka*) is a great note on which to end a yoga class or meditation session. It feels so cleansing. Every time I do it or teach it, it feels as though the whole room, possibly the universe, breathes a collective sigh of relief. This exercise should *not* be sustained or repeated in succession. A couple rounds is plenty. Breath retention is all about releasing the day's mishaps, mistakes, and stress. Its intention is letting go.

- Begin in a seated position, in a chair or on the floor. Focus on your spine being neutral.
- Take a few conscious breaths, culminating in an emptying, complete breath out.
- Then, take a long, slow, steady breath in, feeling the air fill your lungs and rise up your spine as you sit a little taller.

- At the top of the inhalation, *hold* your breath, perhaps counting to four or five.
- Next, sip in a tiny bit more air.
- Finally, exhale all the air out. Feel the dramatic cleansing effect.

Alternate Nostril Breathing

Position: Preferably seated.

Purpose: Balance and clarity.

Practice: Using your thumb and ring (or pinky) finger, seal one nostril while breathing out the other. Alternate sides for several rounds. A round has both sides.

Alternate nostril breathing, or *nadi shodhana*, creates an exquisite feeling of clarity and balance and is said to stimulate both sides of the brain: the left side, characterized by order and logic, and the right, governed by big picture thinking, creativity, and intuition. I am wildly biased, but I think nadi shodhana is a work of art. Hang it in a museum. This breathing exercise is gorgeous!

Hold up your right hand, then fold your first two fingers down. Your thumb, ring finger, and pinky remain extended. This is deceptively hard. If needed, you can just use your thumb and pinky, which is much easier. You will look vaguely like a surfer by doing this.

Begin with a few grounding breaths. Then, take a long slow inhale through your nose. Next, seal your right nostril closed with your right thumb. Exhale out the left nostril. Inhale through the left nostril; close the left nostril with the ring (or pinky) finger, and exhale out the opposite nostril. Each round of this exercise entails an inhalation and exhalation before closing that nostril, then switching sides. Start with five to ten rounds. Try to breathe slowly throughout. When you finish, sit still and breathe through both nostrils. It feels uncannily amazing and balanced, like discovering you have two separate and equally functioning nostrils for the first time. When you open your eyes, notice how your vision feels sharper and clearer. This breathing technique is known to help relieve sinus pressure and pain, headaches, and the cross-eyed exhausted feeling we get after staring at a computer screen too long.

YOU MIGHT GRAVITATE toward one of these breathing techniques or alternate among a few favorites. Use them alone or in concert with formal meditation, for which you generally refrain from manipulating the breath and instead simply observe it. Purists hesitate to call breathwork meditation, and to some degree, that's true. But it's certainly mindfulness practice. It anchors your mind and body in the present moment and decreases stress on just about every discernible level. And you already have everything you need to put it into action. Mindfulness hinges upon the skill of remembering that you are breathing, that you've been doing it all along, and no one had to teach you. It was a remarkable feat when you first breathed air. Remarkable still.

13

Sensing and Structuring

Beauty and grace are performed whether
or not we will or sense them. The least we
can try to do is try to be there.

—ANNIE DILLARD

Into a woven pouch that my brother brought back from Peru I place
a miniature Tibetan singing bowl, a painted rock with the mantra *om
mani padme hum* written on one side and the eyes of the Buddha on the
other, two perfume samples from Sephora, several sticks of Smarties
candies, the detachable hands from my daughter's Mr. Potato Head
toy, a set of earbuds, and a pair of sunglasses. It's a curious assortment,
to say the least. I drop the pouch in my tote bag, strap the tote to the
back of my bike with two bungee cords, and peddle to teach a meditation class downtown.

The class represents a bit of a professional coup. Somehow I managed to convince the most high-profile health club in the world to put a
class on its group fitness schedule featuring no fitness of any kind. We

don't jump, dance, kick, cycle, or punch. No down dog. No squats or push-ups. In lieu of kettlebells or dumbbells, there are meditation bells. Each week, for thirty minutes, we just sit there.

Sometimes there are a handful of us, sometimes a full room. Always the meditators rush in from busy workdays in the nick of time. Many set alerts on their desktop computers to leave the office a few minutes early to make it to class (it's a stretch for most at 5:15 p.m.). The workdays of most industries in the area—finance, law, and advertising chief among them—don't wind down till later. It's not unusual for people to come, meditate in their business clothes, and go back to work.

Beginning, Middle, End

As we approach a more in-depth discussion of formal seated meditation, I'd like to offer some ideas around structuring your mindfulness practice, specifically giving your routines a beginning, middle, and end.

It's important for meditation sessions to have a structure; doing so makes it feel like a complete experience and helps our minds settle. Our brains seek familiarity, and if you think about it, any rewarding experience or journey has a beginning, middle, and end. Great novels, the best movies, our favorite yoga or fitness classes—beginning, middle, end. The mind can relax into the experience because it feels sufficiently held within a recognizable container. It feels safe. Open.

When not in a group setting, it's helpful to create your own beginning, to signify the start of practice and shift your attention away from whatever you were previously doing. A ritual or small ceremonial moment can do the trick. Light a candle. Sit on a special meditation cushion (known as a *zafu*) or a designated chair. Ring a bell or strike a singing bowl. Take a humble bow, hands together at your heart center or pressed against your third eye. If you want to get more creative, draw a card from a meditation, intention, or tarot deck. It doesn't matter so much what you do as long as it speaks to you and helps you concentrate. The ritual awakens your attention. You might feel excited to begin. You are signaling to your mind and body that you are ready. You open yourself to inner wisdom and intuition. You *arrive* in the present moment.

In groups, I typically open with a check-in, which is often as straightforward as saying our names and sharing a little bit about our meditation practice. For those who are shy or taciturn, I offer a fill in the blank option. "My name is Rebecca, and I meditate _____ [fill in the blank: *sometimes*, *always*, or *never*]." The key is to choose a beginning exercise or gesture, whether we are alone or with others, that is low pressure. People often enjoy sharing more. They mention recent meditation breakthroughs, an app that's been useful, or whether they're first-timers. They might share why they've decided to try meditation with these particular people on this particular night. As a group, we take pride in summoning the reliable fanfare. "First time—big night!" I might say, a triumphant arm in the air. It's a big, courageous deal when we decide to pay attention, brave the insecurity of starting something new, and vow to meet the moment. It may not look or feel like much on the outside, but we can trust that it is.

A tone of welcoming, awareness, and belonging is set. The scattered and lethargic energy in the room begins to settle. People feel a sense of relief that they made it to class, that there are other people grappling with the same challenges they are, and that they don't have to go it alone. We spend so much time holding it all together in our lives that there is a palpable sense of relief when we pause to meditate, realizing there is nothing to grasp or clench or cling to for now. Moreover, by being present to what we feel, we realize that we are never alone. Everything we feel, someone else has felt—might be feeling at that very same moment. This point is essential. It's the essence of how mindfulness proves transformative in our lives and relationships. It connects us on a profound level to our humanness, what it means to go through life's vicissitudes, and how to be present for other people and to reality itself.

Meditating in a group allows us to draft off each other's positive energy and steady attention, like runners in a pack or cyclists in a peloton. This is true even when the group or room is conceptual; we're practicing online, for example. What's more, it sets a subtle tone that even when we meditate alone, we never meditate for ourselves alone. We meditate for everyone we know, intimately or peripherally, by choice or happenstance, people with whom we cross paths for a mere blink and people to whom we are bound for life.

Each person reaches into the woven pouch and retrieves a mystery item: Buddha's eyes, the curious white-gloved hands of Mr. Potato Head, the candy. They detect the sensory theme right away: sight, sound, smell, taste, and touch. This prompt is no fill-in-the-blank. Corresponding to the item they draw, each person is encouraged to share one unforgettable sensory experience from their life. This constitutes mindfulness practice because being fully attuned to our senses requires us to be wholly present. Meditation and mindfulness have been shown to improve memory, and it's easy to see why that's true. It's extremely difficult to remember things for which we weren't really *there*. Meanwhile, when we fully inhabit the moment—how it felt, looked, smelled—we're more likely to remember it.

Joy, memory, curiosity, and connection fill the room. It has nothing to do with meditation. It has everything to do with meditation. People realize that they know far more about mindfulness than perhaps they realized. Veteran meditators remember that we're not trying to get really good at sitting still in a dim room not speaking to each other. We're learning aliveness. We're practicing presence. The seed is planted that when we're *not* present, when we're lost in thought or consumed with all that we otherwise could or should be doing, thus avoiding the actual moment, we might use something as simple and standard-issue as our senses to reconnect. We come back to our senses.

A strawberry vacherin family recipe that takes two days to make—you wouldn't dream of scarfing it. The sunset over the ocean as the fiery orange disc slips below the horizon line, taking your breath with it. Music, the relaxing or revelatory kind, not played in the background; you listen with your whole being. A cup of coffee, the ritual of preparing it. A glass of wine, the feel of glass in hand. Smarties candies (the precise ones I happened to bring) from a junior high English teacher, "Smarties for my smarties," she would say as she distributed them before tests. The gesture eased nerves and made young people feel cared for. All these memories poured out. Individual, collective, shared, and felt. We were present when they happened and, again, in their retelling. We are meditating before we are meditating.

Experiencing the moment through your senses is a grounding, accessible way to cultivate mindfulness. We have "sensory impressions" all the time; they're how we experience life, but they can also serve as mindfulness tools. In formal meditation, you might choose one sensory impression on which to focus. A visual anchor, such as a lit candle, patch of sunlight across the floor, or single fluttering leaf on a tree. A specific sound—I love training my ears to the call of a single bird—or let your ears open to the symphony of sounds around you: the wind or whir of the dishwasher, a crackling fire, the cat's purr. Or tune in to a physical sensation: your feet on the floor, hands in your lap, air on your skin.

The theme that day was new and unorthodox, but the formal practice that followed was standard. This was the "middle" of class. We sat and observed our breath. When we got lost in thought or distracted by a sound, emotion, or sensation, for example, we reminded ourselves to return to the physical experience of the moment. The more you can do this, the easier it is to realize how fleeting any one thought is. How frequently desultory and fundamentally impermanent.

To integrate the senses more purposefully, I prioritized sensory-oriented cues, which you can consider on your own.

Sense of Touch:

Where is my body in space? What is the temperature in the room or feel of the air on my skin? What parts of my body touch the floor/chair/cushion? Is the surface hard, soft, rough, or smooth? What physical sensations connect me to this moment? Can I notice these feelings without attaching a story to them or judging them as good or bad?

When you're feeling particularly stressed, you might create a private gesture to yourself using your sense of touch—a hand on your heart center, a hand on your belly, your palm to the side of your cheek as a loving parent or caretaker would do. You may recall the Buddha touching the ground before he became enlightened. "There are hundreds of ways to kneel and kiss the ground," the poet Rumi wrote. Or to sit and touch the earth.

Sense of Sight:

Where is my focus? If my eyes are closed, what is the quality of my eyes, the direction of my gaze, or drishti? Can I relax my eyes, breathe into them, or imagine smiling with them ever so slightly?

Sense of Sound:

Can I open my ears and really hear the sounds around me? Can I listen deeply to quiet or sit with noise, relinquishing the need to control my surroundings in this moment? Try to isolate one sound and then let it fade. Can I hear my own breath? My heartbeat? Do I sense other living beings through my sense of hearing? Can I offer those beings compassion?

Sense of Smell:

Can I feel the breath in my nostrils? What do I smell? This is especially evocative outdoors. Do you smell trees, flowers, a neighbor burning leaves, or that distinct scent of impending rain or snow? If the scent of the environment is neutral, can you notice your sense of smell resetting?

Sense of Taste:

It is possible to do eating meditation, in which you eat a single food as slowly and deliberately as you possibly can. Generally, however, the tongue is inactive in meditation. Let your tongue be soft in your mouth. A helpful approach is to rest the tip of your tongue at the center point behind your top front teeth. Now, feel your molars separate (i.e., relax your jaw). Breathe some space into your neck and throat.

The session ends with three chimes of meditation bells. Meditators learn to rouse themselves gradually. Each chime calls us back to the environment of the room from the interior environment where we've been. You can punctuate your home practice with the same consciousness. Whatever rouses you, from the alarm on your phone, to ringing a bell, to a knock at the door, give yourself a moment to integrate your meditation back into your day. Rather than springing into action, keep the conscious breathing going if you can. Notice the presence of your practice and its replenishment in your day. Take it with you when you answer the door.

It would be ludicrous to suggest that someone could inhale the smell of their grandmother's freshly baked bread the wrong way or should improve their ability to watch a mesmerizing sunset by fixing their eyes on a *better* portion of pink-streaked sky. In the same way, we can't meditate incorrectly. We can meditate *well*. We can commit ourselves to earnest practice and the patient cultivation of presence. We can be more or less honest with ourselves about what we see and feel in the moment. We can be more or less honest about how we hold space for others. Hopefully, we use the knowledge of self-discovery in meditation for skillful action in life. With practice, we improve over time, but we can't do it wrong. The key is paying attention, with the help of our senses.

Sensing the Moment

In the previous chapter, we focused on the breath as the primary tool to center ourselves in meditation as well as moments in daily life. Our senses provide a similar opportunity to hone awareness. Below are a few ways to ground your mind-body, restore your senses, and revive your attention using your physical experiences and sensory impressions.

In Meditation

- SCAN YOUR SENSES AS YOU MEDITATE. What do you feel? Hear? Smell? If your eyes are open, what is the quality of your seeing? If they are closed, imagine breathing into your eyes, sockets, third eye, and temples. Think about all the stimulus and screen time your eyes endure. Allow them to relax and refresh. Feel your tongue resting in your mouth. Perhaps recall the last thing you tasted. Notice how brief that image stays in your mind. It arises and dissipates, as with all thoughts.
- ISOLATE A SENSORY IMPRESSION. Have you ever tried to isolate one instrument in an orchestra or the call of a lone bird in a flock? Tune your ear to just that instrument or just that bird and notice how it stands out, rises on the airwaves above the others. Then, broaden your field of awareness to include other instruments or birds—how they blend. As it relates to meditation, this skill is particularly helpful in less than ideal environments—which is plenty of them.

The next time you find yourself distracted by a sound while you meditate, try to refrain from avoiding it or blocking it out. Just listen. Try to let go of judgments about whether you like or dislike the sound, if it should stop, or how you'd prefer the environment to sound. Instead, feel the sensation of opening your ears and listening to the quality of the noise. Then, broaden your listening so that the sound becomes part of a larger "orchestra." Yes, you hear a lawnmower, but you also hear the joyful shrieks of the neighbor kids playing with a garden hose on a hot day. In the meditation class inside a health club, new students often sense the bumping music on the other side of the wall as disruptive. Sometimes people clang their weights down aggressively or thud a medicine ball against the wall. It's not that these sounds aren't distracting or even unpleasant. However, with practice they becomes less of a factor. And sometimes our judgments and associations change altogether. Of all the things that get stuck in our heads when we meditate—doubt and worry and rumination, old arguments and ongoing to-do lists—suddenly a Lady Gaga song is hardly so bad.

• SENSE YOUR WAY OUT. I love, love, love this simple exercise. It's easily transferable to other contexts, but I use it most often when concluding a meditation (this includes the final seated moments of a yoga class). Let's assume your eyes are closed as you meditate. First, sense the environment around you: the feeling of the surface on which you sit, air on your skin, your hands in your lap. Observe the finest details by becoming aware of your tactile senses. Next, open your ears and *hear* your environment. I frequently do this during a rooftop yoga class that I teach at sunrise. It's fascinating to hear the city waking up twelve stories below: the sound of cars on the street, airplanes overhead, inevitably a construction site nearby revs into action; it's all part of the crescendo from quiet and sleepy to alert and ready for the day. Hear it all. Finally, open your eyes. Take exquisite care to look around *slowly*. In a way that we rarely do, focus on what you see. Note the colors, textures, light, shadow, and movement. Use your eyes like a panoramic camera lens. Allow yourself to take in the moment in this deep way, until your attention clicks back into place within your broader and busier surroundings. Feel, hear, and see where you are—*how* you are—in the world.

If you have the opportunity to meditate in a beautiful setting, you may be moved to keep your eyes open. Go for it! Many teachers and styles of meditation promote open eyes rather than closed. After all, you move through the world with your eyes open; why not maintain consistency and train your focus as you would use it throughout your day? Beaches, forests, parks, mountaintops, starry skies, desert vistas—what better way to appreciate Mother Nature than to sit with her and be still. We've witnessed rainbows during rooftop yoga practice. Can you imagine if we closed our eyes and missed them?

In Everyday Life

When you feel overwhelmed, disconnected, or sense you are operating on autopilot, slow down and feel yourself return to the moment, beginning with your breath or the feeling of your physical body in space. When we're not present, it's probable that we're half-listening to people talk, half-tasting our food, or half-feeling our feelings (the good ones as well as the bad ones, equally), to name a few. Sensory experiences are powerful anchors to the moment. They can awaken, heal, and befriend. Part of understanding mindfulness is learning what grounds you. When you feel off balance, what brings you back? Is it salt air in your lungs and hair? The sound of your breath when you do yoga or rain as you drift to sleep? Do you relax with your hands in the dirt of your garden or kneading dough on your countertop?

Does your soul relax when you sink your body into a hot bath? Clean sheets. The scent of lavender or cut grass. Life is a collection of sensory experiences, each with its unique way of honing our attention.

"Be here now. Be someplace else later. Is that so complicated?" asked David M. Bader, a humorous writer who explores the intersections of Judaism and Zen Buddhism. It's simple indeed, though hardly easy. A sense of humor can help. Remember how to remind yourself. Be in your body. Open your ears. Notice the quality of your gaze. How do you look upon the world? Not: what do you see? *How* do you look upon the world, yourself, other beings? Taste your food, the sensory experience of flavor, texture, and nourishment. Nourish yourself by slowing down, breathing deeply and consciously, and sensing the details of the moment.

WHEN MY DAUGHTER was a baby, I packed the same miniature Tibetan singing bowl I brought to meditation class in our diaper bag before heading to the pediatrician. No one prepares you for how horrible those early doctor's visits are—or at least no one prepared me. These appointments are especially gutting when vaccinations are administered or blood is drawn. The feeling of conspiring in the infliction of pain on your beautiful, unsuspecting baby is visceral, knotted, and nauseating—no matter how necessary. Call me a wuss, but I hated it. I was a wreck for two days in advance of each appointment. If I didn't meditate, I'd need to be tranquilized.

The shots go fine. She cries and howls in a way specific to shots but is easily calmed. The blood draw nearly does us in. As a newborn, she required blood draws every few days with a dastardly heel prick because she had jaundice and needed to be monitored closely. By one year though, the method shifts to an arm tourniquet (her tiny arm!) and then a needle. My husband holds her in his lap. The most terrible part is that our daughter is completely jazzed by the chair. She bounces with delight, holding the armrest as though the enclosure to a ride at an amusement park.

The realization in her eyes as the phlebotomist moves in drops my stomach to the floor. The crying is much worse now. She's hungrier and more confused, too. I reach for the small blue box with the delicate string. Quickly I unfurl the string, open the box, and remove the singing bowl. I strike the wooden mallet to the edge of the bowl, and the gentle chime cuts through the air that carries the sound of her crying. Her eyes widen and the tear-soaked face manages to smile.

She stops crying. The moment is over, and we're grateful to be in a new one.

14

Sitting

"Meditation is not a way of making your mind quiet.
It's a way of entering into the quiet that's already
there-buried under the 50,000 thoughts the average
person thinks every day."

—DEEPAK CHOPRA

The magic of mindfulness is an easy sell. People and products often lead with these promises: of brainpower, productivity, creativity; I've seen great sex boasted as a sales pitch for meditation; I've seen better sales pitches used as a sales pitch for meditation. These benefits may in fact be real for many people, but the myth is that they are instantly available and universally possible. As with any other discipline, we have to commit to the process in order to enjoy its rewards, and such benefits are unique to the individual. There are some, stress-reduction as one example, which are highly plausible and even characteristic, while others we may not expect.

When we don't consider the myths that inevitably arise as we embark on a mindfulness practice, we set ourselves up for confusion, frustration, and disappointment. We often end up thinking meditation isn't right for us or we're not right for it. In reality, our relationship with meditation is more akin to Mark Darcy's with Bridget Jones: he loved her just as she was! Similarly, meditation works for us no matter who we are. It *loves us just as we are*. It works even when we think it isn't working.

But *how* does it work? Presumably, you have some knowledge of how to meditate. We did a quick primer on page 49. This chapter further explains the nuts and bolts of formal seated meditation, which lays a valuable foundation for mindfulness practices of all kinds. Most important, my hope is that this breaking down of the logistics helps you feel more confident putting the practice to work in your life.

Telltale signs of fruitful practice include but are not limited to: better focus, less stress, deeper connections with other people, greater resilience when things go wrong, and healthier boundaries. This last point might seem tangential, but in fact, it's an outgrowth of what happens when you sit long enough to realize you are not your thoughts. You are more than you think! You realize there is a lot in your mind that's not really *you*. The same can be said for a lot of sources of stress. Sometimes, they belong wholly to us. Sometimes, we take on emotional or physical stress that is not ours. All that time watching our thoughts without reactivity helps us realize that we have a choice about the space of our minds, and often the landscape of our lives follows suit.

Some of the information in this chapter might be familiar, but even if you're a veteran meditator, I hope you'll glean new ideas, tricks, or tips to rekindle or strengthen your practice. Cultivating a consistent meditation practice is such a valuable, fortifying resource that it can feel like having a secret superpower. You might not stop a moving train (I do not advise trying), but you'll see oncoming thoughts and emotions from a wiser place. You won't fly through the air like a speeding bullet, but you will be equipped to trust yourself when life's slings and arrows wound you. You won't develop X-ray vision but a clearer, more accurate and empathetic way of seeing the world.

There are many excellent resources and teachers out there, and I encourage you to explore them. I mention many of my favorites throughout. Different techniques and philosophies appeal to different people and fit our varied lifestyles. My experience has been in working with tens of thousands of people from a wide array of backgrounds over a long period of time. I can tell you that, with rare exceptions, they've been busy. Some were running into burning buildings, remember? What I love most is helping each person figure out how to make these practices work for and within their lives. It all starts with the present moment and finding a comfortable seat.

How to Sit

You can sit however you like. Really, truly. The only guideline is that your spine should be long and relaxed. You can sit on the floor cross-legged, as you might be accustomed to seeing in traditional depictions of meditation, or you can sit in a chair. Ideally, the chair should have a back that is straight and of the proper height so that your feet easily touch the floor. A barstool, for example, is less ideal. But if you want to meditate at a bar, who am I to stop you?

For most people, sitting on the floor in total stillness for long periods is not 100 percent comfortable. It's not even 52 percent comfortable (these are my own unverified numbers). Which is why additional tools, such as props like yoga blocks, cushions, and meditation bolsters, are useful. As a general rule, your hips should be elevated above your knees when you sit on the floor. This position can be difficult to achieve if your hips are tight, which is very common. More often, one's knees point up toward the sky. The remedy is usually straightforward. All you need is a yoga block (or two) or a cushion on which to sit. If you are feeling fancy and committed, you can invest in a cushion specifically for meditation, called a *zafu*. Where you sit certainly doesn't have to be anything extravagant, though you can find zafus in beautiful colors and fabrics. Beauty and color can do wonders to zhoosh up our motivation, like being excited to run in a fresh pair of sneakers or make art with new supplies. Otherwise, a couch cushion, throw pillow, or folded blanket will do just fine. When you sit on your cushion, your hips will elevate and, as a result, your lower back will lengthen. This will feel much better.

But maybe now your knees hurt? Or ankles? Dang, no one told you sitting was this complex! Please don't give up, and do be persnickety in the beginning. Finding a comfortable seat is no small thing, and it takes some research. It's not unusual to feel like the Goldilocks of meditation. If you feel like your posture is too slouched or rigid, too high or low, too tight or loose, take the time to investigate how you can sit with greater ease. The shape in which you place your body is important. Because if you can't sit comfortably in your cranky knee joints, how on earth will you sit effortlessly with your unwieldy mind? My perspective on meditation postures is greatly informed by my yoga background, and I feel the same way about body alignment in both disciplines. In short: you shouldn't endure uncomfortable poses for the sake of appearances or an idea of what's right for someone else. With that said, it's true that meditating is difficult at first. You will adapt to sitting still for longer periods over time, and postures that were initially inaccessible will become relaxing one day. Take note that sharp pain or nagging uneasiness is a clear sign to pay attention. Apply a little creativity and compassion, and customize meditation to work for you.

Knees, specifically, generate a lot of complaints and discomfort. I borrow a funny quip from a teacher I once met at a yoga conference who cautioned students to take care of their knees because "You break 'em; you buy 'em." Perhaps you or someone you know had to buy new knees? My dad has an artificial hip, which is a nightmare in airports. All of which is to say that we must accommodate our bodies if we want to befriend our minds. If your feet fall asleep or your knees and ankle joints ache, for instance, there are plenty of adjustments available. Try adding a second block or cushion if one isn't enough (more height, especially if you are tall, can be key to happy knees), adding a blanket (tucking a blanket under your knees or ankles works like a charm), or changing positions (if cross-legged doesn't work, try kneeling or lying down instead).

The main principle is to invoke stillness of the mind by beginning with stillness of the body. If the posture makes you want to run for the hills, then the mind will never be still. Dedicate a little time and some patient trial and error until you find a seat that fits just right. Be willing to change. Experience discomfort with curiosity and without reactivity. Invite ease.

There will be plenty of times when physical sensations feel like distractions. Remember, it's all part of the moment and the meditation. It's all an opportunity for waking up. Distractions, aches, itchiness, and fidgeting . . . no aspect of meditation is separate or a sign of failure. We are learning to pay attention to the moment as it unfolds without judgment. Just awareness. Furthermore, not only is nothing separate; nothing is permanent. If you watch a sensation without reactivity, your itchy nose may subside or the stiffness in your back may relax with breath awareness. This process of watching thoughts, feelings, and sensations arise and dissipate is the training.

Which is not to say that you can't scratch your nose when it itches or you should tough it out if your back hurts. Watch the sensation for a little while. Then, decide how you'd like to respond. You may need to straighten your leg for a few breaths and then bend it back into position. You may decide to use a chair or lie down one day.

Finally, once you've found your seat, try the following subtle adjustment to properly align your spine. Let your torso lean a few inches forward and back. Do this gentle rocking action until you find the point of greatest ease in the middle. That's your neutral spinal position. Take a few deep breaths up the entire length of your spine and back down again. This should feel refreshing and spacious. Feel your chin parallel to the floor. Notice the stability and steadiness held within your physical and emotional being, you sitting with ease and attention.

Where to Look

If you're a yogi, you're familiar with the concept of *drishti*, which refers to the energy and intention of our eyes. Wherever your gaze goes, energy flows, it's said. "Keep your eye on the ball," we hear, regarding things not remotely related to baseball. Referring to someone with "laserlike" focus is the utmost compliment. In yoga poses, the right drishti enhances the likelihood of balance, whether on one foot or both, your hands, or your head.

Yogi or not, we all feel the power of drishti when we sense someone watching us from across a room or use a visual anchor to improve concentration and mental performance. You pick up the pace of your run until you reach the stop sign. You swim to the farthest buoy you can see. A ballerina sets her sights on a singular "spot," holding it in her gaze for as long as possible, before snapping her head around to complete a series of dizzying pirouettes. Without the spot, the room will pitch sideways like a ship in a storm and she will falter. I think of one of the most famous drishti points in all of distance running: the Prudential Center, situated close to the finish line of the Boston Marathon. Towering above the city, the skyscraper becomes visible when runners reach Brookline, the seventh of eight towns along the course, occurring between miles 22 and 24. It has its own motivational couplet:

When you see the Pru, you know you're through. Likewise, an intentional drishti can help get you through tough spots in meditation.

Understanding the concept of drishti and using it to our advantage enhances concentration. It "sets our sights" on success, you could say. Not to mention, with so much visual stimulation in our daily lives, especially in the form of screens, it's important to refresh our eyes regularly.

Most often, meditation teachers prompt us to close our eyes, but if that doesn't work for you, please know that you can always keep them open in meditation. If you keep your eyes open, the key is to relax your gaze and rest your eyelids at half-mast. You don't have to stare at anything in particular; just soften your eyes and allow them to land on one point or in a general direction.

The concept of drishti also applies when your eyes are closed; I encourage you to consider and explore the direction of your gaze in meditation. As an experiment in the energetic shifts of different gaze points, try the following: With your eyelids shut, focus the energy of your eyes on the ground in front of you for several breaths. Then, imagine gazing into your heart or third eye (the inside of your forehead), to name a few. Notice how each focal point—ground, chest, and brow—invites a small shift of your attention.

There are a few reasons why you might opt to meditate with your eyes open as opposed to closed. The most important of which is that you like it better. Say no more. Two common experiences can factor into your preference of where to look when you formally meditate. First, closing your eyes could make you sleepy. Deepak Chopra addressed this challenge at a meditation retreat I attended, and I still laugh at the memory.

"If you feel like you're going to fall asleep in meditation, it means something very important . . ." he said. He then paused as we waited in anticipation for further insight. "It means you need more sleep!" he laughed. Comedy aside, if you feel drowsy or scattered in meditation, opening your eyes can help.

Second, if closing your eyes causes you to feel unsafe in any way, please keep them open. Survivors of trauma, specifically, can experience unwanted imagery from the past or feel vulnerable in their surroundings with their eyes closed. We tend to think of trauma in terms of the most severe cases, but in reality, most of us experience some form of trauma in our lifetimes. I learned a valuable lesson about making meditation more suitable for anyone coping with trauma after giving my first presentation to a group of firefighters. The program director, a former Navy SEAL named Adam, approached me after the session. It had gone well, but I could tell something weighed on his mind.

"Do they have to close their eyes?" he asked.

Of course not. It seemed like such a small issue, but I could tell something deeper was wrong.

"It's just that you have a room full of ex-military guys, with their backs to the door, and you're asking them to close their eyes . . ."

I felt terrible. Of course, no one had to close his eyes. Of course they might see triggering images, the precise kind of stimuli someone suffering from post-traumatic stress disorder is attempting to heal with the help of meditation. Now, *my* eyes are open. I'm extra careful to say that anyone is welcome to close their eyes or keep them open. Helpful focal points include the ground, your hands resting in your lap, or an unspecific open field of vision, as though looking out over the horizon.

Even without meditating, you can use the energy of your eyes throughout your day to recharge. For this reason, you might keep special objects, mementos, a meaningful photo, or inspirational quote nearby so that you can direct your gaze to them when you need a mental reset. Perhaps you have a favorite view from your home or workplace; remember to soak it up. Your senses offer a built-in way to be present and refresh your mind.

What to Do with Your Hands (Mudras)

High-five—we get to talk about mudras! Mudras are hand gestures used in yoga and meditation as another tool to improve concentration. As you know, breath is the most common and effective object of attention. Our senses also help, drishti or our eyes being crucial. Now, you can add mudras. The word itself translates to mean "seal," as in the *sealing* of a letter. Mudras operate as body language you send yourself, sealing an intentional way of being into your body. Here are a few basic mudras for seated practice.

Calmness-Abiding Mudra

If humans were a super chill species by nature, no one would need to meditate. It's that simple. Most people come to the practice to reduce stress. This takes discipline, of course. There's never a place to arrive, only an ongoing process of remembering. What's reassuring is that we never need to manufacture anything new. We don't glaze over hard truths. We don't avoid or deny reality. We notice what is already here. We have choices about which thoughts are useful and which are not. We have a choice about what to bring forth.

What I love most about calmness-abiding mudra is its name. It reminds me of the line from the epic poem *Ulysses* by Alfred Lord Tennyson. *Though much is taken, much abides.*

The line often revisits me when calmness seems improbable. When we are rocked by another breaking news story of tragedy, for example. Each time, I struggle with how to—of all things—show up to teach people to be present, self-possessed, and compassionate toward all beings. How on earth am I supposed to be the steady teacher I think people want when I feel equally lost, angry, or heartbroken? The first time I experienced this professional-emotional struggle was in the days following 9/11. People flocked to yoga. I was twenty-two years old and still recall the air in the room. Blunted. Quivering. Dense. We were dazed with fear, and no one knew what to do. But good instincts, marketing, or both led people to wonder if moving while breathing in and breathing out might help. Maybe being together would help. It did. And I realized I didn't have to be different from how I felt. I just had to be present for the people in front of me. We all have this capacity: to be there for each other. We carry these resources around all the time.

To bring forth abiding calmness, start by sitting comfortably. Next, place your palms on your thighbones and gently press downward. Notice how this action lifts and lengthens your spine. Experience the connection of your hands to your legs. Note any impressions of feeling grounded, steady, and connected. No matter what happens outside, these qualities inwardly abide.

Mudra of Receptivity

On the other hand—forgive the pun—when you feel low energy and need a meditative pick-me-up, it helps to open your hands, turn them upward, and invite that affirming and awakened energy. Try the two mudras now: take a few breaths with your hands facing down, and then flip them upward. The shift is subtle, but you instantly feel it. One is not better or more authentic. Instead, they represent ways to personalize your practice to fit a specific moment. When you sit down to practice, first, check in with yourself. Notice how you feel. What would help you align with what is best for your mind-body? What evokes ease?

According to body language experts, opening or displaying one's hands is a sign of openness and receptivity. Evoking this intention in meditation not only helps us *receive* the meditation but also inspires these qualities in our lives. Rather than focusing on what already exists or abides here, there's a slight shift toward receiving what is to come. This mudra suggests energy, potential, and freshness. We're not holding on; we are opening up.

Dhyana Mudra to Hold Space

Life can be crowded. For some of us, this fact is patently, externally true. We inhabit cities, share sidewalks, cohabit with other people, or take public transportation. We stand in long lines. Our closets are full; our schedules are fuller. Our brains struggle to process evermore information all the time. In fact, the stream of information we process and data we create dwarfs that of any other time in history. And yet, our brains have not evolved to keep up. They can't. We feel squeezed. We start losing the ability to make decisions. We can't hold one thought for, *oh, look at that, the soup of the day is cauliflower*! Whether we are speaking about our exterior or interior environments (or a little of both), we all know the feeling of needing space.

Meditation promotes physical, mental, and emotional space, and dhyana mudra is a way to wire this powerful intention into your seated practice. To do it, lay your dominant hand in your lap and then rest your other hand inside, both palms facing upward. Finally, touch your thumbs together. The hollow shape of your hands will resemble the shape and size of an egg. You are holding empty space. This hand position is particularly common in the Zen Buddhist tradition.

While using this mudra, you might consider the question of what you'd like to hold space for—in the moment or in life. Rather than searching for an answer, use the question itself as an anchor. Ask it, and then hold space for an answer to emerge. Observe what comes up for you. Breathe and feel your hands in the moment. Sometimes with this mudra, when we lose focus, our hands flop open and thumbs come apart. Sealing them together again offers a way to reconnect. It's a beautiful way of using body language to invoke intention.

Jnana Mudra to Connect

Jnana mudra is the most prominent meditation mudra we see in the context of yoga. I bet you are picturing it already. When your friends who've never meditated a day in their lives and are allergic to yoga want to tease you by aping a prototypical yogi sitting in meditation, they rest their hands in a position approximating jnana mudra: thumb and index finger touching to form a circle, backs of hands resting on knees. Palms upward. Expression blissful.

The reason why this mudra is favored in yoga settings is that it's not meant to be held for long. I learned this when I first began attending sessions at a meditation center (sometimes called a Buddha hall). They were forty-five minutes long, which was a significant jump in duration for me at the time. I discovered that holding your hands in such an intricate way gets tiring, which can be distracting.

Jnana mudra is lovely for a few minutes while sitting in lotus pose or sukhasana (cross-legged) at the end of yoga practice, but for an extended amount of time, it fatigues fingers and wrists and becomes difficult to maintain. For this reason, use jnana mudra for shorter increments. If your hands get tired, just relax them in your lap any way you like. This stipulation is true for any mudra.

The prevailing attitude of your meditation posture should be ease. Mudras offer a meaningful way to adapt your practice, center your attention, and seal powerful intentions into our being, but we shouldn't let them overcomplicate things.

To re-create this ancient mudra, rest the backs of your hands on your knees with your elbows bent slightly toward your body. Touch your thumb and index finger together to form a circle. The rest of your fingers (middle, ring, and pinky) will remain extended but not rigid.

Since a circle has no beginning and no end, this mudra represents connection. It conjures our eternal ability to reconnect—to ourselves, to the present moment, and to the wisdom of all the meditators and yogis who came before us. It signifies that we are part of something. We are part of life. We may meditate alone, but we all belong to the human species and planet earth; to families, communities, and friends; to the ocean and mountains and the places where we caught insects or crashed our first bikes. We are part of a mysterious, maddening, breathtaking universe. We contain stardust.

What to Think (Mantras)

Speaking of vastness—oceans and stars and such—it can be a little unnerving to drop into the immensity of your own consciousness with little more than an instruction to watch your breath. *When your mind wanders, come back to the breath.* We understand it intellectually. But practically speaking, it can feel a little like getting plopped down in the middle of the woods and told to navigate your way home with nothing more than a paper clip and stick of gum. Most people need a few more tools in their survival packs than that. This is where mantra meditation (also known as *japa*) is like switching on your headlamp in a dark forest.

A mantra is a word or phrase used to anchor the mind in meditation and an ideal way to channel our attention away from disparate and unproductive thoughts to landing on a single nourishing one, which you purposefully plant in your awareness. The word *mantra* technically translates to mean "mind-protecting." To meditators, these words and phrases offer a vital way to concentrate. A balm. A salve. A path out of the woods. To further explain how this strategy works, I want to take a small diversion to talk about puppies.

When I would address groups, I would often take an informal poll of the dog owners in the crowd. It's a nice opportunity for low-pressure audience participation. More than that, it's an ideal way to explain the concept and pragmatism of mantras. They raise their hands, curious where this tack is going. *Did they have the dogs as puppies?* I press. Many did. *Did they give the puppies chew toys?* Of course.

Why?

You can guess the responses. A puppy without a chew toy is a footwear assassin, book shredder, and fluffy, oversized termite ready to make quick work of the furniture. Oh, you left the garbage unattended? Prepare to find it strewn across the floor. Alas, this is what puppies do. They mean no harm. They might as well be strewing rose petals down a wedding aisle. We're the uptight ones for thinking trash isn't festive.

The mind is a well-meaning, overzealous puppy without a chew toy. It means no harm, and it can conjure up epic trouble when we're not looking. Without proper training or some way to direct its energy in a productive manner, the puppy chews the furniture, gnaws the pillows to expose their fluffy guts, and excavates the garbage as though conducting an archeological dig. The mind similarly gravitates in all kinds of directions that may not be productive or healthy for us. How many of us have some thoughts that are a lot like chewing a couch?

In meditation, all sorts of destructive thoughts arise. You know the thoughts I mean. They constitute the worst things people ever said to us, the worst things we say to ourselves; they dredge the basin of our ego for our emotional wounds, insatiable wants, and conversational loops that have gone nowhere for years. These thoughts, which are just thoughts, which aren't part of the actual moment but rather our habituated projections onto it from the past or future, do not have our best interest in mind. Without guidance, practice, or mindful presence, it's easy to keep acting out those conditioned responses. We are chasing our tails. A mantra is like a chew toy for the mind: a safe, sanctioned, nourishing thought on which the mind can gnaw to avoid more menacing patterns. You see, mantras *protect the mind* as chew toys protect the furniture.

Mantras can have literal meanings or none at all, profound significance or be a semblance of syllables that's difficult to translate, harder still to explain. Nevertheless, the sound or energetic vibration that mantras create outweighs their literal meanings. Consider how you can be deeply moved by a piece of music sung in a foreign language. You may not understand it word for word, but its emotion unlocks something within you. You respect its origin, context, and ability to convey truth.

Because my language skills beyond my own mother tongue are extremely limited (how did I study French for *so* long to no avail?), I mostly use English words and phrases. I also believe it's important to honor the original traditions and languages in which these mindfulness practices started, so I reference mantras in Pali, the original language of Buddhism, and Sanskrit, the original language of yoga, often. If you speak other languages, please translate and incorporate as you like.

Historically, it was commonplace for a guru to "transmit" a mantra to a student but withhold its meaning. As modern practitioners, we typically want to know what we're saying. It helps affirm what we're doing. Here's how to choose your own mantras and do japa meditation on your own.

How to Do Mantra Meditation (Japa)

The most important thing to remember about mantras is that we're not trying to recite them like robots. The key is to use the word or phrase you've chosen only as much as it is helpful to you. One option, which we mentioned in Chapter 12, is to link the mantra to the flow of your breath. Or you can begin with basic mindfulness meditation watching the breath, and if you get stuck, then you can use the mantra as a tool to bring your mind back into focus. Meditation need not be a scripted experience. Say the mantra a few times. Become aware of how it makes you feel, what it brings forth. If it becomes no longer useful, you can let it dissolve. If you get stuck, pick it back up again.

THINGS TO REMEMBER:

• Incorporate the mantra as much as it is useful. When your mind wanders, you have something productive to which you can return. When you don't need it, let it go and simply watch your breath.

- If you become lost in thought or feel stuck, you can count the repetitions of your mantra as you recite them. Besides being stylish accessories, mala beads are made for this purpose. In Buddhist and Hindu traditions, malas contain 108 beads. As modern meditators and yogis, we're often pressed for time; 108 may take too long. Still, we can opt for a factor of 108 (e.g., 54, 27, or 9) as a nod to tradition, as well as time-saving.

- You can silently "say" the mantra so that you hear it in your own mind or visualize the actual word. Our brains are unique. Some of us are more literal than visual and vice versa. Give yours the best chance for staying on task by noting what works for you.

- It's best to choose short mantras to start (i.e., one, two, or three words), especially as a new meditator. Two-word mantras work beautifully with the breath. Say the first word on the inhalation and the second word on the exhalation.

Examples of two-word mantras to try:

I Am

We are so programmed to identify and quantify ourselves. Most often, this is the ego talking or, rather, society's conditioning speaking through our ego. And it can be very tiring. When we say *I am* as a mantra, its power is contained in the openness of not filling in the blank. I am a mother. I am a writer. I am exhausted. I am scared. I am running late. Instead, leave it open. Let it be nonjudgmental and unquantifiable. Let the soul utter it. How does it feel just to be?

Just This

One of the most powerful and popular mantras, "just this" fits any moment or situation. What can change if we are able

to pause and tend to *just this*, the moment unfolding before us?
Everything.

Let Go

If you have nothing in your life that you need to let go
of—no doubts, regrets, limiting beliefs, or mistakes—then this
one will be useless to you. But chances are you may have a few
things weighing you down that you're ready to part with, and it
may come in handy. Inhale: *Let*. Exhale: *Go*. Repeat as needed.

This Too

The truth is that even the things we need to let go of *belong*
in the moment. Put another way, they're there anyway. How
can we work with them from a place of wisdom? Rather than
blocking or avoiding, the practice might become *letting it be* as
much as letting go. The scared wolf sleeps at our feet by the fire.

I Can

Mantras align your mind with what is nourishing,
constructive, and possible. If the voice of doubt echoes loudly
inside your mind, consider replacing it with this resolute two-
word response.

I Will

In the space between stimulus and response, we can choose.
Who will you be in this moment? Whatever you will do next
begins right here.

Om Shanti (in Sanskrit; in Pali: *Santi*; translation: "Peace to All
Beings")

This ancient mantra holds the essence of it all: Peace to all
beings. No exceptions.

One Last Note

That's it? you might be thinking. Sit there, eyes open or closed, and watch my thoughts and the sensations in my body? Hold my hands this way or that. Say some meaningful words to give my mind a task, or skip the mantra altogether. *What if that's not enough?*

These are enough.

You sit and breathe, using basic tools, and the transformative, stress-reducing, creativity-boosting, peace-inducing benefits avail themselves to you. It's exquisitely simple but also, you're right, deceptively hard. The reason why it's so hard is that we prefer instant gratification and we're programmed, deeply conditioned, by our thoughts about the past and the future.

OK, there's one more tool for when you get stuck. It's a technique called mental noting, which helps us sort through the internal chatter. If you keep coming up against what to do with all the commotion in your mind—thoughts, distracting noises, your stomach growling, people who want to take away women's bodily autonomy, whether you'll ever be able to go to your favorite restaurant again—you might need reinforcements.

Mental noting works by acknowledging thoughts as they arise so that you reduce their momentum. Then, you return to the breath. I once heard this approach described as watching your thoughts as though guests arriving at a dinner party. People mill about. Small groups cluster in the living and dining areas. Introductions are made. Friends chitchat. Most of us arrange our whereabouts in proximity to the North Star of every dinner party: the cheese platter.

When a new person arrives, the rest of the partygoers take note. We might nod hello, wave the new guest over to join our conversation. We let her take off her coat and make her way across the room in her own time. There might be a warm hug or stylish air kiss. All of which is to say there is a presumption of space, an invisible boundary that allows the person to arrive and settle in without intervention.

You may know the guest intimately or not at all. Either way, you don't drop your plate of Brie on the floor, leave the person with whom you're talking in midsentence, race across the room, and seize the person who's arrived for your personal benefit. Sure, there are some exceptions. Epic and unexpected reunions with friends from bygone chapters of life come to mind. But generally, we allow space and appreciate the same in return.

When a new thought arises, it's helpful to address it in a similar fashion, by acknowledging its arrival without rushing toward or latching onto it. Give it some room. Allow it to show up, take off its coat, and move through the party. This practice cultivates what's known as the "perspective of the witness," which is the invaluable ability to notice our thoughts and perceive them from an outside perspective. You'll hear this term more later.

In noting, you acknowledge whatever you're aware of by giving it a label, a one-word name to describe what you are experiencing: "thinking," "planning," "hearing," or "feeling." You can name the emotions: happy, sad, worried, angry, enraged . . . it's important not to make your feelings bad; just notice and name them. This skill is especially useful for understanding emotions and discerning how we'd like to respond, as well as untangling disparate emotions from one another when they're in a jumble. You can also describe sensations. The temperature in the room: warm, hot, cool, or cold. Or the feeling on the tip of your nose: itch. Earlier we talked about japa meditation, the use of mantras, to give the mind a job. The principle here is similar. An idle mind, like an unattended puppy, can get into trouble. Instead of substituting your thoughts with a phrase (i.e., mantra), you're recognizing where the mind has gone and returning it to the breath.

Some people love this technique, especially beginners and people trying to meditate with a restless, overwhelmed, or anxious interior state. Sitting with mental chaos is uncomfortable, which is why it's beneficial to incorporate an organizing technique like noting. Living in our minds, which we do 24/7, is like living in our homes—it's easier when the house is in order. Even if you decide noting isn't for you, trying it can be illuminating, and you will have one more resource to lean on in case you need it.

If the technique feels tricky or awkward, it's usually because we have trouble choosing which word best fits its corresponding thought. We get caught up in our judgments about doing things right. Should I say I am "thinking" or "planning"? Maybe "ruminating" sounds better? When I hear a noise in the other room, should I describe it as "noise," "hearing," or "sound"? The mind is cunning this way; it takes something perfectly simple and overcomplicates it. Please don't blame yourself. It's just the mind doing its mind thing. Keep turning toward inner stillness. And whenever you can, have a sense of humor. If it becomes too exacting, let it go. You can always try again later.

NOTING TIPS:

- Describe sensations: warmth, coolness, hunger, noise, tightness, space, relaxation.
- Name emotions: happy, sad, worried, anxious, content, grateful, angry, excited.
- Organize activities: thinking, planning, remembering, avoiding, desiring.
- Name the thought; return to the breath.

MY LAST SPEAKING engagement before the COVID-19 pandemic forced a lockdown in early 2020 was a magazine event where I spoke on a panel with other professionals. We were talking about mind-body recovery, for athletes specifically. The moderator opened by asking plainly why meditation was important.

There are a zillion answers, but one struck me as most essential that night, not just to athletes but for anyone listening. Meditation is important because your life is important. Meditation is important in direct proportion to how it supports your life, aliveness, humanity, capacity for goodness, and courage to face the moment.

I remember how close together the chairs were in the audience that night. How a line of people formed to ask questions after we spoke. Handshakes. Hugs. Selfies. I signed a book, borrowed a pen. Servers with hors d'oeuvres on silver trays weaved through the room. None of us could have known the radical new territory into which we'd be thrust in a few short weeks. *Because your life is important* was such a presumption that night that it warranted a gentle reminder. It was less obvious. Then, all at once it was the thought that consumed our unfamiliar days. Staying—being—alive was the most important thing.

You can meditate formally by setting aside the time and using the tools discussed here. Or you can informally integrate mindfulness techniques within your daily routine. You can take a deep breath before picking up the phone. You can meditate for two minutes or twenty while waiting in your car for soccer practice to let out. You can pause. You can pause. *You can pause.* It means you're here and you get to choose.

15

Walking

I arrived at the Bridge of the Gods and finished my
1100+ mile hike on the Pacific Crest Trail. The thing I
thought then is the thing I still think about almost every
day: how grateful I am for every single mile: the hard
ones, the easy ones, the beautiful ones, the wretched
ones, the ones that reveal ourselves to ourselves, the
ones that teach us to change. Keep walking.

—CHERYL STRAYED[1]

I just can't sit still. These are the frequent words of would-be meditators, and they're not wrong. It can be exceedingly difficult to sit still,
especially as it's become deeply ingrained in our psyches that our worth
is contingent upon busyness, incessant doing, productivity, and multi-
tasking. Before the coronavirus pandemic became our nation's most

---

1   Cheryl Strayed commemorating the twenty-fifth anniversary of the hike that inspired
her bestselling book *Wild* via social media on September 15, 2020.

menacing public health crisis, the condition of burnout was reaching epidemic proportions and threatening our mental and physical health. One can surmise we've not made many gains on this front in the face of challenges of historic proportions.

While sitting still is one way to practice mindfulness, sometimes the best way to find stillness is through movement. Often you will hear the term *embodiment* used in reference to this type of mindfulness practice, which means the object of our attention becomes the movement of the body—an awareness of the body moving in space—and includes activities such as walking, yoga, running, and other forms of fitness. For all its emphasis on various mind states, meditation and mindfulness can admittedly get a little heady. All this thinking—about thinking! Sometimes the most effective way to allow the thinking mind to settle is by feeling it drop down into the body. This area of practice is relatively new, given that contemplative practices have been practiced, taught, discussed, and debated for thousands of years across many cultures and spiritual traditions. One reason for this fresher, embodied take is that modern life is much more sedentary than any time in history.

My port of entry into meditation was yoga, often referred to as "meditation in motion." The progression from this mindful movement practice to a sitting practice comes naturally for many people, particularly yogis in the West. All those years of all those sun salutations, of holding poses and breathing our way through them, finally make it possible for us to sit still. Ancient yogis devised the plan precisely this way, creating and prescribing poses to prepare the body to sit peacefully in meditation for long periods.

Walking is not only the humble precursor to yoga but also a powerful movement practice that we spend much of our lives doing already. It requires no special skills, equipment, or expensive pants. You can do it with or without shoes. You can break a sweat or not. And once you get the hang of it as a toddler, it's virtually impossible to be bad at it.

On average, we walk about five thousand to seven thousand steps each day, making it an ideal opportunity for anyone to practice on-the-go mindfulness. What's more, walking of all kinds—whether modest transit, form of fitness, creativity boost in lieu of a caffeine break, or spiritual pilgrimage—has scientifically proven health benefits. Just twenty minutes per day of walking has been proven to make people feel happier, improve cognition, and boost immunity. Mentally, it helps us resolve conflicts and sparks creativity.

Mindfulness includes formal and informal practice. Meditation is the formal practice, while cultivating presence in everyday life is our less structured approach. One reinforces the other. Walking meditation is similar, in that it can be done as a formal ritual in a secluded area or as an informal element of your day—as you walk to the post office, perhaps—one step at a time, one breath at a time. In the latter example, you're not walking as slowly and methodically as a monk, absorbed in each foot strike; you're walking like yourself; throughout your day but with fewer distractions and more presence. Both styles of walking, both expressions of mindfulness, use the kinetic experience of the body to shift state of mind.

The Latin phrase *solvitur ambulando* seems to capture this sentiment best. It translates to mean "It is solved by walking."

Walking is so natural that we do it largely without thinking, which is what makes it a perfect vehicle for mindfulness. It's an accessible activity with which we're intimately familiar, *and* because we're so familiar, we often do it on autopilot. This is the crux of informal practice and the core of mindful living, to take anything we do unconsciously and make it conscious. The goal is to stop sleepwalking through life, as it were.

Socrates walked as he taught. Meanwhile, President Thomas Jefferson's diaries read like analog versions of today's wearable fitness trackers: how many steps he took, at what pace, where he went, and his state of mind before and after. Those who walked before us have shaped, for better or worse, every moment in history. Meanwhile, we shape our lives in real time by how we move through the world. How we move forward. When we speak of being less stressed and more mindful, we often visualize new or different things we might do, often separate from the flotsam and jetsam of daily life. Seldom do we consider opportunities when we are in motion, the in transit and in between moments. Folk singer Ani DiFranco said it well: "When I look down I miss all the good stuff. And when I look up, I just trip over things."

Walking gets us where we need to go on a daily basis, but in a grander sense, it has also played a role in movements of social change, from suffragettes marching down Pennsylvania Avenue in Washington, D.C., to civil rights protesters bravely walking across the Edmund Pettus Bridge in Selma, Alabama. More recently, we've witnessed—and perhaps participated in—demonstrations like the Women's March, the March for Our Lives, Climate Action Strikes, or one of many Black Lives Matter marches. The act of walking is utterly plain yet radically powerful. One foot in front of the other demonstrates how progress of any kind begins with a single step. Paying attention and moving forward one step at a time. It sounds ordinary, but it has always been the path to progress. It's also another route to accessing the magic contained within a mindful life.

What to Know about Walking Meditation

The first thing you need to know about walking meditation is that, of course, it counts as "real" meditation! The heart of both is the same, whether sitting on your bum or ambulating on your feet (or in a wheelchair or with the assistance of any other mobility device). However, walking meditation differs from seated practice in a few key ways. Here are some considerations before you take the first step:

- Walking meditation requires a slightly broader field of awareness than seated meditation. For example, you will need to be aware of where you are going, who or what is nearby, and when you need to avoid obstacles in your path. You may need to slow down, speed up, or turn.
- Please keep your eyes open.
- Choose an area to walk that is enclosed or protected from too many other people, traffic (i.e., cars, bikes, runners, or dogs), and general busyness that might cause distractions or endanger safety.
- Walking outside in nature is especially inspiring and healing, but that's not feasible all the time. Walking meditation areas don't need to be particularly big, scenic, or even take place outdoors. Walking in circles in a relatively empty room works equally well. Local sanctuaries you might try include: yoga, dance, fitness, or martial arts studios when classes aren't in session; an unoccupied basketball court at the local Y; school gymnasiums or cafeterias; empty conference rooms at the office or hotels on work travel; or church and community rec rooms, to name a few.
- Consider merging a period of walking meditation with your typical fitness or running routine. Cooldown is the perfect time for this. Your mind and body will be more open to the contemplative pace.
- This one is key: walk for the sake of walking, as opposed to trying to get somewhere. Savor not having an agenda but instead using the physical experience of walking as a sensory anchor. This action allows your mind to rest. Some people relax in meditation by watching the flicker of a candle flame. In walking meditation, your physical experience becomes the primary focus of your attention. This shift can be difficult at first. We are so conditioned to walk to *get* somewhere. I am a classically impatient Bostonian; trust me, I understand.
- Consider your footwear. If the weather and surface permits, go barefoot. If not, it's important to wear shoes that have flexibility and

accentuate your connection to the ground. This may sacrifice fashion. Walking meditation not *werking* meditation, for now.

- Think of each step as containing three parts: heel, midfoot, ball of foot. Feel the transfer of weight as you move. Notice your feet in contact with the earth. The knee rising up as the foot leaves the ground, its time in midair, and the careful placement back to earth. Become curious about the sensations throughout your entire body as you move through space.

Walking Home

My first exposure to walking meditation occurred in environments separate from the hustle and bustle of real life, notably yoga and meditation retreats. There was also the idyllic college campus where I first studied Buddhism, and our professor assigned us to walk through a secluded corner of the quad on a fall day when the sun illuminated each leaf a glowing autumnal hue. Our peers were in Accounting. We knew just how lucky we'd gotten. Later, on countless retreats, whether I was teaching or attending, a group of us would tread silently down powdery beaches at sunrise or through verdant forests overlooking lakes and mountain ranges. For years (decades, actually), I didn't think to use walking meditation in my actual life. Until I had to.

The Mother of Innovation

For five years, I dutifully sat in meditation every day. I rotated between a few favorite spots: the living room floor on a woven rug, a loveseat chosen to fit the specific measurements of my small one-bedroom apartment; a renowned meditation center with a handful of other people at sunrise, each throat clearing in the room or passing car on the street below singularly audible; or my parked car if I was pressed for time. I highly recommend car meditations, by the way, provided you're parked and in a safe, well-lit area with the ignition turned off. My daily practice wasn't a big deal, but it was consistent. Consistency is the entire point. Over time, I grew deeply grateful— and a tad dependent—on the time each day spent in stillness.

Then, I had a baby, and maybe you can guess what happened.

I stopped meditating because carving time for it became absurdly, laughably, *are you kidding me?* difficult, especially in the first few months. Which is ironic because I was sitting still for twelve hours a day breastfeeding, and yet, seated meditation was impossible. Not to mention, there were plenty more things that I needed to do to keep the baby alive while not sitting, more things to do than hours in the day, as any parent can vouch. I bounced her in my arms and pushed her in a stroller. I changed a thousand diapers before noon (slight exaggeration). We went to a new mothers' group together, where all these beautiful babies and their stunned mothers became friends because we were strangers marooned in a foreign land at precisely the same life-altering moment.

I took my infant daughter on long walks all over the city, for hours at a time. We'd depart the house and roam, stowing ourselves in department store dressing rooms or on park benches to nurse. I sang songs that were not quite lullabies because I couldn't remember the words to many lullabies. Sleep was not one of the things I was doing when I wasn't meditating.

Sometimes, after putting her down for a nap or bed in her basinet or crib, I'd attempt to sit on the floor and meditate. Just for a few minutes I'd tell myself. A little goes a long way. *You can do this*, my internal pep talk at 3 a.m. or 3 p.m, or does it matter if you never go to bed anyway? I'd close my eyes, feel my body in space, and notice my breath. A familiar calmness would rise to the surface, but then my body would begin to sway, as though rocked in a boat at sea. My eyes stung and fluttered. I was thirsty. I was hungry. *Why is it a mere footnote that the Buddha had an infant son and wife, whom he left in search of enlightenment?* I would snap awake. *Is this why so few pioneers of the mindfulness movement were women? Is it true that horses sleep standing up? Sleep deprivation is a form of torture.* Some thoughts I had.

The surprise of going from my daily sitting to almost-nothing was that I didn't miss it, *at first.* The situation at hand, also known as life, was so new and all-consuming that there was no space for anything other than stone cold survival. Feeding the baby, putting her down, rummaging for a snack, guzzling a tall glass of water, and going to the bathroom. Sleep in durations greater than twenty minutes was nonexistent. The bright side was that I no longer took showers for granted; they became luxurious holy ablutions. Water meditations. And yet, each of us has our version of life "getting in the way" of our practice. No matter how many times we hear that life *is* practice, it can be hard to recall, especially when we find ourselves in the primal state of survival mode.

"Darling, I'm off to the spa!" I'd call down the hallway to my husband before closing the bathroom door, and I could hear him laughing from the kitchen.

I didn't miss meditation because I knew *this* was the purpose of meditation. If meditation is preparation for the urgency of life, I had never been more unstintingly present than in those first months. This feeling of emotional preparedness is among the most affirming gifts of practice. Reality changes drastically, but we stay grounded.

I was intoxicated by a ferocious new love that recast everything and beholden to an entirely new set of mind-blowingly intricate, tedious, and tender responsibilities. I felt at once righteous and patient but also like I could lift cars or grow fangs and bear them at anything posing a threat. Motherhood is supposed to do this, biologically speaking. I felt lucky for the mindfulness reserve I'd created. I felt it holding me up, nudging me along. I sat watching my daughter for hours, marveling at how she existed solely in the present moment. When she was hungry, there was only hunger. When she was tired, there was only sleep. She was meditation personified. I held her and simultaneously felt held by something bigger. There was no other moment.

Until I no longer felt held but dropped like a carton of eggs on asphalt.

This is what can happen after spending too much time in survival mode. The source of survival mode, of major life events happening, can be any experience of monumental change: welcome change, like a new baby, big move, or new job, or unwelcome and sometimes traumatic events, such as serious illness, death, individual or community violence, natural disasters, or losses of any kind (i.e. relationships, jobs, financial catastrophe, loss of a home or social or spiritual community). Either way, we can exist within great intensity for a period, but chronically high levels of stress and lack of basic self-care eventually become destructive.

I began to miss meditation desperately. I missed it like food or a friend. If meditation is a savings account into which you deposit with daily practice, my account was overdrawn. I had experienced complicating postpartum health issues with lasting immunological effects, as well as the anxiety of financial free fall as one half of a self-employed family unit, with no access to subsidized parental leave or childcare (a grave reality for most new mothers in America and exceedingly worse for BIPOC mothers). I contended with a nagging fear that time away from my job would cause irreparable damage to my career. The details are specific to my experience, but the themes are universal. What mother on earth, what person, has not been walloped by parenthood, illness, or life altogether?

I knew there was something I could do to help ground me, if I could just find the time. Not a wholesale solution or cure but a refuge. An anchor. When the cycles between my daughter's feedings lengthened and I began to sleep again, I started stealing a few minutes of meditation here and there. I grew more comfortable leaving home without the baby, and I meditated in the midst of errands, work, or going to the gym. It was a start. Mini sessions serve an important purpose, like a snack to tide you over till dinner. Eventually, I wanted a meal. And yet, I had no interest in sitting still for a minute longer than absolutely necessary.

A solution presented itself on a Saturday morning in September. Our daughter was about five months old, strapped to my chest in a baby carrier. She was still extremely small and light, and we had to pad the bottom of the carrier with rolled blankets to boost her to the proper height. The air held the anticipatory coolness of not-quite fall as we stepped outside together. I draped a light blanket across the top of the baby's head to shield her from the sun and wind; delicate gray stars dotted the gauzy fabric.

My husband and I walked through our old neighborhood, where we'd been strangers, then not a couple, a couple, then married, and now a family of three. We nodded or waved at neighbors and friends, people who shop at his running store, people who take my yoga classes. On the way home, I held the blanket to the back of our daughter's head with one hand and a cup of tea in the other. Dan carried a takeout breakfast sandwich from a favorite bakery and a coffee. Occasionally, he'd drape an arm around the two of us—Edie and me—a reminder of the cocoon of our still new family. The sandwich in its white paper bag bounced on my shoulder with our stride. We gazed down at our daughter lovingly. We were mesmerized. She was fast asleep.

Next began the age-old parenting conundrum of whether to keep moving and hope she stayed asleep, passing ambulance sirens and blaring car stereos notwithstanding, or continue home and gamble the precarious transition to her crib. Movement or stillness, which one?

We kept walking. Dan was hungry. The egg sandwich was warm, and it prevailed. We noticed a bench in a park set back from the street, just enough so that we'd never bothered to enter before. There was a low, wrought-iron gate providing the illusion of privacy, but it was a public park on a quaint street lined with brownstones and dogwood trees. We detoured. A giant urn stood in the center filled with fuchsia-colored flowers; around it wound a circular walkway resembling a mandala. Dan sat on the sun-dappled bench and peeled the silver foil from his sandwich.

I slowed down. The little stone path transformed into an impromptu labyrinth. I was two streets away from our apartment and in an entirely new realm. My daughter breathed against my chest, emitting soft snores like a sublime baby dragon, and I bathed in the sound. I walked under trees with the sun beaming above and across the patterned shadows of their leaves on the ground below. Each piece of gravel under my shoe released its own sound. I sensed my heart rate drop, drop, *drop*. The minutes ticked by. The sandwich was devoured. The sun shifted. Our shadows lengthened. Everything about it felt like a homecoming.

Words to Walk By

I know I used a mantra that day to get started. I don't know if it was two words or three, if I used it the whole time, or let it drop. It doesn't much matter, only that it worked. As in seated meditation, using a mantra is a great way to further focus your attention while you walk. It's not mandatory but can be a meaningful, grounding option, especially for beginners.

If you consider each footstep as containing three parts comprised of the heel, instep, and ball of foot, then a three-word mantra is a natural fit. With each touch-point of your foot to the ground, you'll silently say the corresponding word of your mantra. For example, take a step onto your right foot, placing the heel down first, and say *Be*. Slowly shift the weight across your foot to the arch, and say *Here*. Finally, push onto the ball of your foot and finish the mantra, *Now*. Repeat on the left foot: *Be* (heel), *Here* (midsole), *Now* (ball). Conclude your walking meditation by standing or sitting in stillness for a few breaths or minutes, letting the benefits of the meditation land. Meditation can feel more accessible after a period of walking. We get the ants out of our pants, I think.

THREE-WORD MANTRAS

- Be here now.
- I am _____ [fill in the blank]. For example: enough, strong, here.
- Walk with _____ [fill in the blank]. For example: grace, peace, love, purpose.
- Let it go.
- Trust my journey.

IN SOME SCHOOLS of meditation, sitting perfectly still is the only way to practice. However, this traditional philosophy might not sync with the circumstances of your life or mental and physical health needs. Throughout the day, it's rare for the mind and body to be in the same place at the same time. You might be sitting at your desk in the morning, but your mind is home in bed. You're in shavasana, but your mind is perusing the fridge for dinner ideas. When we experience mind-body connection—whether the body is still or in motion—it's an opportunity to recognize inner peace. The more we do this, the more intimate that connection becomes. We begin to trust it. We know ourselves on a deeper level. When we practice this kind of presence, pockets of magic open within the mundane. We can do this wherever we are—or wherever we're going.

In formal practice, you walk *slowly*, and it's best to do in an enclosed area. You can say a mantra silently or focus your attention solely on the experience of walking. You can link your steps to your breath, as though they were yoga poses. You might uncover a perfect walking meditation spot near home or create a short-distance personal pilgrimage during your next vacation. Walk in the ocean shallows as the waves wash underfoot or along mountain trails with the scent of pine and spruce in your nostrils, in your lungs, in your hair.

But nobody can walk in such a slow, monastic way all the time. You'd never catch a bus and probably cause several altercations on the sidewalk. There are also exceptional physical, mental, and emotional benefits to picking up the pace, including a dose of stress-busting endorphins.

As much as we love meditation, it's also OK to acknowledge that in some circumstances and for some people, more sitting is less ideal; we are not aiming to become entirely sedentary creatures, after all. Walking is beneficial to mental and physical health, and we already do it. What's more, you probably enjoy it much more than you realize, a revelation that comes when we pay attention to its physical sensations, mechanics, and perspective. Unlike running, which we'll discuss later, walking allows us to enjoy a less pressured pace. It offers our mind the ability to slow down to match the pace of our steps or the body the option to move briskly or leisurely depending on what the mind dictates. *Solvitur ambulando.*

So, let's not overthink it. Just take a walk! If you feel moved by your inner or outer environment to sit and meditate before, during, or after, go for it. If you want to slow down and meditate on foot, you now have the tools to do a proper walking meditation. Whatever helps untangle your thoughts and shift your attention to the present moment is a giant step in the right direction.

When you walk mindfully but not necessarily as meditation, consider the following tips to make the most of your mind-body connection on foot.

- Unplug from your smartphone. Or, at minimum, put it away. Free your hands. Feel them open and lightly swinging at your sides with your step. If you're in nature, touch your surroundings. Touch a giant tree. Trail your fingers through leaves or grass. Imagine nature breathing with you. (She is.)

- If listening to an app, podcast, or music (perhaps conducive to restoration), disable other applications such as social media. Consider a quiet period from texting or calls.
- Notice your posture. Experience a spacious, tall spine allowing for optimal energy and ease.
- Use sensory impressions to anchor yourself: notice the sights, sounds, and smells you encounter.
- Feel your feet touch the ground, the transfer of weight from heel to toe, and honor all the miles over all the years that your feet have carried you.
- Become aware of the temperature without judging it as good or bad.
- Offer compassion to sentient beings as you pass: people, dogs, birds, geese, ducks, rabbits, squirrels, and tiny bugs. Some Buddhist monks use small brooms to sweep a harm-free path as they walk to avoid crushing insects. You may not go to this length, but you can silently send any and all sentient beings your wishes for peace as you encounter each other. Notice how this practice changes your perspective and experience. How does it feel to do this?
- Honor the land on which you walk and the Indigenous people for whom it was home first.

Any type of walking can be a doorway to better concentration, more contentment, and less stress. Our minds enjoy space to wander, our skin absorbs much-needed vitamin D if we're outdoors, and our eyes are spared evermore screen time. We breathe fresh air. We move our body in the most natural way it knows. We move forward. It's a myth that we need to be still as statues to experience stillness.

16

Yoga

Chitta vritti nirodha.
[The purpose of yoga is to still the
fluctuations of the mind.]
—PATANJALI

Segue: an uninterrupted transition.

One way to merge walking and yoga is to do walking meditation on your yoga mat. This is a grounding way to begin a yoga practice, and I do it with my students often. I must credit yoga teacher, Buddhist chaplain, and author Cyndi Lee for the inspiration. Start at the back edge of your mat. Fold your left thumb into your palm and make a fist. Wrap your right palm and fingers around your left fist. Hold this mudra in front of your navel. Walk the length of your mat as slowly as possible, feeling your heel, midfoot, ball of foot, and toes connect with the earth. When you arrive at the top of your mat, begin yoga practice as you normally would.

THINK OF YOGA as an extension of walking. A next step, so to speak. Both use the physical movement of the body as the primary object of our attention. We *move* into stillness. Mindful movement practice has profound benefits for our bodies and minds and can be used as a complement to formal meditation or at times a substitute. What excites me most about teaching yoga and meditation has always been their real-life application. I am most interested in helping people figure out what works within their daily reality.

Yoga class was my first exposure to formal mindfulness practice at the age of sixteen. At the time, it had yet to explode into its current popularity in the United States. I like to joke that I started doing yoga so long ago that we didn't have yoga pants. We had only pants. You could wear them to yoga.

Yoga was more meditative than what you tend to see in studios today. The styles were slower (and there were fewer of them from which to choose), environments quieter (there was no music, for instance), and more integrated with mindful living, if for no other reason than because you had to go out of your way to find opportunities to practice. Dedicated studios were not commonplace until the early 2000s. My first class took place in a renovated fire station turned community hall. Today, just about everyone seems to do yoga or at least knows of a place where other people do yoga. More likely, *many* places. Or no place at all because a wide range of online offerings exist. The early experience was more underground, sometimes literally—two of my yoga communities began in basements, of a church and hair salon, respectively. My fondness for white twinkly lights has little to do with Christmas decor and everything to do with a hair salon basement in Richmond, Virginia, where strands of lights demarcated the space for yoga and plain white sheets were draped into makeshift walls.

The more popular yoga grew, the more physically demanding it became. We turned up the heat, too, both on the thermostat and in yoga's imagery. Classes sped up. We called yoga "meditation in motion," which is demonstrably, viscerally true; however, there was much more emphasis placed on the motion. If you asked yogis to sit still for too long, sometimes even during shavasana at the end of class (the most important and meditative part of asana practice), they would huff and puff and fidget and sometimes check their phones. *Sometimes.* Not never.

There's no denying that our approach to yoga practice has changed, but it's hard to pin down the cause and effect. Did yoga speed up in response to modern life? Or did modern life—the Internet Age, the Digital Revolution—speed up the pace of life so alarmingly fast that yoga had no choice but to keep up? I suspect it's a combination of both. Yoga evolved to match the needs of modern yogis, as has always been the case to some degree. Consider, for example, that women were once not allowed to practice yoga or that classes were once taught exclusively in Sanskrit, yoga's language of origin. Modern life innovated who had access to yoga, how they found classes and teachers, how classes and teachers were marketed, how payment was given and received, and much more. All of which is to say that for thousands of years, yoga changed little. But in the span of a few decades, it radically transformed.

Yoga was not a workout in the beginning. It was laughable then gauche to suggest as much. Then, it became one of the hardest physical workouts humanly possible. Madonna famously threw out her treadmill and pledged to do only yoga to maintain her legendary physique. But, still, we didn't *talk* about these superficial benefits. Fast forward a few short years and yoga became the largest fitness trend the world had ever seen, inspiring offshoots that bore little or no resemblance to the original incarnation. Without yoga's proliferation, you do not have the boutique fitness craze that followed.

It was exciting and it was cringey. It made yoga accessible to millions of people who needed its magic. It raised deep concerns of cultural appropriation. It woke people up, got them out of their heads and into their bodies; it asked that we think about, really consider, causing less harm in the world. Doing more good. Countless gurus caused irreparable harm by manipulating, exploiting, or abusing students in the name of yoga and other spiritually adjacent practices. In short, yoga mimics, reflects, and reinforces life.

More, more, more. Faster, hotter, harder. Look at me. Yoga fixed me. I am getting what I want. This will make everything OK.

Yoga is the state of missing nothing.

That's one of my favorite definitions of yoga, from Brahmananda Saraswati. It captures that feeling at the end of a class, of utter contentment and ease, of not needing to jump up and do the next thing and the next. Of not needing to be anything other than who and how we are in the moment. We're not missing previous versions of our selves or an unlived life of the imagination. Of belonging to each other, which we recognize in the collective hush or hum or heartbeat of everyone resting so still at once. To connect, unite, or join. To yoke together as one. If you've felt it, you know.

Things have changed for yoga. And they will again. And yet, the meaning remains. We do yoga to join together our minds, bodies, and souls. We do it to remember, at once, how small and infinite each of us is.

The key is to understand *how* we are using the yoga. Are we using it to avoid the moment, or inhabit it? Is it helping us to become kinder and more conscious, or is it just another thing to check off our to-do list? Is our kindness genuine or performative? Are we perpetually speeding up and never slowing down? When was the last time we embraced stillness on our mat? Like walking, you can dash around not knowing your feet touch the earth, or you can walk as though praying with your feet. From the outside, it can be hard to tell one from the other, but *you know*.

When we speak of yoga, it's important to recognize that we are not speaking solely of the postures, though that is what we associate with yoga in popular consciousness. It is underpinned by a philosophical structure, a many-limbed tree. Eight limbs, to be precise. The entire tree grows from the soil of mindfulness. One branch represents our postures. The rest of them largely relate to meditation and mindful living. Here's a quick review of each limb. Perhaps take a moment to pause on each one, however briefly, considering what it means to you.

Yamas | Attitude toward the world
    These include: ahimsa (nonviolence, nonharming),
    satya (truthfulness), asteya (non-stealing), brahmacharya
    (abstinence), and aparigraha (greedlessness).
Niyamas | Attitude toward the self
    Namely: saucha (cleanliness), santosha (contentment), tapas
    (discipline), svadhyaya (self-inquiry, self-study), and ishvara
    pranidhana (surrender to god, have faith).
Asana: Practice (i.e. the poses)
Pranayama: Breathwork
Pratyhara: Withdrawal of the senses (i.e. turn inward and
    replenish your senses)
Dharana: Concentration
Dhyana: Meditation
Samadhi: Enlightenment

For the sake of simplicity, let's begin with physical poses to support mindfulness practice. We'll return to the broader philosophical overlaps later. If you don't do yoga already, you have some options. If you'd like to try it, you can use the following poses as a beginner-friendly starting point. If you don't like yoga or have no interest in trying it (no offense taken; I promise), you can skim the rest of this chapter or read along as a tourist of sorts. I recently read an entire article on pigeon racing. I have no interest in racing pigeons, but it was fascinating! Decide what you'd like to do with the information later.

Yoga Poses for Formal Meditation

The following poses are favored for formal meditation practice. The purpose is never to force our bodies to fit the poses. Instead, create a fleet of options that you might use depending on how you feel.

1. SUKHASANA: Also known as easy pose, sometimes confused with lotus or half lotus, this pose is how you sit cross-legged on the floor. Ideally, instead of crossing your ankles, which causes pressure or loss of circulation, try to align one shin in front of the other. Most people benefit from sitting on a cushion, block, or bolster.
2. PADMASANA: Also known as lotus pose, this is an advanced posture not meant to be trifled with. It's very intense for the knees, and even yogis who can perform lotus shouldn't hold it for extended periods of meditation.
3. VIRASANA: Also known as hero's pose. For meditation, it should be done with one or two yoga blocks, a cushion, or folded blankets beneath one's bottom. There are also specialized meditation stools for this. In short, you kneel, while separating your feet and shins enough to place a block or cushion between them on which to sit. If the knees disapprove, please obey them. The spine, as with all meditation poses, should be tall and relaxed. Think of sitting with dignified posture.
4. SHAVASANA: Also known as corpse pose. Lie down flat on your back and extend your legs straight ahead of you; let your arms drop below your heart. You can allow your feet to flop outward and your arms to drift away from your sides. You may choose to support the back of your head with a blanket or pillow or place a rolled blanket

behind your knees. The only stipulation is that if you are here to meditate you don't fall asleep. Remember, the purpose of meditation is to "wake up."

Yoga Poses as Preparation

Yoga poses were invented to prepare the body for meditation. Think of this ancient inspiration before you sit down. Perhaps one of these families of poses might help you sit more comfortably.

- Standing forward folds
- Sun salutations
- Neck and shoulder stretches, including shrugs
- Gentle twists
- Cat and cow poses

Restorative Poses to Heal and Recharge

Say you are mentally and physically exhausted. Your body aches. You don't even have the attention span to attempt meditation. You have been crying all day (or night). You have been on your feet all day (or night). You can't. You *just can't* . . . But maybe you can with the help of one of the following restorative yoga poses. You don't need to force it. These moments of meditation are like medication. Use as directed. Their purpose is healing, stability, and replenishment.

- SUPPORTED FISH POSE ON A BOLSTER: Place a bolster, couch cushion, or rolled blanket behind your midback (think: if you had wings, the area from which your wings would sprout). Recline backward with your head touching the floor or resting on a low pillow or yoga block. Feel the expansion in your heart, chest, lungs, and throat.

- SUPPORTED CHILD'S POSE ON A BOLSTER: Place a bolster, couch cushion, or rolled blanket(s) on the floor and come into child's pose. Your head, chest, and abdomen will rest on the bolster. Spend equal time with your head resting to each side.
- VIPARITA KARANI: Legs-up-the-wall-pose. This one is like a spa treatment without the price tag. Sidle up to a wall. Lie down. Swing your legs up and rest them on the wall. If you like, you can rest your low back on a yoga block or bolster. Do not pass *go*. Do not read anymore. Just do it. Trust me. Your achy back, tired legs, throbbing feet, and frayed nervous system will thank you.

ANY YOGA PRACTICE can be mindfulness practice, as long as you pay attention while you're doing it. What's ideal about the preceding postures is that they do some of the work for you; they gather your attention by virtue of how the body is aligned. They are deliberate; they embody stillness. They are perfect places to start. Whereas they prioritize alignment of the body, the following tips align the mind. They keep yoga's focus on practicing presence, cultivating compassion, and refreshing attention.

Slow Down

The most popular yoga style around the world is vinyasa, which means "to flow with breath." It moves, glides, floats, and hovers. It flows, flows, flows. It's my favorite and can be deeply meditative. The rhythm of it feels at times like dancing. But it can also be yet another way never to slow down, never to be truly anywhere, always to be in transit. It can deepen the grooves in the mind's neurological wiring toward rushing, competing, and "keeping up." Rather than expand, as is the purpose of mindfulness, we might further truncate the pause between stimulus and response. We don't have time to pause or notice because we are chaturanga here, chaturanga there, chaturanga every-where. Turn up the volume. Turn up the heat. Go, go, go. We are so programmed to add stimuli that removing it can be very difficult.

Have you ever been running late to a yoga class? Stuck in traffic or circling for parking. Stymied behind a slow walker. "Hurry up! I GOTTA GET TO YOGA!" a voice shouts in our heads. It's even more stark as a teacher, "GET OUTTA THE WAY; I GOTTA TEACH THE YOGAAAA!" The voice is quite obnoxious. And funny. The key is to catch ourselves in our impatient patterns of condi-tioning, maybe laugh, and then choose more wisely.

Take a breath. Hold the door open to the studio for a fellow yogi. Take your shoes off slowly, place them neatly in the cubby. Hang your coat. Leave your phone. No, seriously, leave your phone. Stay for the whole class. Be in your life while it's happening. The traffic is life, too. The parking. The frustration. The noticing. The remembering, slow-ing down, and waking up.

Make Your Mat a No Phone Zone

Most modern yogis spend an absurd number of hours per day looking at some kind of screen, our attention spans whittling with each scroll, swipe, and click. This data is sure to increase exponentially when it accounts for life in and after the pandemic, as work and school envi-ronments will be altered for the foreseeable future and screen time further rises. Ideally, yoga is a reprieve from these incessant and rival-rous demands on our attention. Though there are a few reasons why yoga practice might add to that digital-time tally. They can be neces-sary and even productive. Like taking an online class, for example.

Occasionally, while taking an in-person class, you may need to keep your phone nearby in case of emergencies. But in my experience, the vast majority of yogis with phones at the ready do it out of habit rather than necessity. I include myself here, by the way. I define necessity as relating directly to the health and safety of you or someone reliant on you.

There are always exceptions to the rule, but generally the rule is that if you're doing yoga to reduce stress and foster mindfulness, having that hot little device peering at you from beside the top corner of your mat the whole time usually does more harm than good. If you're alone, it will almost guarantee you stop saluting the sun in favor of checking social media. Next thing you know, *whoops*, we're shopping for shoes in half pigeon. If you're in a studio setting, your phone also distracts *all* your neighbors, whether they say anything or not, and perhaps whether they realize it or not. It definitely distracts your teacher. It's disrespectful to the teacher and disrespectful to your good intentions, which brought you to yoga in the first place.

But what about music, you ask? That's next.

Skip the Soundtrack (Sometimes)

Originally, yoga classes (like meditation halls) were quiet places. They fell into the same category as libraries and holy temples (libraries qualify as holy temples if you ask me). Can you hear the sacred hush? Yoga environments are much more bustling, chatty, and musical now. Music infuses joy and energy into yoga classes, and it's a key way to summon momentum when you practice alone. But it's also added stimuli, when sometimes we need less.

It has become rarer to find yoga classes without music, but I predict this could change. Give the quiet classes a chance. If you're a teacher, have enough confidence in yourself and your students that you can hold space for silence. Sometimes, music fills an important need, softening noisy surroundings or shifting the mood, but it can often take us out of the moment. Instead of experiencing the yoga, we're thinking about a song we like or don't like, the volume of the music, or a memory associated with the melody. What I mean to say is that music is a "nice to have" but it shouldn't be a "have to have" in yoga. Try it. With a little practice, the extra quiet in your life might become music to your ears.

Set an Intention

Yoga without intention is stretching—a bit of fitness thrown in—which is perfectly fine but doesn't graze the scope of the practice's origins nor all the mind-body benefits it offers. Put another way, yoga without meditation isn't yoga.

Intention setting is an important aspect of both practices, as well as a skill you can use elsewhere in life. It should be noted that intentions are not the same as goals. They may often support our life goals, which are important to have, but their nature is not based upon productivity, execution, or "doing." Rather, intentions articulate a desired way of being. They are more holistic in nature, helping us to fashion how we show up for the world and ourselves. Mallika Chopra, who has written several books on the topics of meditation and intention and founded a website to help people all over the world set powerful intentions, puts it this way: "Intentions represent who we aspire to be and what values we want to embrace in our life. [They] come from the soul, from that quiet place beyond thoughts and emotion."

To set an intention for a yoga practice or formal meditation session, or perhaps to start your day, consider the following questions. If helpful, write down your answers. From your answers, let an intention naturally arise. Try not to scrutinize or edit too much. Just ask yourself the questions and listen for a response from a place of inner stillness and quiet.

1. What is my deepest desire for this meditation/yoga practice/my day?
2. How do I want to feel?
3. What quality do I want to bring forth in my practice/day/life?

Remember Roots

The roots of yoga and mindfulness originated in the same geographic vicinity (i.e., India and Nepal) in overlapping eras thousands of years ago. The former sprung from within Hindu tradition. The latter is rooted in Buddhism. Today, yogis around the world, representing a vast array of spiritual communities and mind-body intentions, use these practices to live fuller, happier, and more awakened lives. No one is expected to become Hindu or Buddhist, though it's important to acknowledge, respect, and honor the traditions that created and are the primary caretakers of these practices. They must make sense in our lives, yes. *And* they must align with basic principles of presence, goodness, compassion, and connection. Furthermore, we must continually question our own intentions, blind spots, and biases, never claim another's inspiration without attribution, and continually investigate how to cause less harm in the world, through our words, actions, and, yes, mindfulness practices.

WHEN I WALKED into my first class at sixteen, yoga was not cool or popular, two qualities that tend to guide a young person's life and extracurricular choices. I admired an older friend who did yoga, which factored into my decision to give it a try; but it wasn't why I kept going back. I stayed because something happened to me just a few minutes into that first class.

I heard a voice. I heard the voice when the teacher, a deeply wise woman named Carol Dubin, looked at me. "This kid needs to be here," the voice said. But it wasn't Carol's voice. It came from within me.

Each of us contains this clairaudience. *We contain multitudes*, as Walt Whitman wrote in *Leaves of Grass*. We contain obnoxious, judgmental, doubtful, and foreboding voices, but we also contain deeply wise, kind, and loving ones. We contain the voice of the Buddha and the ancient gurus, our first yoga teacher or favorite grade-school teacher, our closest and most trusted friend or spiritual elder whom we've never met, only read about. We contain pep talks and poetry, soothing support and steely resolve. Sometimes we need to bring forth these voices. We must sit quietly long enough for them to come through, as though tuning into a radio frequency.

Remember, many of us arrive on a yoga mat or meditation cushion because something is out of balance. The competing, scared, or anxious voices have grown too loud. They are exhausting, indecisive, or mercurial. Truly, there should be a noise ordinance for the interior racket to which they subject us all day. So, we sit still or move deliberately through some poses. We breathe. Quiet spaces unfold and gentler voices emerge. *This person needs to be here.*

Yoga classes all close the same way, regardless of their style, pace, or origins. Always, they end in meditation. First, reclining in shavasana. Then, seated upright. *Shavasana* translates to mean "corpse pose," which can feel a bit macabre initially. We lie unmoving, as though dead. Until you realize how freeing it is to let go of everything that is not this, specific, living, breathing moment. How else can we handle the loss that life contains if we don't listen to the loving voices around and within us?

17

Running

Go to the limits of your longing.... Let everything happen to you: beauty and terror. Just keep going.

—RAINER MARIA RILKE

An excited student once told me, "Your yoga class is really helping my running!" She continued, "but not the other way around." We both laughed. As a runner myself, I knew what she meant. Yoga bestowed her with fluidity, mobility, and a sense of ease in her body. She could stop, pop down to tie her shoelace, bounce back up again, and be on her merry way. Additional physical benefits of yoga for runners include greater flexibility, fewer injuries, and shorter recovery time. Meanwhile, any amount of running leaves many of us feeling like the Tin Man after rusting solid in the rain. "Oil can!" we plead-squeak from the corner of our oxidized mouths. This can make sitting cross-legged on a cushion a little challenging. As runners who meditate, it's important to be diligent in our approach to finding ease in the body to promote peacefulness in the mind. The good news, of course, is that running is known to cultivate diligence and discipline, and many runners possess these qualities in spades. What's more, meditators who run make the mind an ally, letting our legs, as opposed to our thoughts, race while our minds enjoy some much needed rest.

The truth is, meditation and running make a great pair (as long as we remember to throw in some yoga stretches to make sitting easier), and they have a great deal in common. In this chapter, we'll focus on physical expressions of mindfulness, especially running and other forms of fitness. If you're not a runner or fitness enthusiast, you can think of these practices as relevant to any movement done mindfully.

The mind is similar to the body; it, too, gets rusty, dusty, and cramped sometimes. Stiff and unbending. And naturally, the two are inextricably linked. What we do with the body affects the mind; what we do with the mind affects the body. The mind is the container for all our experiences, but instead of taking deliberate care of it, we sometimes forget and leave it out in the rain, so to speak. Mindfulness opens and aerates the container. Running lends itself to mindfulness practice for the same reason anything does; you have to do it with attention and intention. And yet, there's something particularly special and synergistic about the meditative terrain that running provides, how we fall into a flow on a long run, glimpse that peak athletic experience of "being in the zone," or perceive within ourselves a quieter, more spacious interiority on the days we run. Runners learn in a practical and profound way that you can only run the mile you're in. This is no small thing. In fact, it's just about everything.

The body is nourished by movement while the mind is nourished in stillness. And vice versa, of course. For many people, a certain amount of physical exertion is required to become still. Put another way, when the body is relaxed, it's a better friend to the mind. It's one less distraction. Again, this was the original intention of yoga's asana practice—to move, bend, and prepare the body in deliberate ways so that it could become steady and centered in meditation. Part of mindful living involves creating the favorable conditions you need before sitting down to meditate.

Too often the myth goes that meditation, commonly referred to as "sitting," is diametrically opposed to movement, running, or fitness. From the most basic, literal standpoint, I suppose that's true. But you will also find plenty of people who describe running *as* their meditation. What they mean is that running provides ideal space for mental solace, solitude, and silence. Thoughts are clearer. Problems can seem to solve themselves. Bright ideas burst into existence, carried perhaps on a cresting wave of endorphins. In my extensive work with runners, I've often said that marathoners intuitively know how to meditate. One cannot run a marathon if our legs are at mile 5 and the mind is at mile 20. You must run one mile at a time until you reach 26.2. So, are running and sitting alike or different? They share more common ground than you would think, but they're not substitutes for each other. Being a runner is healthy physical preparation for the demands of meditation, but only mind training (i.e., meditation) prepares us to meditate. For example, God help anyone who shows up to the starting line of a race without logging the necessary miles but instead having done plenty of seated meditation. The best approach is to use one to enhance the other. Most important, they both enrich how we engage with the moment we're in, also known as life.

Just Begin

In running, the hardest part is getting out the door. In meditation, it's sitting down and becoming still. Even when the time has been set aside, our sneakers are on or we've dragged our cushion or folded blanket on which to sit to its position, we dawdle. A snack, another bathroom break, a scroll through the latest social media circus on our phones, let me just redo my ponytail, change my shirt, charge my GPS watch, check the weather one more time. . . I don't know about you, but I can do this all day.

Running and meditation can be demanding and lonely. This, too, is part of the training. When we train—the body in running, the mind in meditation—we build endurance, forbearance, and resilience, as well as self-compassion and the ability to keep ourselves company. Getting out the door or sitting down with a willingness to look inward are familiar, reoccurring, sometimes tedious battles, but we do it. We value how we feel afterward. We sacrifice instant gratification in favor of long-term discipline and sanity. Running, with its more direct, endorphin-rushed state. Meditation, offering a gradual but cumulative effect; we may not notice a dramatic shift after a single session, but our relationship to the mind changes, which in turn can change, improve even, just about everything else. Both journeys are powerful, generative, and often joyful. But nothing can happen or change unless we begin.

Warm Up

What can you do to set yourself up for a productive session? In running, you'd dress for the weather, maybe create a motivational playlist, and make sure you're well fueled and hydrated. In meditation, you choose your space and posture, remove distractions, and set an intention. Either way, it helps to warm up and start slow. Warming up to meditate might be as simple as taking three or four deep breaths to begin, or you might do a more involved breathing exercise, like one of those in Chapter 12. Allow the initial awkwardness of getting started. Be gentle and supportive with yourself. Remember, "It's a meditation not a sprint." Something like that . . .

Build Momentum, but Don't Judge It

Some days you dash out the door with pistons for legs and feet so light you could swear they've been infused with espresso. Other days, your body feels leaden, head foggy, mood *blah*, and the environment emits only resistance. It's pouring rain, whipping wind, or oppressively hot. Most of the time, it's somewhere in between. The first minutes or miles have a life and quality all their own no matter how experienced the athlete. The sensory experiences of the body deliver all kinds of information, suggesting how this run may go. The information is helpful, but outside of sharp physical pain or discomfort, the resistance is overwhelmingly colored by thoughts, which are not permanent and change like the weather. How often has the first mile been narrated by *I hate this, I want to stop, good lord, I think I'm dying. Why do I do this to myself?* As runners, we learn to listen to our bodies, discern important information, but ultimately stay the course. Thus with meditation, sometimes it takes a little while to find your "legs," but it's important to keep going.

The mind is wily in the first few minutes of meditation, too, but as with all minutes of meditation practice, we are cultivating the essential skill of nonreactivity and starting over. Of course, you want to jump up after three minutes and go make a sandwich, do a load of laundry, or pull out your hair one strand at a time. If you're not accustomed to this feeling, you might heed it or think you're doing something wrong, as we've said before. You are not. The mind just needs to settle. The mind is unaccustomed to releasing its conditioning, all the things it thinks it *has* to do, all the incessant judgments it makes allowing for so little space, quiet, and choice. Give it some time. Explore patience. Test your compassion muscles. Maybe you need to adjust your pace or refresh your posture with a few deep breaths. Runners stop and walk for a bit or linger at a stoplight for extra recovery, perhaps you have a meditation session equivalent. Then, we begin again. Do this as many times as you need. You are getting stronger, often without realizing it.

Train for the Terrain

Elite runners go to great lengths to simulate the conditions of racing. Distance runners travel to courses to familiarize themselves with each section, turn, and hill. Many train at elevation to get the most out of their lungs. They track sleep patterns so that they will be well rested on race day. They eat the same thing for breakfast before competition no matter what. They wear the same shoes and socks. Contrary to superstitious sports lore, the socks are usually clean.

Every single one of us, runner or not, meditator or not, lives inside our own mind 24/7. Try as we might to escape, we will always be right where we left ourselves. And yet, most of us overlook how helpful it is to train for this terrain, how to navigate our own minds. In this way, regularly meditating is like studying the course map. Do we know where we're going? Are we acquainted with the downhills, weather patterns, and crowds? When we sit with our minds, we learn its habits, tendencies, and conditioning. Some thoughts, emotions, or feelings test us more than others. Very few are new. None of this means the journey won't be hard; it means we are better able to trust ourselves when it is.

The Voice in Your Head Should Be in Your Corner

You'll recall the process of becoming aware of the voice in our heads from earlier chapters. The many voices. We learn they are not actually "us." Through practice and careful attention, along with a generous dose of kindness, we observe the voices piping down a bit. Sometimes, it helps to replace them with healthier, gentler, and more supportive voices—the voice of a loving parent, coach, spiritual teacher, or wise elder, for example. Through conscious practice we also increase the likelihood that those voices will be available at other times, perhaps when we need them most.

Some towns are known for their famous chocolate factory or U.F.O. sightings or giant pumpkins that win the state fair each year. My hometown is famous for running, specifically a road race that snakes along an ocean road for 7.2 miles. The number 7.2 is not an official distance in competitive running; it was the distance between two beloved bars in the 1970s. A bunch of runners who liked drinking beers together thought it would be fun to run from one watering hole to the other. The race began on my birthday. Not the year but the day. (I lag a few years behind.) Needless to say, my affinity for running lore started early.

The story of Billy Mills's gold medal at the 1964 Tokyo Olympics is one of the greatest upsets in all of sports history. A moment of victory so improbable and magnificent that after he crossed the finish line, even Mills couldn't believe it. As a race official held up a single finger to indicate first place, Billy, utterly gobsmacked, thought maybe he missed a lap. "Do I have one more lap to go?" he asked. "First place, gold medal!" the official pointed at his singlet and said. He remains the only American distance runner to win Olympic gold at the 10,000-meter race.

Years earlier, before Billy mounted the winner's podium as the anthem played and cameras flashed, he stepped onto a chair in a hotel room wishing to end his life. Orphaned by the age of twelve and frequently discriminated against for being Native American, his heart—and to hear him tell it, his wings—were broken. While posing for a photo as a first team All-American, the photographer once asked him to step out of the frame. Half Lakota Tribe Native American and half white, Billy was accustomed to being told that he didn't belong. He came to believe it.

Before stepping off the chair, though, Billy heard a voice. More like an energy or a flutter overtaking him inside. Mills recognized the voice to be his father's.

Don't, it said.

Don't.

Don't.

Don't.

Four times. What followed was the memory of advice his father had shared when he was alive, after Billy's mother died. Billy was only nine then. "I'm going to share something with you and if you follow it, someday, someday, you may have wings of an eagle," his father told him. Billy recounts this story often, in interviews and speeches. I had the honor of meeting Billy and hearing him tell the story in person in 2016, days before the Boston Marathon. "He told me to look beyond the hurt, the hate, the jealousy, self-pity," Billy recounted of his late father's words. "All of those emotions will destroy you," he went on. "Look deeper where the dreams lie. You've got to find a dream, son. It's the pursuit of dreams that will heal broken souls."

This memory, this voice, was enough to convince Billy to step down from the chair and away from the precipice of self-destruction. In that moment, he wrote down a dream: Olympic gold medal, 10,000 meters. It was the start of his spiritual journey.

Sometimes, our thoughts cannot be trusted. Discerning this wisdom is life-changing. In Billy's case, it was life-saving. When we practice consciously inviting kind and wise influences into our thoughts, especially in times of challenge, we wire our minds away from painful patterning and harsh habituated responses, and instead invoke qualities like love, acceptance, bravery, healing, and compassion. To keep these voices close means they can arise when we need them. What's more, as we practice the skill of noticing the voices in our minds and bringing forth those with our highest good in mind, our own voice shifts. Our authentic self, the deep "us" beneath all the superficial layers usually used to describe a person, becomes gentler, kinder, and wiser, too. We no longer need to bring the voice in from the outside. It exists from within. It wants only what is best for us. It may keep us safe or inspire us toward bold action. It is exceedingly patient and firmly in our corner. This voice always roots for us.

"Look at Mills! Look at Mills!" the broadcaster screams as Billy makes his move in the final lap of the historic race. The journalistic remove is gone from the announcer's voice. The audio online is gravelly, accompanied by grainy footage. But you imagine Dick Bank, who died in 2020, on his feet jumping wildly, giving way to the raw emotion and stunned magic of the moment. The joy of it. He would later be fired for his "unprofessionalism," and it's hard to believe racism was not a major factor. Against all odds, Billy—also known as Tamakoce Te'Hila, member of the Oglala Lakota tribe—had bested everyone in the world. He won. On wings of an eagle, he soared, just like his dad said.

Something Is Better than Nothing

Consistency and practice are the keys to success for just about anything. You can also think of this as the something is better than nothing principle. Too often, we can't carve out our preferred amount of time needed for meditation, so we avoid it altogether. Running can also be this way. Many healthy habits we hope to create can suffer similar all-or-nothing fates. The problem is that we need something and too often end up with nothing. Eventually, we learn to salvage a short run. We feel better. Or we take a five-minute breathwork break in lieu of a full meditation session. These small victories work wonders. There are times in life when we aim to go the distance, build endurance, or be all in, but there are also plenty of times when a little goes a long way. The key is not to quit on yourself.

Body Scan

Anyone who has a body can benefit from doing a body scan meditation. You don't have to be a runner. You don't have to go to the gym. You don't have to be a yogi who enjoys twisting herself in all manner of curious and delightful knots. You just have to lie down (or you can sit) and rest your awareness on various parts of your body. Imagine breathing into and exhaling from that part of your body. Note the sensations you experience without judgment. You can even thank your body for all that it does. Here is a basic structure for how to guide yourself through a body scan. There are many guided versions available elsewhere, but the gist is the same.

1. Begin by bringing your awareness into your body. A phrase I often use is to feel your mind "dropping down" into the body, as opposed to racing around in the ether. Spend a few breaths feeling your breath in your body. Be sure your spine is straight and spacious.
2. Start with your feet. Feel any sensations in your feet: tightness, tingling, tension, ease. If you're lying down, let them flop outward a bit. Imagine you are breathing out the soles of your feet. Relax your ankle joints.
3. Next, let your awareness travel very slowly up your legs, landing on each section one by one: calves, shins, knees, and thighs. Notice the parts of your body in contact with the floor, your chair, or your mattress and blankets. Think of all the ways your legs support you. Perhaps thank them. Allow your knees to relax; breathe from your kneecaps. Feel the weight of your thighs, containing some of the largest muscles and longest bones in the body.
4. Bring your attention to your hips, buttocks, and pelvis. If there is any tension in these areas, encourage them to soften. Can you invite length and space into your hip flexors?
5. Breathe deeply into your lower back and belly. Notice your belly

rising and falling. Feel the breath rising into your lungs and chest. Invite ease into your heart, the back and front. Let your shoulders melt.

6. Arms, wrists, hands, and fingers—unfurl them. Soften. Open. Relax. Relinquish. Practice letting go with your hands but also your heart.

7. Allow your neck and throat to be long and neutral. Things said and unsaid dissolve. Feel your neck as a clear channel connecting your heart and your head.

8. Relax your jaw, sinuses, eyes, and third eye. Your brow is smooth and open. Maybe there is the gentlest smile on your lips or in the corners of your eyes.

9. Breathe out the crown of your head.

Relaxation Is Power

The following is not a running story, but it contains a surprising mindfulness lesson that I learned in the realm of fitness, a boxing ring, specifically. Sometimes meditation gets a bad rap for being passive or weak. And yet, for those of us who practice regularly, we quickly learn that everything about mindfulness is quite the opposite: how hard it can be, how much courage it takes, how brave one must be to face the moment, no matter what shows up. I'd like to tell you about the time I got into the ring with George Foreman III. Yes, undefeated professional boxer George Foreman III, son of one of the greatest boxers of all time, world heavyweight champion George Foreman, and namesake of the most famous kitchen appliance in history.

What was I doing in a boxing ring with George Foreman III? Learning. Learning new activities changes our brains, promoting neuroplasticity. Not to mention learning anything new requires deep concentration. Moving my body has always helped calm my mind.

Yoga and running have been my preferred forms of fitness for most of my life. Before that, I was obsessed with ballet, swam competitively, and played field hockey all the way into college. But I was in a workout rut in early 2016. My yoga felt lackluster. My running was ho-hum. The presidential election was stressing me out, and I needed a physical outlet. OK, I wanted to punch things.

I didn't punch George, and he didn't punch me either. He trained me, holding up padded mitts, calling out punch combinations, and teaching me how to fight. From my first lesson, I was hooked. A gloved fist makes such a satisfying *thwack* against the mitt. The new movement patterns—thinking patterns—required total focus. In the one-hour lesson, I never looked up. And maybe after so much time in tidy, bright yoga studios, it was refreshing to be in a dark boxing gym with graffiti on the walls and hip-hop blaring through the speakers.

Thwack!

1 . . . 1 . . . 1 . . . 1–2. 1–2, 1–2–3–4. 2–3–2, slip-slip-duck! 1 . . . 1–2 . . .

Thwack, thwack, THWACK!

Maybe I took the catharsis too far. My form grew tense, my shoulders climbing toward my ears and punches extending from my shoulder joints rather than my core and hips.

"Relax," George said.

"Relax your shoulders."

It was a technical cue but felt psychological, too. I took a breath to reset, returning to my basic stance. I rolled my shoulders down my back, just as I would in yoga class. I angled my body slightly, my left foot in front. The point is to conceal as much of your torso from your opponent as possible. I raised my gloved hands to protect either side of my face. The cushy gloves grazed my cheekbones, and it soon became reflexive to bring them back to this position as fast as possible after throwing a punch. The goal is readiness, yes, but also efficiency. I was wasting energy by being too fired up.

"Relaxation is power," George added.

It was so simple. A practical instruction. But it rang in my mind like a meditation gong. I still laugh at the irony of a boxer teaching the yogi how to relax.

STRENGTH RESIDES IN the present. Likewise: relaxation, peace, and, in sports and other physical feats, peak performance. In formal meditation, we train our minds to relax into the moment no matter what arises. In this safe and practical setting, we develop a willingness to get in the ring or toe the starting line and courageously and compassionately face the moment. This technique of resting in awareness and observing what is going on, without judgment, trains our minds to be in the moment and *not* run. We learn not to exist so frequently in *fight, flight, or freeze*. In life, though, running and other forms of movement don't necessarily take us away from the moment. With intention and attention, they might be vehicles for inhabiting it more fully. We appear on the move when in the ring, dancing in the living room, jumping rope in the driveway, or out for a run. We may be kinetically fierce, but inwardly, we embody relaxation and stillness.

18

Nature

In nature, nothing is perfect and
everything is perfect.

—ALICE WALKER

How is your breath? Where is it in your body? If you haven't checked in lately, let's take a moment.

Ah, that's better.

No matter where we are, we owe our breath to the natural environment, specifically the ocean. 71 percent of the earth is covered in ocean, and it contributes more than 50 percent of the oxygen we breathe. Put another way, that's every other breath you take.

Communing with nature is excellent mindfulness practice. Perhaps second only to breathing, being present in the natural world offers the most intimate and innate connection to who we are at our core. You can sit and become still on a pristine beach or practice walking meditation in freshly fallen snow or unroll a yoga mat in your backyard under a blue sky. You just need to go outside and be present in the moment. Even city dwellers, which the majority of us now are, maintain deep, biological, emotional, and evolutionary bonds with nature. Michael McCarthy, an environmental journalist and author of the book *The Moth Snowstorm: Nature and Joy*, explains it this way:

> For we forget our origins; in our towns and cities, staring at our screens, we need constant reminding that we have been operators of computers for a single generation and workers in neon-lit offices for three or four, but we were farmers for five hundred generations, and before that hunter-gatherers for perhaps fifty thousand or more, living with the natural world as part of it as we evolved, and the legacy cannot be done away with.

The ocean and trees provide the air we breathe, meanwhile natural experiences of all kinds can take our breath away. However seemingly ordinary or rare and majestic our exposures to nature may be, each bestows myriad mind-body benefits. One notable study showed that hospital patients who had a view of green space healed more quickly than those who didn't have the benefit of such a perspective. They didn't even have to go outside; the sight alone lessened the severity of their symptoms and expedited recovery. Observing the natural world invites us to slow down. It takes us out of the artificial stream of being caught in the past or worrying about the future and, instead, roots us in the present. "Nature does not hurry yet everything is accomplished," wrote the ancient Chinese philosopher Lao Tzu.

This chapter derives its mindfulness inspiration from Mother Nature, from humble houseplants to the great outdoors, from meditating in nature to honoring her elements no matter where you are. It goes without saying that to be a mindful resident of planet Earth, we must protect it. Thoughtful action, including climate action, is not contradictory to stillness; it is the essential and urgent by-product. It's also important to note not only how interconnected we all are, how entwined our fates are to the planet's, but also how inextricable the links between environmental justice and other forms of justice, namely racial and economic justice as well as gender equity. To be mindful means we do not close our eyes to hard realities. We see clearly and act with courage and compassion to change things for the better.

THE APEX EXPERIENCE of my life in sixth grade was a field trip to the Cape Cod National Seashore: forty miles of protected beaches, teeming marshes, and lively ponds filled with tiny hermit crabs and hulking sea lions and birds so lovely they drop your jaw. The whole grade went, our lives that year measured in relation to the overnight trip. There was life before the National Seashore, and after.

We, boys and girls together, would stay in hostel accommodations, while learning about sea life, climate change, and more. We would stay in separate cabins, of course, but we would be in the same vicinity well after school hours. Can you imagine? We would eat dinner together, actual dinner. There might be a joint session of tooth brushing. Rumors circulated of popcorn and entertainment. Not a movie—there were no TVs—but something. Something!

The rumors were true. There was popcorn and a production of Dr. Suess's environmentally minded *The Lorax* performed by the camp staff. So, it was off-Broadway, but excellent.

The defining moment of the trip was going to the beach at night. The cold sand sifted through our sneakers as we walked closer than usual. Rather than a straggling, ambling amoeba of adolescents teasing and jostling each other, we bound together like a school of silvery fish. We were still kids walking toward the raging ocean after dark, whether we wanted to admit it or not. Development near the National Seashore is strictly regulated, so there is little light pollution or artificial noise. When we arrived at the ocean's edge, our teachers instructed us to crouch down and trail our hands through the icy water, swishing them back and forth several times. It was like the technique one uses to brush crumbs off the couch. Withheld from us for the briefest moment was why we were doing this. What would happen?

Thousands of glowing specks illuminated from our fingertips like magic. Embers but in water, not hot or dangerous like fireworks but brilliant all the same. Instead of shooting skyward, they appeared in the ocean, before our eyes. Shrieks of delight bounced between the dunes in the open fall air. We had witnessed bioluminescent phytoplankton for the first time.

I will be twelve years old forever in this moment. The joy is so visceral that it feels possible that the adult me was somehow there, recording the experience for my future self: this spectacular and singular moment of being dazzled and dumbstruck by nature. The middle school years are often characterized by the race to be a teenager, to get braces, to go to awkward school dances, to drive a car someday. But, in this instant, I couldn't have imagined being anywhere other than where I was. I believe this is what Buddhists mean when they say we are awareness itself, how the self is not fixed or tethered to temporary or superficial characteristics. Every cell in our bodies turns over multiple times between childhood and adulthood and again multiple times throughout life. Awareness remains. Without attending to our awareness, life happens to us with the volatility of crashing waves. With attention—the waves don't cease, and they can still be vicious—we recognize that we are much more than the surface water. We have calmer, deeper, quieter depths. We are not the waves but the whole ocean. Or, as Thich Nhat Hanh says, "Enlightenment is when a wave realizes it is the ocean."

Bird's-Eye View

Cultivating a bird's-eye view perspective is not just a form of expression; it's a key meditation technique, also referred to as the witness perspective. The guiding principle is to witness the moment as though from the outside looking in. You see yourself in the moment as though perched in the eaves like a wise old owl peering down. Undoubtedly, you have experienced this state. This sensation often occurs in times characterized by intense emotions, whether positive or negative. Either way, something about the moment signals that it's time to pay close, careful, uninterrupted attention, and you do.

Writers, musicians, and artists rely heavily on this perspective and try to cultivate it intentionally. It's a conscious "click" as the mind begins to process a moment about which it might write or make art later. Details become finer, the point of view sharpens, and words in a sentence or notes in a song emerge with ease. The song or poem "wrote itself," an artist might say. Michelangelo famously admitted that he didn't so much sculpt a statue as free it from the stone.

A spacious perspective in meditation helps refine our attention. It sounds slightly counterintuitive, that to gain closer attention, it helps to zoom out. Think about what it's like to be immersed in the tedium of your day, on autopilot, zoomed in tight to every gaffe and glitch and little thing. We might feel stressed, bored, reactive, or overwhelmed. We lose perspective, as it were. Meanwhile, the view from higher ground shows us what we miss. It offers more space and time for us to choose how we want to respond. This heightened attention benefits everything we do, from the quality of our work and relationships, to opening the channel for creative inspiration to lessening risk factors of prolonged stress. Sometimes it occurs naturally. Like anything else, this mind state improves with practice.

To cultivate your internal bird's-eye view (also known as zooming out), begin with a few minutes of meditation, sitting tall and breathing deeply. Let your attention rest on the spot within your body where the breath is most prominent. Perhaps it's your belly, chest, or tip of your nose. Zoom in to see and feel that sensation as closely as you can. Rather than judge, evaluate, or manipulate, simply watch. Think of placing your attention on this spot as a piping plover touches down on the sand, its small feet barely leaving a trace.

Then, zoom out a bit so that the field of your attention includes the rest of your body. Observe the outline of your body in space as a silhouette. Notice what is happening within its perimeter: your breath moving through your body, the posture of your spine; your bones and muscles in contact with the chair, cushion, or floor; the feeling of your clothing touching your skin; any tingling, tightness, warmth, or coolness moving through your body. Your heart beats. Your blood circulates. Physical tension arises and dissipates. Next, as though a movie camera zooming out, see yourself in the room or natural environment in which you are seated. Experience the sounds around you, presence of other people or objects nearby, and boundaries of the space. Do this without getting too caught up in any one particular sound, surrounding, or boundary. Now, zoom out farther, to include not just the room you are in but the whole house or building that contains it. Keep seeing yourself within the meditation and continue zooming out. In your mind, visualize the rest of the neighborhood you're in, and then the town or city, state or region, country, continent, and, finally, the entire planet. See it from above like an epic National Geographic documentary. Notice the feelings in your body as you do this. Has whatever gripped you before meditation loosened a bit? Is there more space? Instead of quibbling with things up close, can you step back and experience a fresh point of view?

Honor the Elements

The system of Ayurveda, a holistic practice of health care originating in India before modern medicine and alongside yoga, is based upon the idea that we are each comprised of all five elements, namely: earth, water, fire, air, and ether (or space). Commonly said, we are made from the earth and eventually return to the earth. Biologically speaking, 60 percent of our bodies are comprised of water. Anatomically, in our nasal cavities, lungs, and between each vertebra of our spines, we contain space (to name a few). In these real and palpable ways, we not only connect with nature or find solace when we inhabit it. We *are* it.

To align with our own nature and connect to the slower, selfless pace of the natural world, we might meditate with the concept of the elements. This exercise is inspired by Ayurvedic and yoga practices. It's especially powerful when done outdoors, but you can do it anywhere. Similar to a body scan, you will let your awareness rest on various parts of your body, as they relate to the earth's elements.

Begin by sitting quietly for a few breaths or minutes.

- Earth

First, notice what is most solid within your body, particularly your bones, all 206 of them. Feel your sitting bones connected to the chair, cushion, or floor; your shinbones touching the ground; the entire length of your spine, from tailbone to the base of your skull to the crown of your head; the bones in your hands as they rest in your lap. Try not to create a story about what you observe. Just scan your body for the ways in which you feel grounded to the earth.

- Air

Second, notice your breath. Locate your breath in the most predominant spot within your body. You have practiced this key skill before. Next, bring your awareness to the precise quality of the air within your body. Does it have a shape or texture? The more you do this, the more intimately you will know your breath and what it can teach you in the moment. Sometimes, the breath is sharp, hard, or firm. Other times, it's buoyant or diffuse. It can be soft or nebulous. What about its pace? Is it fast, slow, level, or varied? And temperature—is it warm or cool? Feel your breath deepen; imagine oxygen reaching each of your trillions of cells. Become aware, too, of the air *around* your body. If you're outdoors, feel the quality and temperature of the breeze. As within, so without; the proverb goes. Feel the texture and pressure of the air on your skin. Can you breathe with the environment, as Mother Nature breathes? Can you experience the environment breathing you? Are you aware of the beauty and irreplaceability of this most essential part of your existence: air?

• Fire

The heat in your body, especially your body temperature and metabolism, represents the element of fire. Observe your body's heat or coolness. Most of us tend to run hot or cold. If you are outdoors, observe the climate's direct influence on your body. Our body temperatures naturally drop when we meditate—do you need a light blanket or meditation shawl? Can you feel your digestive fires, as they're known in Ayurveda, your belly growling or satiated by the last thing you ate or drank? Are you energetic and alert or sluggish and tired? Are you hungry? (An inordinate amount of the mind's meanderings in meditation are spent meal planning, by the way.) Bring awareness to these sensations without judging them or getting lost in thought (or recipe ideas).

• Water

Our bodies are mostly water. Meanwhile, bodies of water (i.e., oceans, lakes, and rivers) make ideal points of focus for meditation. See your mind as a still lake. Feel the wavelike quality of emotions passing through your awareness, arising, accumulating energy, cresting, and dispersing. Physically, notice how blood flows through your body. Can you feel warmth, pulsing, or tingling beneath the skin's surface? How miraculous that we were born with a mere pint of blood but by adulthood contain several quarts. The careful quantity and balance of it is crucial to our health and survival. Feel your heartbeat, as the body's reliable engine pumps blood through our bodies, circulating it through our organs. Blood, sweat, tears—all water.

- Space/Ether

   We meditate because we need space. We crave it somewhere in our interior or exterior lives, whether we can articulate as much at any one point in the mindfulness journey. This spaciousness of mind (heart, too) is the barest benefit of practice. "You may not control all the events that happen to you, but you can choose not to be reduced by them," Maya Angelou wrote. Moreover, if we want to bring forth specific qualities or gifts of the practice, say, peacefulness, generosity, courage, or clarity, we must make space for them.

   Whether the stimulus is the actions of another person, a foreboding thought, strong emotion, distracting sound, or intense sensation, we can choose our response. With practice, we train our minds toward insightful and productive responses. Of course, this skill building does not happen within the heat of the moment. We don't *learn* how to create space when the stimulus is already upon us. We don't learn the protocol to put out a fire when something is ablaze on the kitchen counter. We must learn these skills in advance.

   To encourage mental, physical, and emotional openness, notice the physical space within your body: between your fingers and toes, between your ears and shoulders, inside your forehead (the home of your third eye); in the hollows of your nostrils, the expanse of your thoracic cavity, and between the vertebra of your spine as you sit upright. If you are outdoors, you may feel a broader, bigger sense of space as the ground stretches out around you or the sky opens overhead. Take a moment to look around. See yourself in space, as well as an expression of it.

Take Care of Your Animal

While we are here, when was the last time you drank a tall class of cool water?

Even small durations of meditation and other types of daily mindfulness practice can have a profound and positive impact on your life and well-being. And yet, none of it supersedes the importance of taking good basic care of ourselves. If I am honest, I don't love the term *self-care*. The concept is vitally important, and on balance, the words themselves are fine. However, too often it seems like coded marketing language used to sell products and services or convince people, women in particular, that we are falling short in yet another vague and systemic way.

Being equally paid to our male counterparts, for example, would alleviate more stress than, say, a facial. It's not that these examples are mutually exclusive, only that self-care can start to feel either like luxury or yet another obligation.

Before the runaway behemoth bestseller *Eat, Pray, Love*, Elizabeth Gilbert spent a lot of time deriving inspiration from nature. She wrote about fishermen and cowboys. She slept under the stars, swam in freezing rivers, and honed the ancient oeuvre of storytelling by a fire. Nature is not so much a setting in much of her work as it is its own awesome character.

She tells an incredible story of floating down a river only to come face-to-face with a giant moose. Initially, she panics. Surely, there will be a collision. An adult male moose can weigh up to 1,500 pounds. Thankfully, at precisely the necessary moment, Elizabeth Gilbert realized that the rushing river was shallow enough to stand. So, she did. Crisis averted.

I appreciate a particular animal metaphor that Gilbert uses to cut to the heart of what self-care really means. I was lucky enough to hear her recount the story[1] at a book signing.

"I don't understand what people mean when they say we're supposed to love ourselves . . . How do I do that?" a reader once asked her. The woman began to cry, and Gilbert describes this moment as one where her heart broke for another human being, unknown to her until seconds before.

"You need to take care of your animal," Gilbert tells her. To explain what she meant, she used the image of a frightened dog in a rescue shelter.

"Pretend you've just adopted that dog from a kill shelter. You don't know anything about this animal's history—and you don't need to know. You can see she's been abused, and she's afraid of being abandoned or hurt again. Now imagine this: It's your first night home alone with that dog, and she's trembling in fear. How would you treat her? Would you scream at her and tell her she's an idiot? Would you kick her? Would you lock her in a dark room all alone? Would you starve her or let her binge-eat a bunch of garbage? Would you let her stay in an environment where other dogs attack her every day?"

"No," said the woman. "I would take care of her."

Aha! Gilbert says, her tender point so clear. We all intuitively know how to love an animal, a defenseless creature. We'd make a warm, safe bed, give healthy food, walk in the sunshine, and ensure fresh air and clean water. Our animal bodies are no different.

Sometimes, meditation is daunting. Sometimes, we try but our

---

1 Gilbert has written about the experience for O, The Oprah Magazine in an article, "What Taking Care of Yourself Really Means."

thoughts volley like they're in a tennis match. We're busy, exhausted, or overwhelmed. Maybe it is hitting the fan in our life or in the world. In these moments, it's important to remember that we, too, are animals. Approach with care. Speak softly. Use the voice you need to hear. Maybe a nap, bath, or walk around the block turning your face toward the sunshine like a lemur. Drink the tallest glass of the coolest water you can find.

Meditation soothes our deepest and most natural instincts: to be safe, to be seen, and to belong. In this way, we belong to the moment. But if meditation isn't coming easily or it's not useful for us to be with ourselves in a deep way, we can take refuge in basic, gentler things. It may sound ordinary, but small things, like the tiniest plankton, sometimes alight the whole ocean.

Mindful Action

It goes without saying that if we love the earth, our only home, we must protect it. Moreover, our collective fates are inextricably linked to the fate of the environment. *There is no Planet B* read the signs at climate strikes around the world. *Respect your Mother,* with an illustration of Earth in place of the "O." Our fortunes or lack thereof, unfortunately, too often and unjustly determine how much or little of the natural world we get to enjoy. For this reason, we must use the skills and clarity of paying-attention-practice to preserve as much of nature as we can on behalf of not just ourselves but all beings, especially those most vulnerable to the real and present dangers of the climate crisis. We can't sit in nature, communing with its sacredness remarking on how present and whole we feel, embodied version of the elements that we are, without taking aligned and corresponding action. In other words, we cannot "just sit there." Well, we can. That's how we meditate, but then we have to get up off our butts and do something.

"I want you to act as though the house were on fire," climate activist Greta Thunberg famously said at the World Economic Forum in Davos, Switzerland in 2017, ". . . because it is."

All the meditation and breathwork and yoga in the world won't matter if we can't breathe clean air, or extreme weather forces millions of people from their homes, or we don't have enough clean water and nourishing food to eat. We can't claim to care for the Earth and its inhabitants but act in a manner that suggests the opposite. That is the opposite of being mindful.

What good is all of this contemplation if it doesn't clarify the most essential components of our lives? When we practice in earnest, right action becomes clearer. Meditation brings us home to ourselves. The trees bring us home to ourselves. The ocean breathes us into being. Sunrises and sunsets, how utterly common, and yet, they continue to enchant us and take our breath away. But we cannot merely take breath from the planet without giving it back. Next time you find yourself in nature or enjoying its gifts, whether going for a walk in the woods, swimming in a cool body of water, or admiring cloud formations in the sky, ask yourself what it means to you to be in that place, in that moment. Then ask, what am I doing *right now* to protect it?

19

Creativity

All the arts we practice are apprenticeship.
The big art is our life.

—M. C. RICHARDS

One Christmas, I baked cookies with my friend Coeli and her two children, Luca and Evan. They are now astonishingly grown adults, but at the time, they were the age of peak holiday cookie decorating. We gathered the icing and our selection of standard food dye colors: red, yellow, blue, and green. We sprinkled sugary glitter on yellow stars. We trimmed green trees with tiny silver pellets, likely the bane of any dentist. We began mixing colors and getting creative. Luca, feeling particularly inspired, began mixing all the colors together.

You can imagine the result: a mauvey brown, more suggestive of upholstery than festive frosting.

"No, no, no—don't do that!" we said.

"It will be yucky," Coeli told her. But Luca saw things differently.

"I like it," she said satisfactorily. "It's modern," she added.

At five, she was invoking the perspective of the artist. The avant-garde color palette was intentional. She liked it. Her mom and I shrugged, and everyone carried on making an array of cookies, some of which shared the color scheme of couches in the 1970s.

People who regularly spend time on creative pursuits such as art, music, movement-based expression, and writing experience psychological benefits of all kinds. "Creativity in and of itself is important for remaining healthy, remaining connected to yourself and connected to the world," says Christianne Strang, a professor of neuroscience at the University of Alabama-Birmingham and the former president of the American Art Therapy Association. For bona fide artists, this urge comes naturally. For the rest of us, the key is broadening our definition of what art and creativity look like and doing them in a way free from agenda or evaluation. If, as we say, mindfulness is *paying attention on purpose without judgment*, then the mindful practice of creativity is characterized by creating without judgment—for a sense of joy and aliveness alone. To some, you may be doing it all wrong. *No, no, no, not like that!* a critical voice (inwardly or outwardly) might say. To which you can smile and reply, "I like it."

Art Is in the *Brain* of the Beholder

"Anything that engages your creative mind—the ability to make connections between unrelated things and imagine new ways to communicate—is good for you," says Girija Kaimal, a professor at Drexel University and researcher in art therapy who leads art sessions with members of the military suffering from traumatic brain injury and caregivers of cancer patients. Here's an overview of some activities that can engage your attention in deep, meaningful, and restorative ways.

- BEADING: From the friendship bracelets we made as kids at camp to the woman who left my meditation lecture with a rekindled love for jewelry making, beading offers a concentrated yet low-pressure way to string together something from nothing. *Ex nihilo* is the Latin phrase meaning "out of nothing," and it is the essence of all art, from humble and homespun to hanging in a museum. And once you live long enough (or wear enough bracelets), you learn things have a penchant for coming undone again. Something snags, the string breaks, and all the delicate little pieces ping off the walls and spill onto the floor. Beading represents a colorful, patient manner of gently kneeling down, scooping them up, and being able to say, *Oh, yes, I can fix this.*

- CERAMICS: A kiln regularly reaches two thousand degrees Fahrenheit, imbuing the creative act of pottery with a karmic quality. Potters must balance just the right amount of force with their hands and speed with their feet to take the rawest of elements—earth—and shape it into a thing of beauty or utility or both.

- COLORING: When friends in publishing revealed that adult coloring books were the industry's life raft for a period in the 2010s, I confess to laughing ruefully. But I'm the parent of a toddler now and ideally less of a jerk, and I *get* it. That regular class for busy professionals that I taught at a tony health club? My students were most excited the day I set out a box of freshly sharpened color pencils and meditative coloring books. The experience is soothing. Artful without art's angst. It engages the mind but doesn't make demands on it, all while indulging our senses—the feel of fresh paper beneath open palm, satisfying scribble of the pencil's spiked tip, and vibrant colors to conjure nature and imagination. I guess what I'm trying to say is, don't knock it 'til you try it.

- COOKING (also known as culinary *arts*): Cooking engages all of our senses and nourishes body and mind. A quotidian mindfulness exercise is to prepare and/or eat a meal with total presence. Breaking bread is a timeless way of connecting with other people. Sustenance is the source of life. We can't exist or thrive without it. When we pay attention to it, the experience feeds much more than the body.

- CRAFTING: My friend Joslyn is a master of what she refers to as "stress crafting." It's how she copes while simultaneously entertaining twin kindergartners. Together, they've made soap, artisanal spices, herbal teas with flower petals that burble in your glass, linen sprays with lavender, and hanging mobiles made of fall leaves dipped in beeswax. To open my online yoga class during the pandemic, we once "visited" Joslyn in Vermont. She showed us her view of the foliage and the mobiles she'd made that week with her girls. Stress may have catalyzed them into creation, but their effect on her and us was soothing.

- COLLAGING OR CUTTING OUT IMAGES THAT YOU FIND VISUALLY PLEASING: Think of it as throwback Pinterest. Instead of vying for likes or followers, this analog process of curating photos is for artistic pleasure alone. Not for the whims of an algorithm designed to keep you online, syphoning moments away from you with each mesmerizing scroll. Cut some pages of a magazine. Make some shapes. Glue them to a vision board; form a collage, or make homemade greeting cards, or nothing at all. Recycle them. Upcycle them. You decide!

- DANCE: Is there anything more primal, graceful, and evocative of embodied joy than dancing, even comically bad dancing? More on this later.

- DRAWING OR DOODLING: The oldest artwork in humanity is cave drawings dating back more than sixty-four thousand years ago. Each time we translate our thoughts into shapes and shadows, no matter how elegant or rudimentary, we reconnect to some of our most basic needs as humans—namely, to make and record meaning of life.

- JOURNALING OR WRITING: Ernest Hemingway famously gave the following writing advice, "There's nothing to writing. All you do is sit down at a typewriter and open a vein." Which is a bit dark, *and* great writing. And yet, not-great writing is also extremely valuable, sometimes more so. Hear me out . . . For writing to be healing, affirming, and generative of countless intellectual, creative, and emotional benefits, it doesn't have to be good. Rather, like meditation, it can be wildly liberating, not to mention more productive, to take the pressure and performance-based metrics out of the equation. Instead of sitting down intending to rip open the deepest parts of our soul, we just need to sit down with our thoughts. Jot them down as they come. Forgo the computer. Slow down and pick up a pen. Write to write, not to bleed or judge. More on this in a moment.

- KNITTING: We begin wanting to knit a cozy hat or sumptuous scarf. I tried mittens once and, alas, ended up with just one the size of a cooking mitt. We continue knitting because it soothes us. It gives the hands something to do, some softness to hold. My friend Sarah whiled away time during the pandemic knitting a blanket depicting the most charming Bohemian llama you have ever seen. Another friend, Claire, has been meeting with the same knitting group for more than a decade. They started when their kids were small and now are in college. Like most mindfulness routines, we begin because we want to *get* something. That's OK! We stay because we experience something transformative and true. Something exists now where once there was nothing. We know because we can see it with our eyes, touch it with our hands, or wrap it around our neck and go for a walk, protected from the chill.

- PAINTING: We talked about finding loving and supportive voices when we need them, and perhaps you'd like to add Mexican painter Frida Kahlo to your list, who said, "You deserve the best, the very best, because you are one of the few people in this lousy world who are honest to themselves, and that is the only thing that really counts." Whether painting for artistic or therapeutic purposes—or a bit of both—the driving force is honest self-expression.

- POETRY: You have to slow down to read poetry; the form requires it. Cadence, line breaks, and intentional pauses, to name a few, all purposefully give the effect of total presence in the experience of reading. You cannot skim a poem like a news article. You don't read a few stanzas and skip the rest to get the gist. You read poetry to *feel* something. Or, you can write it.

- QUILTING: One of the biggest current trends in contemporary art is the embracing of works and mediums previously relegated to the territory of the home, as opposed to the hallowed halls of museums. Quilting and other textile forms are chief among these art forms, traditionally viewed as less noteworthy on account of their domestic context and who created them (mostly women).

- SEWING: You can make your own clothes or mend a humble button. Either way, you are making or mending.

- SINGING: The first time my daughter heard the voice of Whitney Houston she was about six months old, sitting on the floor playing with her toys. The first notes of "I Will Always Love You," began, and my baby was transfixed. I am not kidding. She stopped, she *stopped* everything to listen. How ingrained music is to the soul. More on this later in Chanting (page 215).

- WOODWORKING: The cardinal rule of any woodwork is *measure twice, cut once*. Put another way: are you paying attention? Are you sure you're paying attention? Which is, as you know, the whole point.

It's easy to demote or discard hobbies and passions within the ruthless hierarchy of daily life. There's work to do and school lunches to make and the car needs a new inspection sticker. There are piles of laundry and you have been on hold with the insurance company for eight days and seven nights—it *feels* that way at least. Initially we may not miss our creative hours. Until we desperately miss them. Until something fundamental to our being feels lost. As you can probably guess, my preferred form of creative expression is writing. But you don't have to be a published writer or ever share your work with anyone else to benefit from time spent putting the thoughts in your head down on paper.

The Artist's Way: A Spiritual Path to Higher Creativity quickly became a cult classic for creative types when it was published in 1992. Author Julia Cameron's call to arms hinges upon the act of writing "morning pages." Three longhand pages to start each day. No excuses. This time for reflection and uncensored honesty serves as a disciplined daily act of meditation in writing. The result? "As we work with the morning pages, we begin to treat ourselves more gently. Feeling less desperate, we are less harsh with ourselves and others." The purpose of mindful or expressive writing is its catharsis, comfort, and self-companionship. We process our feelings and experiences, whether by calling them morning pages, keeping a journal, writing poetry, telling stories, or writing letters. Any of these artistic-spiritual practices can heal the heart and refresh the mind. The following is a mindful writing exercise you can do to ground yourself. I learned it from writer Dani Shapiro at a writing and meditation retreat she teaches annually. Shared here with her permission.

Step 1:

Find a sheet of blank paper or journal. Start by dividing the paper or page into quadrants. You can do this by folding it in quarters or drawing a vertical and horizontal line with an X-Y axis. In each quadrant, write the following word at the top along with the corresponding numbers. If you enjoy this exercise, you can add more items to each category.

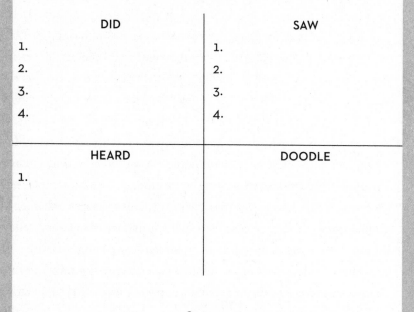

DID	SAW
1.	1.
2.	2.
3.	3.
4.	4.

HEARD	DOODLE
1.	

Step 2:

Turn the sheet of paper to its reverse (blank) side or to the next page of the journal. Right in the middle of the page, begin to settle your mind by drawing a slow, tight spiral, like a seashell or mandala. Start with a dot in the middle of the page and gradually spiral around in tight circles without the lines touching one another. The purpose of this exercise is to give your mind a low stakes way to concentrate and quiet the external noise. Now, this is the fun part . . . keep spiraling until an inner voice tells you you're ready to move on to the next thing. Don't rush. Truly, listen and wait for prompting from your inner voice. You have to slow down and become quiet enough to hear it. Wait for the "click" of your attention.

Step 3:

Fill in your quadrants one at a time, enumerating four things you did today, four things you saw, one sound that you heard, and then let loose with a doodle. Tap into the sensory details of what you did, saw, and heard, and be sure not to edit as you go. Just riff and flow and see what arises. It may help to set a timer. This can be done in seven to ten minutes. Remember not to evaluate your art, especially the doodle. Have fun with it. I am a comically bad doodler, but there is freedom, too, in being bad at things. It's wonderful for your mind to be immersed in an activity for the act alone, rather than a performance-derived goal. Does this principle remind you of anything?

This mindful writing activity is an ideal gateway to formal meditation or purposeful writing. Whenever I share it with a group, the overwhelming response is that people feel more ready and able to meditate now that they have put their thoughts and feelings *somewhere*. I wrote many chapters of this book by starting with this exercise. Or let the exercise stand alone as an amuse-bouche for your brain, a small morsel that awakens your senses to what's happening around and within you.

Music

No one gloriously jams out to their favorite song and wonders *Am I doing this right?* Nor do any of us in the throes of a broken heart play our chosen anthem of angst on repeat while debating if we are fully experiencing the agony of the moment. We are fully experiencing the agony of the moment; that's the problem. But in another way, it's also the remedy. "Music is the best means we have of digesting time," the legendary composer Igor Stravinsky said. Not to mention, listening to music is healthy for your brain, leading to a potpourri of benefits, from reducing stress, pain, and symptoms of depression to improving cognitive and motor skills, as well as enhancing spatial-temporal learning and neurogenesis,[1] which is the brain's ability to produce neurons.

Most of us don't need any help integrating music into our lives. We can pipe it into the background of our day at just about any moment, if we desire. Making it part of our mindfulness routine is different. It's not about whether we're listening to music; it's *how* we're listening. Music can be a catalyst for healing, empathy, connection, and joy. Generally speaking, it's best to meditate without music. However, listening to a piece of music with total focus can be a great gateway exercise to formal meditation. In practice, this might mean listening to a track to help focus your mind, transitioning out of what you were previously doing and into the present moment. A useful exception would be if the piece is quiet in nature and conducive to meditation (think: ambient sound as opposed to anticipatory lyrics and catchy choruses), which could exist as a buffer against the noise in your natural environment. Plenty of meditation-specific tracks exist for this purpose. Tibetan sound bowls, specifically, provide a traditional meditative musical backdrop. The key is that the music offers an immersive experience, rather than entertainment or distraction out of the moment. This type of deep listening stands in stark contrast to how we typically listen to music: while coexisting with other things we are doing. Remember, mindfulness is less concerned with doing and more invested in *being*.

How to Listen to Music Mindfully

1. Select a piece of music. For simplicity, you might begin with something instrumental. Don't play the track immediately. Pause.

---

1 "Your Brain on Music," *Pegasus: The Magazine of the University of Central Florida*, https://www.ucf.edu/pegasus/your-brain-on-music/

2. Check in with yourself. Notice your posture. Spend a few breaths allowing your mind and body to meet up in the moment. What emotions and sensations are you feeling? Notice without judging.

3. Just listen. It may be useful to close your eyes to focus your awareness on your sense of sound. You may also want to wear headphones or earbuds to block external noise. Resist the urge to fall into old listening habits by doing something else in conjunction with listening (e.g., scrolling through social media, checking email, doing the dishes). Instead, open your ears and hear the music as if for the first time.

4. Observe. Notice the experience of listening this way. How does it feel to listen with your whole body? Are your hands open and listening? Are your shoulders listening? Can you listen to the music with the soles of your feet? What emotions and sensory experiences do you feel? Where is your breath?

5. Reflect. Once the music concludes, sit quietly. This might be a natural segue to formal meditation. Check back in with yourself. Now, how do you feel? Has anything shifted?

The absorbing experience of listening to music is one of the oldest and most relatable mindfulness practices we as human beings enjoy. Beginning tens of thousands of years ago—likely with clapping hands, chanting, and instruments fashioned from bones—until present day, music has comforted and connected us. It pleases our brain chemistry and delights the spirit. It takes us on a cascade of memories and sensory experiences, based on where we were and the sounds that traveled on the air.

Chanting

Music and meditation have long been combined in the deeply traditional, spiritual practice of chanting. Buddhism, Hinduism, Christianity (i.e., Gregorian), Judaism, and the Muslim faith (among others) all chant in some way as part of worship and ritual. If you are coming to meditation from yoga, it is likely that you have already taken part in the most popular Sanskrit chant: *om*. The purpose of chanting is to unite with the divine, whether that divinity is perceived as an external God or internal source of love and kindness.

You know how people have secret talents? Singing is not mine. My singing is the opposite of a secret talent. It is a dirge. Chanting *om* I can handle, but devotional chanting in the ritualistic reverie it evokes is not my forte. It makes me a little squeamish actually. And yet, still—I love it. I do it anyway. I listen to traditional chants on my iPhone. I play them in yoga classes. I sang them to my daughter as lullabies, I knew so few true lullabies. What matters in chanting is its vibration, not how beautiful the voice is or even the literal meaning of the words. You will recall this principle from mantras. Here are three basic ways to appreciate traditional chants as part of your personal practice.

- Listen.

    Choose a chant and listen to it in the manner suggested. A few of my favorite devotional artists include: Beautiful Chorus, Craig Pruess, Donna De Lory, East Forest with Ram Dass, Krishna Das, Sacred Spirit, Tina Turner (yes, the one and only), and Wah!
- Sing or recite.

    Try learning a few meaningful chants and practice them. You can do this alone with recordings or in meditation or yoga class settings. If you're not comfortable singing, you can recite the words. Oftentimes these chants will be in Sanskrit or Pali. While you can, of course, chant in any language you choose, bear in mind the importance of honoring the originating cultures and languages of these traditions.
- Read or use as an object of attention.

    You can use a chant as you would a mantra, poem, or prayer.

Read it aloud or silently before you meditate to help ground you. Or you can keep it printed somewhere in your environment where you will see it and be reminded of its power and intent.

Dance and Other Movement-Based Expression

"Dance is the hidden language of the soul of the body," Martha Graham said of the discipline that made her name synonymous with the art of modern dance. The same can be said for any type of movement-based expression, from the primordial act of cathartically shaking off nervous energy and trauma (more on that later) to the languid, methodical movements of tai chi. How we move influences how we feel, how we experience the world, and, put another way, who we are. Using creative movement as mindfulness practice prompts us to ponder: How does my soul move through the world?

Before I was the awkward young adult who strolled into my first yoga class in the mid-1990s carrying a beach towel in lieu of a mat (like yoga pants, mats didn't exist yet either), I was an avid ballerina in my childhood and early teens. I remember a specific Saturday morning class, looking out the window as we moved through a routine at the barre, when I first recognized that dance was not purely something I *did*; it conjured a *way of being*. It felt like being in a house of worship except the hush was contained inward rather than entered through a doorway. There was music playing, but I heard a total quiet. We were moving, but I felt still. I didn't have words for it, only this alchemic reaction of being wholly absorbed in the moment. The windows fogged with the warmth and effort of the perspiring bodies in the room, and I remember snow fell outside. When I found yoga a few years later, it was this feeling that I recognized, this essential aliveness, a blurring of the lines between the moment and me.

Dance doesn't have to be rehearsed, elegant, or comprehensible to access aliveness. The sacred tool of moving our bodies in rhythm is one we possess naturally. Of course, we can develop fancy footwork skills over time, but the essence is primary and exists long before choreography. We may become self-conscious over time, but can any of us truly say that there isn't some rhythm deep in the marrow of our bones, *somewhere?* Think about babies and children. Their rhythm is innate. They learn best through song. They often dance or bop or kick their chubby legs in time to music well before walking. Conversely, in elderly patients who suffer from neurodegenerative disorders such as Alzheimer's, music can stimulate vocabulary and cognition in a way that nothing else does. The effect lasts for a short period even after the music finishes.

If you can remember that dancing is embodied mindfulness practice, you might do it more often. You might make time for it, even in your own kitchen as an intermission between cleaning the countertops or turning the potatoes. You might release the judgment around how good it is. You might be the slightest more likely to ask, "Would you care to dance?" If you don't want to dance, that's OK, too. You might move in another expressive way that works for you. Some people refer to yoga or fly fishing as church. Church doors opened in my heart that day in ballet class. The point is to get out of your head and into your body and sometimes perhaps onto the dance floor.

It's not my place to tell anyone how to dance. I trust you have your moves. I trust they are awesome. But I can share a couple techniques to soothe the mind by moving the body in a rhythmic manner akin to dance. You can think of them as dance adjacent activities. It's possible these exercises feel so good, natural, and conducive to letting the spirit move you that they lead to dancing. Do what feels good. Crank up the music. Get out of the thinking mind and into your body—it knows what to do.

Breath of Joy

The breathing exercises in Chapter 12 are traditionally performed from a seated posture and appropriately soothing for beginning or closing formal meditation. Breath of joy is spectacularly different. Without music, it feels musical, like you are the conductor of a symphony. Without technically being dancing, it contains irresistibly invigorating breath-movement choreography. Here's how to do it.

Begin by standing up straight with your arms at your sides. For this breath you will do a three-part inhale followed by a giant, emphatic exhale, along with the flowing movements of your arms.

INHALE 1: As you inhale, raise your arms to the level of your navel while bringing your hands to touch.

INHALE 2: Inhale again while raising your arms to the level of your shoulders in wide V-shape.

INHALE 3: Bring your arms together and straight overhead.

EXHALE: Now, for the finale . . . As you exhale, bend your knees like a downhill skier, fling your arms behind you, and exhale out your mouth while sticking out your tongue as you would in lion's breath. Think: *HAAAAA!*

There's nothing timid or contained about breath of joy. It's buoyant and big, and the beauty of it is you really gotta let your freak flag fly. With its bold breath, energetic sound, and wild facial expression complete with extended tongue, it feels reminiscent of the traditional Haka dance of the Indigenous people of New Zealand, as well as the country's infamous All Blacks rugby team. The ceremonial dance often marks life milestones like weddings and funerals (and rugby matches, of course). Throughout history and across cultures, dances of all kinds have heralded life moments. They help human beings cope and celebrate. They move us to the music or to the joyful beat of our own breath.

Shake It Up

Most of the time, we live in our heads. This isn't a bad thing or a good thing; it's just a thing. You're not a bad meditator or person incapable of focusing on one thing longer than a goldfish. You're OK. You're a person, operating in a modern world largely incentivized to distract you. However, spending too much time up there, invested, ruminating, and reacting to things that aren't necessarily happening in the present moment increases stress. Which makes us less competent at choosing skillful responses. It can lead to anxiety and depression, and being too stressed for too long can also make us sick, sometimes chronically. We hold all this tension in our bodies, of course. Maybe we chalk it up to sleeping awkwardly on our neck, tweaking that bum shoulder again at the gym, or sitting with poor posture at work resulting in an achy lower back. All these things might be true, but the underlying emotional stress causing the tension in those muscles to begin with isn't helping. On a daily basis, it can make everything feel harder and heavier than needed, like wearing a suit filled with sand. Which is precisely why it's good to shake things up.

You can shake things up as a solo act or as a follow-up to breath of joy. Energetically, these two moving meditations make excellent dance partners. OK, dance-adjacent, like we said. They provide an instant energy boost, which carries over to mood. Shaking or trembling practices are so powerful that they are sometimes used to treat trauma, which wires painful experiences and emotions into our bodies. Meanwhile, studies show that the act of voluntary shaking dislodges tension and stress. Above all, shaking out the stuff that weighs us down, whether physical or psychological, feels really good. Here's how to do it:

Begin by grounding yourself in a standing position with your feet hip-width apart and your arms relaxed at your sides. In the following order, you will shake your whole body gently. Think of politely shaking sand from a beach towel with other beachgoers nearby to start; you don't want to snap the towel or whip sand in anyone's eyes. As you let go of tension, increase the intensity slightly as feels good and helpful. Remember to stay conscious of your breath. If possible, keep everything loose and unserious. Envision yourself as a peaceful one-person mosh pit at a Pearl Jam concert in the nineties. Stagnant energy, worldly cares, and cell phone: be gone! (No, but really, you have to put your phone away for this one.)

- Start wiggling the fingers of your right hand and then shaking out your whole hand, wrist, arm, elbow, and shoulder. Keep your entire arm loose and your joints soft. Remember to start slowly.
- Move on to your right foot. Wiggle your toes, feeling each toe joint loose and relaxed. Next shake out your ankle, lower leg, and thigh. Feel your femur bone move easily in your hip socket.
- Now your left fingers, hand, wrist, arm, elbow, and shoulder. Loosey-goosey, just go with it.
- Next your left foot, all your toes, ankle, lower leg, and thigh. Loosen this hip joint.
- Finally, shake out your whole body. Add a bounce to the balls of your feet, but keep them connected to the ground. Move and shake your torso and head. Relax your face. You might even close your eyes. Stick out your tongue. Whatever lets go of the things weighing you down.
- When you're finished, stand quietly and feel the flood of energy through your body, cells dancing and practically pinging around, singing at the tops of their little cell lungs.

Martha Graham famously said that a dancer dies twice. First, when she stops dancing, and again, upon death. The first is more painful. Dance is this synonymous with life, she wanted us to know. For most of us, not dancing is not tragic. And yet, for any one of us, creative movement and dance bring us alive.

20

Silence, Prayer, and Service

Only a soul that ventilates the world with tenderness
has any chance of changing the world.

—FATHER GREGORY BOYLE

It's important to acknowledge and honor that mindfulness derives from Eastern traditions, predominantly Buddhism. In this way, Buddha was the original mindfulness teacher. It's also true that every major religious or wisdom tradition dating back centuries or millennia contains some form of mindfulness practice—prayer, contemplative silence, and meditation among them. What's more, at the foundation of all of these traditions, you might say the most direct way to Buddha nature, or godliness, or humanness is through compassionate action and service to others.

Catholics like my ancestors pray the rosary, pausing on each bead as a touch point to track God's grace in real time. Muslims prostrate toward Mecca five times per day, a whole-body prayer performed over and over again, as though embedding reverence and humility into muscle memory. What a profound way of remembering to pause. In

Judaism, the Hebrew words for "soul," *neshama*, and "breath," *neshima*, are uncannily close; they share the same root. Breath follows soul; soul follows breath.

To breathe is to be alive, and to be alive as a human being is to be a social creature grounded by our daily routines and connections to other people. Humans have always needed ways to pause within the bustle of earthly existence and connect to something bigger. This chapter explores a few ways in which secular mindfulness intersects with practices common to spiritual tradition such as prayer, contemplative silence, and selfless service.

It's said that prayer is when you talk to God, while meditation is when you listen. In either scenario, it is essential to access a space within ourselves that is quiet and still. This is where we assimilate information, reflect, and *rest*. It is where sacredness resides. In his poem *Keeping Quiet*, Pablo Neruda opens, "Now we will count to twelve/ and we will all keep still." Poetry is so often its own form of prayer.

We can get caught up in the idea of meditating *correctly*. On some level, this is just more noise. Noise we might quiet if we thought of meditation simply as sitting in silence for a time each day.

It's not your imagination that we have less silence than ever before. Life is noisier today, with fewer places throughout the world insulated from artificial sound. Acoustic ecologist Gordon Hempton treks deep into volcanoes and other natural environments to study and record their audio landscape. He describes silence as a think tank for the soul and an endangered species. Silence is not the absence of sound but rather the absence of noise. Warblers singing and leaves rustling and rain pelting the roof are unmistakable auditory impressions but hardly noise.

What's clamorous is the endlessly stimulating onslaught of competing sounds in the form of an ebbing and rising din in the background at all times. Traffic outside, the buzz of lights inside, everywhere a ping, ring, or vibration that however fleeting takes our attention elsewhere. Takes it nowhere. How uncomfortable we are sitting silently with another person before one of us must say *something*? And yet, how unreservedly healing to the soul to sit silently with another person and not have to say a word?

Contemplative Silence

We relish quiet. We crave it. But we also avoid it at all costs. If we're unaccustomed to silence, it can feel unnerving, lonely, or boring. For this reason, it's fruitful to take time to remove external noise and simply listen. With practice, you can learn, first, to tolerate and then to savor silence. Finally, you feel restored by its existence. You "interrupt," as Neruda put it, whatever is keeping you from understanding yourself.

One famous figure who captivated many of our childhoods was fiercely dedicated to promoting the importance of silence, slowing down, and listening deeply. Can you guess who I might be describing, *neighbor*? That's right: Mister Rogers. Of the qualities that typically make for good television—action, conflict, and more action—*Mister Rogers' Neighborhood* had few. Do you remember how long he took to change his shoes? How carefully he selected a sweater, put it on, and zipped it up just so? How meticulously he fed the goldfish? The goldfish! And for this (and more), we loved him.

To Fred Rogers, a television personality, educator, puppeteer, musician, writer, and ordained Presbyterian minister, silence was a form of love. Demonstrable, unembellished, unmistakable: love. Paying attention was love. Slowing down was love. Listening to whoever was speaking as if it was of utmost importance, even if who was speaking was a small child (especially a small child), was love. In a world obsessed with speeding up and growing up, he was quietly revolutionary. In many ways, he remains a beacon of mindfulness. He educated on what is right in front of us, how to find wonder in it, and, above all, how to treat each other. This low-tech program, aired alongside

Sesame Street, beamed love's humblest rituals into people's homes. He spoke out against war and racism at times when it was personally and professionally inconvenient but wholly right to do so.

He brought his reverence for contemplative silence to audiences of children and families for decades and to a less expected venue at the Daytime Emmy Awards in 1997 when he accepted its Lifetime Achievement Award. The following profound moment was captured in journalist Tom Junod's famous *Esquire* profile and is shared here with his generous permission.

[Rogers] went onstage to accept Emmy's Lifetime Achievement Award, and there, in front of all the soap-opera stars and talk-show sinceratrons, in front of all the jutting man-tanned jaws and jutting saltwater bosoms, he made his small bow and said into the microphone, "All of us have special ones who have loved us into being. Would you just take along with me, ten seconds to think of the people who have helped you become who you are . . . Ten seconds of silence." And then, he lifted his wrist, and looked at the audience, and looked at his watch, and said softly, "I'll watch the time," and there was, at first, a small whoop from the crowd, a giddy, strangled hiccup of laughter, as people recognized he wasn't kidding, that Mister Rogers was not some convenient eunuch but rather a man, an authority figure who actually expected them to do what he asked . . . and so they did. One second, two seconds, three seconds . . . and now the jaws clenched, and the bosoms heaved, and the mascara ran, and the tears fell upon the beglittered gathering like rain leaking down a crystal chandelier, and Mister Rogers finally looked up from his watch and said, "May God be with you" to all his vanquished children.

I wouldn't dare pretend to do it better than Mister Rogers, and I don't want to overteach his fundamental point. Taking time to honor sacred silence within yourself and your life is an affirming mindfulness practice all its own. It brings us closer to the truth of who we are, the nature of love, and the essence of being. Some people call these things the presence of God; it's one option but not a requirement. Which is not to say that cathartically loud music, or the cacophony of your favorite restaurant on Saturday night, or the burble of the coffeemaker on Sunday morning, or the neighbor kid practicing cello, or the hubbub of your city returning to life after lockdown are not deeply satisfying sounds that, also, border on holiness. It means that occasionally the burble and bray and buzz must cease so that we can truly hear.

QUESTIONS FOR QUIETUDE

- When was the last time you sat in silence and contemplated the people and experiences that *loved you into being*? How does this make you feel when you do it? (Perhaps you could try it now.)
- When, in the course of your day, do you experience silence? Is there an opportunity to do this more often? For example, in the morning when you first wake, upon getting in the car, or after arriving home: before reaching for noise, music, TV, artificial company, or distraction, can you listen for a while?
- In the absence of noise, what do you hear? What do you notice? How does it feel in your body? When it's uncomfortable, lonely, or boring, can you watch and observe these feelings without impulsively reacting? Can you allow them some space?

Prayer

The mindfulness movement emerged as a modern phenomenon, in part, by removing overtly spiritual aspects of its Buddhist roots. But secularization didn't change the deep spiritual connections people have to their experiences of meditation and mindful living, or to their existing faiths. It's both possible to be religious and a meditator or not religious at all. It's possible that mindfulness practice of any kind connects you more deeply to the spiritual world. To feel more connected to our spirit is a common side effect, to comprehend humanness more fully an inevitability.

Meditation and prayer look, feel, and function in similar ways. Of course, they are still different. They can reinforce each other, and as with any form of personal mindfulness practice, prayer can be used in conjunction with other spiritual and worldly rituals to find solace in daily life. Lovingkindness meditation sounds like a prayer. Truth be told, it feels like a prayer. Its origins are Buddhist, but its essence is nondenominational and applicable across faiths. It worships no God beyond the transcendence of our own capacity for kindness toward ourselves and the world.

We begin inwardly, which is significant. The reason is that we must cultivate lovingkindness toward ourselves so that we may offer it more skillfully and powerfully to others. In plainer terms, the relationship we have with ourselves affects all our other relationships. First, take a moment to sit quietly, letting your mind settle into your body and into the moment. Next, you will recite the following wishes silently or aloud. Take your time with each phrase, allowing it to land within your being. There are many translations and permutations of this blessing, but the following represents its beautiful intention.

> May I be safe.
> May I be happy.
> May I be healthy.
> May I live with ease.

In the second verse, you will direct your heartfelt wishes for safety, happiness, health, and living easefully outward to another person or being. To begin, it's best to choose someone whom you love in an uncomplicated way. (This can be a daunting criterion. Pets also count.) Over time, we strengthen this capacity for lovingkindness by broadening our focus from uncomplicated and easy relationships to harder-to-love people, neutral people, and eventually people who challenge us or who have harmed us. Please note: You can extend compassion to someone while maintaining firm, clear, and safe boundaries for yourself. This person doesn't need to be in your life. Instead, lovingkindness meditation can be a vehicle for your healing and growth. If this exercise feels triggering in any way, please stop. Revert back to people who are easier or neutral. There is no shortage of people in the world who need your lovingkindness. During the pandemic, I taught an online yoga class with participants joining from around the world. Each week, we closed with this same blessing. Sometimes we visualized friends and family we missed most. Other times we focused on healthcare and essential workers. We sent lovingkindness to teachers. We channeled it to marginalized people suffering most. Yogis selected the gallery view setting, looked into the faces and homes of each other—lives that had suddenly become so interior—and without knowing who they were held love for them in their hearts. All you do is say:

> May you be safe.
> May you be happy.
> May you be healthy.
> May you live with ease.

This practice is transformative, internally and externally. You can do several rounds dedicated to different people. When you are finished, sit quietly and notice how you feel. As you progress, remember to continually broaden your circle so that you not only wish well-being for yourself or people you love or like, not just people who look like you or are familiar to you, but as many people as you can.

It must be said that the lovingkindness work of our generation is racial justice. We cannot, as yogis, meditators, or decent people, say that we believe in practices based upon the premises of peace, connection, and compassion, and not live them. To ignore or overlook the reality of the moment, especially people who need love, support, and solidarity most in the world right now, is not mindfulness. It's not helpful, just, or heartful. In many languages a single word exists for both mindfulness and heartfulness. There is no distinction. Please do this meditation with your whole heart. That is the only way.

Another mindfulness routine that invokes feelings of heartfulness is gratitude practice. Studies also show that gratitude is linked to happiness by age five. Here are a few ways to incorporate this practice into your life:

- Try gratitude meditation. Each time you inhale, think: *Gratitude to* . . . As you exhale, allow an image, name, or feeling to come to mind for which you are grateful. Don't force or filter your answers, just allow space for gratitude to arise.
- Keep a gratitude journal in which you write three to five (or more) things per day for which you feel fortunate.
- Keep a jar in which you write one thing down on a small piece of paper each day. When you need a boost or at year's end as your own ritual, you can reach in and recap all your previous blessings. Notice how you feel when you do this.
- Invite friends and family to recount moments of gratitude as part of sharing your days or making conversation. No need to reserve this for Thanksgiving only.
- Before you go to sleep, recount a small triumph of the day you're grateful you experienced. Please be generous; nothing is too small.

Selfless Service

The point was never to excel at sitting perfectly still with our eyes closed not talking to each other. The purpose of mindfulness, of meditation, of yoga, of paying attention on purpose without judgment to life, was always to understand who (and how) we are being in the world. Buddhists consider their *sanghas*, or communities, to be one of the three essential jewels of practice. Yogis take part in *seva*, also known as selfless service or community work. What you offer your community might come in the form of something you teach, making art, taking part in community building initiatives, planting a community garden, or engaging in public service or volunteerism, as a few examples.

There's an anecdote about a father who starts meditating regularly. It was going great, and he stuck with it. He felt amazing! But the novelty waned, he got busy, and he wondered if the meditation was "working" anymore.

"I think I'm going to stop," he announced one morning over breakfast, in the way that we do when we talk to ourselves aloud in the presence of others. We're not expecting a response.

"Please don't," his daughter answered.

The people closest to us feel the effects of our meditation first, and then the ripples cascade outward to coworkers and neighbors; the person who bagged our groceries, delivered our mail, drove the car that nearly backed into ours; people we affect by how we vote, people whose lives are a lot like ours, people whose lives are unimaginably different from ours.

Ventilate the world with tenderness. Empathy. Kindness. Mindfulness without awareness beyond our own needs and wishes is not mindful. Then, it might be navel-gazing, self-indulgent, or passive—or willful ignorance. The good news is that it's difficult to practice in such an insular or self-interested fashion because people are intrinsically good and inextricably connected. Mindfulness builds courage to face reality, nourish inner goodness, and zoom out to see life from more than our own singular perspective. The story of the Buddha is perhaps meant to illustrate the lengths to which we can be sheltered or deluded, or shelter and delude ourselves, until we must wake up to the truth of suffering. This is what just about every wisdom tradition teaches: to alleviate the suffering of others is sacred and vital work.

I FIRST HEARD Nancy Taylor speak while sitting in a pew of one of the oldest churches in America, Old South Church, which was founded in 1669 in Boston, Massachusetts. I was not there to worship but to take part in a gathering of one thousand other women, mostly moms, to organize against the gun violence epidemic on behalf of the activist group Moms Demand Action. It was the first time I'd gone out at night for a nonwork event while leaving my daughter, who was not yet one year old, at home with a babysitter. Minister Taylor rose to the lectern.

What she delivered was part welcome remarks, part sermon, and part slam poetry. Her message was selfless, fearless, and filled with love. She hearkened back to the church's roots in activism, which boasts famous congregants in history such as Benjamin Franklin, Phillis Wheatley, and "Sam Adams and his Tea Partyyy," Minister Taylor all but sang the line for emphasis. And then, "We're not afraid to wrangle with authorityyy!" she roared. The crowd burst into cheers, which echoed up the historic cathedral's vaulted ceilings.

It reminded me of lines from Naomi Shihab Nye's poem "Different Ways to Pray":

Hear us! We have pain on earth!
We have so much pain there is no place to store it!

It's true: there is no place to store all the pain we might feel in a lifetime. Which is why we pray. Or meditate. Or do yoga. Or make art. Or take long walks. Or turn pain into activism. Or commune with trees. Or collect shells. Or swim in freezing cold water. We need a vessel to contain all that we feel, a place to put it or channel it, so that it's not stored in our bodies, lodged in our hearts, or wreaking havoc on our immune systems.

The next time I heard Nancy Taylor's voice it was over the phone when I was working on a newspaper column. The news had become relentlessly devastating, and I was charged with writing articles for the *Boston Globe* that offered some solace or perspective or steadiness. The inhumane policy of removing children from their parents at the border had recently come to light, and when the audio recordings surfaced of babies and toddlers wailing for their mothers, I felt a rancid combination of anguish and rage. It seemed nearly impossible to function, let alone write something uplifting. I asked Nancy what to do. How can we be OK when the world is so demonstrably not OK? I thought I had known but I'd forgotten. Thankfully, the spiritual path is one of remembering. We cannot pretend things are OK when they're not. We must acknowledge the suffering of others, which has always existed. We don't need to avoid how we feel. We can cultivate the steadiness and resilience to do something about it. We can choose where and how to direct our attention. Her answer came like an incantation: *You are not helpless. You are not without agency. Provide comfort. Provide solidarity. Give money. Communicate your outrage and pain.* "It's not unimportant for people to hear that stuff," she added. *This is not right. This is not OK. We do not accept this.*

Ventilate the world with tenderness. Neshama, neshima: soul, breath. All that we have for certain is this breath. Are you aware it carries your soul everywhere you go?

The idea of selfless service takes shape across spiritual traditions, cultures, and communities. Yet, it doesn't have to be spiritual at all. One silver lining from the pandemic has been the collective recognition of how fundamentally we need each other. Everywhere we turned there was loss, grief, and injustice. What can I do? What am I supposed to do? Who needs me? How can I help? What skills or gifts do I have to share? Money is one powerful way, but it is far from the only way. Where we don't spend money also speaks volumes. At the risk of sounding glib, we must pause to ask not what mindfulness can do for me but what can I mindfully do on behalf of others. We can give food or friendship. Generosity. Forgiveness. The bigger tip. The kinder word. The box of diapers to the new mother. *I am here in the hospital lobby. If you want a hug, I'll be here for the next hour. No pressure.* In our neighborhoods, we can repair something or make a spot lovely. Then, do the same thing in someone else's neighborhood. Witness and repair. Repair and witness. We can collect the peace found on a cushion, in a practice, and put it into the world: into the soil to grow things, into our kids' hearts so that they grow up to be brave and caring adults, into antiracism work so that the world reflects what we say we value as yogis and meditators, into our jobs, families, and communities.

21

Life Practice

The world is full of magic things, patiently waiting for
our senses to grow sharper.

—WILLIAM BUTLER YEATS

We need the power of myths. The kinds that teach, motivate, and inspire. They tell of fantastical journeys, undaunted or unlikely heroes,
and insurmountable odds. Till they are surmounted! Great myths
unlock something sacred but perhaps dormant within and serve as a
catalyst to wake us up. They comfort or entertain, enlighten or heed
caution. Myths that explain the world can save people; they demon-
strate that we are not alone. We are part of this magnificent, harrow-
ing, complex human experience, and no matter what we feel in the
moment, someone else has felt the same. They might be feeling the
same right now, which allows us to better understand and relate to
each other. This connection and awareness makes us more empathetic,
compassionate, and wise. Myths may offer moral clarity. They always
bid *pay attention.*

The story of the Buddha reckoning with self-doubt before enlightenment. *Celebrities: they're just like us!* Two wolves battle in my heart, yours, too. Icarus, who flew too close to the sun, felled not by heat but hubris, another name for ego. Meanwhile, the phoenix regenerates itself in flames. The same things that take us down can alternatively lift us from the ash, transformed. Who among us hasn't felt (on one day or many) like Sisyphus pushing a boulder uphill for eternity? Life is full of boulders, but also purifying fires, gentle wolves, and buddhas everywhere you turn.

The world needs people who show up fully, who pay attention, who are present and kind and awake. It needs people who know themselves and can discern thoughts from reality. It needs people courageous enough not to evade reality. These are not merely nice words. It is also science. To strengthen the parts of our brains governed by reason, logic, and leadership, we can meditate. To enhance compassion and empathy, we practice mindfulness. We put our devices down and lift each other up. We can signal to the impulsive, primal, smoke detector portion of our mind that all is clear. We await no mythical saviors because it serves no one to play small or stay silent until feeling 100 percent ready or comfortable. Meditation doesn't do anything, skeptics say. Until you witness life as a meditation on lovingkindness in action.

Meanwhile, we can let go of those myths that keep us small, whether they arise in mindfulness practice or the rest of life. Pesky falsehoods about who we are or how to do it "right" abound, dictating too much of the journey before we begin. Who gets to tell the story? You do. This is one more reason why attending to the moment and watching it unfold, over and over again, is powerful. We learn to self-reject less. Listen to your heart. Apply for the job. Create the art. Pitch the idea. Run for the office. Speak up. Save the earth. Send the email or love letter or apology. *I hope you can forgive me*, the letter could say. This is what we say to ourselves each time we become quiet and still and listen inward. I forgive you for forgetting the power and wholeness of your being. I remember now.

We may swear it doesn't work, we're too busy, or we have too many thoughts. We're doing it wrong. It doesn't feel blissful. It is *so hard* sometimes. We are wrong. We are bad at it . . . None of that's true. These are various thoughts, and you are more than your various thoughts. You are much more than you think. *I hope you can forgive me.* I left you for a while. Things were nuts. Life happened. I'm back now. I'm still here. You can take a deep breath in and say, "I am." As you exhale, you can say, "here now."

I am

here now.

IF YOU ARE ever embarrassingly late to an appointment, one helpful scenario is that the person you're meeting is a patient Buddhist monk from Tibet. Such was the case when I ventured to the center where the Venerable Geshe Ngawang Tenley lives and works at the Kurukulla Center for Tibetan Buddhist Studies in Medford, Massachusetts. Like my conversation with Minister Nancy Taylor, I wanted to talk about how to be OK when the world is not OK. This was long before the COVID-19 pandemic, but there were plenty of other tragedies and indignities unfolding around us every day. It seemed as though to be conscious was to be, in turns, enraged or gutted. There was no amount of meditation or yoga that could penetrate the darkness or reduce the suffering.

The traffic snaked through the city endlessly. My hands gripped the steering wheel. I flicked the radio up and down, on and off. I tried to breathe. Finally, I arrived, parking beneath a shady tree. Across the center's porch, Tibetan prayer flags fluttered.

I entered a bright, tidy, sparsely decorated room where Geshe Tenley sat on a low dais. Behind him hung an ornate *thangka*[1] of the Buddha in rich colors of maroon and gold painted on canvas surrounded by silk brocade. The colors complemented his traditional maroon robes and added to the room's warm, welcoming atmosphere. I sat opposite on a similar but plainer dais. I wore a long black and white dress that previously belonged to my mom. I had showered and washed and combed my hair, which might seem unremarkable, but I assure you it was not. I was late because we'd recently moved, and I had yet to acquire sufficient wisdom about the location of our new home in relation to anything else. Meanwhile, traffic was abiding its typical patterns, and I'd scheduled the interview for an altogether brutal place on the space-time continuum known as late afternoon on a Friday. My husband and I had traded the baby like a relay baton in a 4 x 400-meter relay. I didn't realize I'd skipped lunch until I was on the highway rummaging through the door-side compartment for the dregs of a bag of trail mix. All of the good stuff was gone; a disappointing surplus of raisins remained.

Geshe-la asked about my daughter, whom he had blessed the year before in a tiny, casual ceremony. I tried to answer cordially but quick, wanting to be sensitive of his time. *She's wonderful, thank you. So big!* Maybe the monk had weekend plans. So, I launched into the heart of things. Big, grappling, leading questions, life questions that spiritual leaders get all the time. One of the *sangha* members was ill, and Geshe-la had been at the ER the night before. He was distraught by what he saw, and his tone was firmer than I'd ever heard from him. The waiting area was crowded, and people who were sick were triaged in hallways and on the floor. Pay attention when a monk gets mad, I thought.

"If this woman were the mother of the mayor . . . some important

---

1 A *thangka* is a traditional piece of Tibetan art painted on cloth, usually depicting Buddhist deities, mandalas, or other sacred symbols.

person . . . they would not make her wait on the floor, sick like that!" he would say.

But not yet. That would come later in the conversation. First, he listened to my questions, observed my intention to write practical solutions on paper in the small notebook in my lap. The monk was upset, too. This didn't make him less of a monk. It made him more of a human being.

Around 170 B.C.E., the ancient Greek playwright, Terence, wrote, "I am human; nothing human is alien to me." *Homo sum: humani nil a me alienum puto.* This was well after the Buddha beneath the Bodhi tree but more than two millennia before this moment in the company of the monk.

He nodded. He smiled. "Yes, yes. Not OK. We can talk . . ." he said.

"But first, tea."

A small pot of tea sat on a low table beneath the window. Steam rivulets wound toward the sill. Beside my cup, I noticed a basket; inside a cloth napkin kept something warm. Homemade Tibetan pancakes. More like a crumpet than a pancake. More like heaven fluffed into dough about the size of your palm. I inhaled the smell. My stomach growled, and a memory of my grandmother panged my heart. The scent was of a warm kitchen on a cold, rainy day. It was the politesse of a gracious host or a spiritual offering. Are they very different?

Paying attention to people is our magic. How we wrap the cloth around the bread. How we unwrap the bread and eat. How we listen. How we observe. How we hold space for all our feelings, not just the pleasant and comfortable ones. How we make space for others. How we sit in the waiting room holding hands. How we care. How we comfort. How we say hello and good-bye. Who we are. Who we are *being*. What we fight for. What we write down. Who we lift up. The sounds we hear. The words we say. The words we do not say. How we nurture the best in others and ourselves. How we live.

"Not OK," the lama said it like a pronouncement, after I'd outlined my whopping question. All the suffering I described, the state of the world, maybe the harried energy he could sense beneath my voice—he wanted me to know he felt it, too. It wasn't OK, the injustice and pain and hatred that are too often part of life. But, then, he added something as exquisite as it was plain.

"But . . . human nature is not negative. Human nature is positive."

I don't mean plain as in ordinary. I mean in that moment, with the June air wafting in carrying the scent of tea and flour, the sight of the monk sitting in the sun under a painting of the Buddha, a notebook in my lap and questions in my head, my hair still wet and my stomach hungrier than I realized, it was plain to the eye. Obvious. I could see, feel, and hear the care and attention all around me. Wherever I looked, it was there, and because I felt it, I would take it with me like seeds transported on wind.

When I listened to the recording of our interview to write this, I became instantly choked up. I can't explain precisely why. Only that it had something to do with a depth of kindness, to have nothing in a notebook then and now a book to give you, or to have spent this year without the company of friends (or interview subjects) in the same room. How special it is to be together—only that—to be human beings together.

"GOD IS CHANGE," writes Octavia Butler.

"Change is the only constant," Heraclitus said.

Whatever our mind state in this moment, it will soon change. Whatever the external state of matters, however daunting, glorious, or ordinary, it, too, will shift. This is what the Buddha taught 2,500 years ago. The essence remains.

I am here now.

Whatever change, purpose, or grace we hope to find in life, it begins with being here now. You're still here. No magic. It is all magic. You are the magic.

acknowledgments

Meditation and mindfulness can save lives, but writing a book about them, as a new mother during unprecedented political and social turmoil with a global pandemic and economic crisis thrown in at the homestretch, almost killed me. I kid! (Sort of, mostly . . .) The stress was, at times, profound, which made me worry I must be doing some part—or all of it—wrong. Still, in moments of personal doubt or collective darkness, mindfulness was my anchor, and meditation and yoga, in particular, were often how I stayed connected to other people from afar. My head could tell me I was a fraud; this is the nefarious setting of imposter syndrome. But my heart would send me to my cushion or the floor as I leaned against the living room couch or onto Instagram Live to meditate with friends and strangers from around the world, and I would emerge steadier. I could begin again. I could keep going. I remembered the innate goodness and beautiful obstinacy of being alive.

Thank you to everyone who buoyed me through the long process of writing this book, especially my family, friends, mentors, and writing inspirations. I thought the second time would be easier, but I stand corrected. That calculation was uproariously naïve. The second book is *much* harder!

Thank you to my editor, Julie Will, who has seen me through it all with a level of clarity to which I'm now accustomed but still in awe and admiration. Your candor and compassion kept me going. Thank you to everyone at HarperWave: Karen Rinaldi, Emma Kupor, Penny

Makras, Laura Cole, Yelena Nesbit, Andrea Guinn, Bonni Leon-Berman, Lydia Weaver. I feel absurdly grateful to have landed in your care. Like the books you steward, you exude creativity, intelligence, boldness, and vision. I am inspired and indebted once again. Thank you to Jennifer Jill Araya for lending her mellifluous voice to the audio recording.

I met my literary agent, Stephanie Tade of the Tade Agency, via phone on Valentine's Day, and coincidentally knew I'd met the one. Stephanie, you make me a better and more resilient writer and human being. Whenever I hang up from our calls, I exhale. (Still, I try not to call too much.) Thank you, also, to Colleen Martell and Gretchen Van Nuys, who believed in and supported *Still Life* with unwavering kindness and insight from the beginning.

An early reader is the most tender of writing relationships, requiring the finest combination of holding work gently while offering incisive direction. I am extremely lucky to entrust my friends: Priscilla Warner, my doyenne of early drafts; Serena Kabat-Zinn, my arbiter of authenticity and art; Joanna Rakoff, my esteemed, new(ish) writer friend who instantly felt timeless and true; and Joslyn McIntyre, with whom I share a rare and treasured personal/professional simpatico.

Thank you to my visionary yogi-friend multi-hyphenates, Christine Needham and Michael Alba, who checked in, kept me sane, and helped choose this book's beautiful cover. Thank you, Wendy Cook and Nicholas Ribush, for being my Buddha buds and facilitating my experiences with the Kurukulla Center for Buddhist Tibetan Studies.

My new mom duo: Abigail Prague and Ann Altman. Together, we inadvertently formed the most unlikely book club while breastfeeding, which met via group text between the hours of midnight and 4:00 a.m. You helped me navigate an unknown and intense life chapter, which requires a lot of sacrifices, but in our case, reading and sharing great books was never on the table.

One of the greatest boons of my academic life was studying with

Dr. Miranda Shaw at the University of Richmond. Dr. Shaw fostered my curiosity (OK, obsession) with Eastern philosophy and religion. I was humbled and delighted to have her careful scholarly input on the story of the Buddha, as well as her support all these years later. She retired the same week she reviewed that chapter—a final assignment for us both! Thank you forever, Dr. Shaw.

To the meditation teachers and spiritual leaders who have inspired me personally and professionally: Jon Kabat-Zinn, Sharon Salzberg, Tara Brach, Pema Chodron, Thich Nhat Hanh, Deepak Chopra, Roshi Joan Halifax, and Cyndi Lee: thank you for sharing your wisdom. In particular, I want to thank Jon and Myla Kabat-Zinn for reading and endorsing my first book before it was published. It meant the world then and still now.

I was fortunate enough to speak with two remarkable religious leaders for this book: Minister Nancy Taylor of Old South Church and Geshe Tenley of Kurukulla Center for Buddhist Tibetan Studies. Thank you for your time and wisdom. Our conversations are etched in my mind and heart.

Billy Mills—athlete, activist, wise elder—is a category unto himself. I am humbled by your and Patricia's generosity. I first heard Billy's voice on NPR and am now fortunate that it visits my thoughts regularly. Thank you for your work, wise words, indomitable spirit, and showing others how to fly. I am grateful for the friendship and mind-body motivation of Kim Vandenberg and George Foreman III.

Thank you to Dani Shapiro for being a writer I admire and allowing me to share her writing exercise, which appears in Chapter 19. An excerpt from Tom Junod's now famous profile of Fred Rogers for *Esquire* magazine appears with Tom's generous permission and was facilitated by Ayla Zurod-Friedland of the David Black Agency and Laurie Feigenbaum of Hearst Magazine Media, Inc.

One of my writing heroes, Zadie Smith, writes, "Time is how you spend your love." Thank you to my family most of all: my husband,

Dan Fitzgerald, and my daughter and guiding, brightest light Edie Fitzgerald; my mom and dad, Rita and Robert Pacheco; my mother-in-law and father-in-law, Joanne and John Fitzgerald; and my brother and sister-in-law Reece Pacheco and Annie McBride. You spent your love and time in ways that allowed me to follow my dreams. I love you.

To my teachers of writing, yoga, and life: You have made me the person and writer that I am. To my students, this is my favorite part—this thing I wrote now belongs to you.

bibliography

Books

Das, Surya, and Lama Surya Das. *Buddha Is as Buddha Does*. New York: HarperCollins, 2007.

Harris, Dan. *10% Happier*. New York: HarperCollins, 2014.

Kabat-Zinn, Jon. *Full Catastrophe Living* (Revised Edition). New York: Bantam, 2013.

Kabat-Zinn, Jon. *Wherever You Go, There You Are*. New York: Hachette Books, 2009.

Kolk, Bessel A. Van. *The Body Keeps the Score*. New York: Penguin Publishing Group, 2015.

Lamott, Anne. *Bird by Bird*. New York: Anchor Books, 2007.

Nestor, James. *Breath*. New York: Riverhead Books, 2020.

Satchidananda, Swami. *The Yoga Sutras of Patanjali*. Buckingham, VA: Integral Yoga Dist., 2012.

Walpola, Rahula. *What the Buddha Taught*. New York: Open Road + Grove/Atlantic, 2007.

Warner, Priscilla. *Learning to Breathe*. New York: Simon and Schuster, 2012.

Articles

Beth Harris, "Dick Bank, Who Called '64 Olympic Track Upset, Dies at 90." AP News, February 25, 2020.

Diana Raab, "What is Spiritual Bypassing?" *Psychology Today*, January 23, 2019.

Drake Baer, "The Father of Mindfulness on What Mindfulness Has Become." *Thrive*, April 27, 2017.

Malika Garib, "Feeling Artsy? Here's How Making Art Helps Your Brain." *NPR Life Kit*, January 11, 2020.

Mary Grace Garis, "Science Says Sighing Is Involuntary Self Care—Not Your Inner Angsty Teen Being Rude." *Well + Good*, June 7, 2019.

Robert H. Shmerling, "Keeping Your Smartphone Close May Not Be So Smart," *Harvard Health Blog*, August 2017.

Tom Junod, "Can You Say Hero?" *Esquire*, November 1998.

Will Johnson, "Full Body, Empty Mind: Embodied Meditation Practice." *Tricycle*, Fall 2007.

"Your Brain on Music." *Pegasus: The Magazine of the University of Central Florida*, Summer 2017.

Video

"How Mindfulness Empowers Us: An Animation Narrated by Sharon Salzberg." *Happify*, January 19, 2016.

Lazar, Sara, *How Meditation Can Reshape Our Brains*. 2011; Cambridge, MA: TEDx Talks.

Podcasts

Tippet, Krista, host. "Gordon Hempton: Silence and the Presence of Everything." *On Being* with Krista Tippet, August 29, 2019.

index

about the author

REBECCA PACHECO is the author of *Do Your Om Thing*, which was named one of the "top ten yoga and meditation books every yogi needs" by *Yoga Journal* and is used in teacher-training programs across the United States. Previously, she founded and wrote the popular blog Om Gal (2008–2015). She's the creator of the Runner's World Yoga Center as well as videos for *Women's Health*. She has appeared on NPR and the Canadian Broadcast Company, has been featured in *Forbes*, the *Huffington Post*, the *Hindu*, *Reuters*, and *USA Today*, and frequently contributes to the *Boston Globe*, covering a range of topics including mind-body health, the natural world, culture, feminism, mindfulness amidst modern chaos, and parenting in the present. She lives in Boston with her husband and daughter, where she enjoys stillness and movement in equal measure. You can connect with her @omgal.